Regression Analysis

Advanced Quantitative Techniques in the Social Sciences

VOLUMES IN THE SERIES

1. **HIERARCHICAL LINEAR MODELS: Applications and Data Analysis Methods, 2nd Edition**
   Antony S. Bryk and Stephen W. Raudenbush
2. **MULTIVARIATE ANALYSIS OF CATEGORICAL DATA: Theory**
   John P. Van de Geer
3. **MULTIVARIATE ANALYSIS OF CATEGORICAL DATA: Applications**
   John P. Van de Geer
4. **STATISTICAL MODELS FOR ORDINAL VARIABLES**
   Clifford C. Clogg and Edward S. Shihadeh
5. **FACET THEORY: Form and Content**
   Ingwer Borg and Samuel Shye
6. **LATENT CLASS AND DISCRETE LATENT TRAIT MODELS: Similarities and Differences**
   Ton Heinen
7. **REGRESSION MODELS FOR CATEGORICAL AND LIMITED DEPENDENT VARIABLES**
   J. Scott Long
8. **LOG-LINEAR MODELS FOR EVENT HISTORIES**
   Jeroen K. Vermunt
9. **MULTIVARIATE TAXOMETRIC PROCEDURES: Distinguishing Types From Continua**
   Niels G. Waller and Paul E. Meehl
10. **STRUCTURAL EQUATION MODELING: Foundations and Extensions**
    David Kaplan

Introduction to the Series:
Advanced Quantitative Techniques in the Social Sciences

The volumes in the new AQTSS series consider quantitative techniques that have proven to be or that promise to be particularly useful for application in the social sciences. In many cases, these techniques will be advanced, not necessarily because they require complicated mathematics, but because they build on more elementary techniques such as regression or descriptive statistics. As a consequence, we expect our readers to have a more thorough knowledge of modern statistics than is required for the volumes in the QASS series. The AQTSS series is aimed at graduate students in quantitative methods specializations, at statisticians with social science interests, and at quantitative social scientists who want to be informed about modern developments in data analysis.

The AQTSS series aims to be interdisciplinary. We prefer to publish volumes about techniques that can be used, and have been used, in different social disciplines and, in some cases, in the behavioral, medical, or physical sciences. This also is reflected in the composition of our editorial board. The board consists of scientists from many different disciplines, all of whom are involved in creating the Department of Statistics at UCLA.

The series also seeks to be practical. Although a good mathematical background may be essential to understand some aspects of the techniques, we insist on an emphasis on real data, real social science problems, and real analyses. This means that both data structures and computer packages get a great deal of emphasis in the volumes of this series.

Statistics present us with a series of techniques that transform raw data into a form that is easier to understand and to communicate or, to put it differently, that make it easy for the data to tell their story. In order to use the results of a statistical analysis in a responsible way, it is necessary to understand the implementations and the sensitivities of the transformations that are applied. We hope that the volumes in this new series contribute to quantitative social science applications that are both persuasive and precise.

—Jan de Leeuw, UCLA
—Richard Berk, UCLA

For information:

Sage Publications, Inc.
2455 Teller Road
Thousand Oaks, California 91320
E-mail: order@sagepub.com

Sage Publications Ltd.
6 Bonhill Street
London EC2A 4PU
United Kingdom

Sage Publications India Pvt. Ltd.
B-42, Panchsheel Enclave
Post Box 4109
New Delhi 110 017 India

Printed in the United States of America

Library of Congress Cataloging-in-Publication Data

Berk, Richard A.
Regression analysis: a constructive critique / by Richard A. Berk.
p. cm. — (Advanced quantitative techniques in the social sciences, v. 11)
Includes bibliographical references and index.
ISBN 0-7619-2904-5 (alk. paper)
1. Regression analysis. I. Title. II. Advanced quantitative techniques in the social sciences; 11.
QA278.2.B46 2003
519.5′36—dc21

2003046500

03 04 10 9 8 7 6 5 4 3 2 1

Acquiring Editor:	Lisa Cuevas
Editorial Assistant:	Alicia Carter
Production Editor:	Diana E. Axelsen
Copy Editor:	Connie Adams
Typesetter:	C&M Digitals (P) Ltd.
Cover Designer:	Sandra Ng Sauvajot
Indexer:	Judy Hunt

Regression Analysis

A Constructive Critique

Richard A. Berk
University of California, Los Angeles

Advanced Quantitative Techniques in the Social Sciences Series 11

To Susan

Contents

Series Editor's Introduction

It is a pleasure to write a preface for the book *Regression Analysis* by my fellow series editor, Richard Berk. It is a pleasure in particular because the book is about regression analysis, the most popular and the most fundamental technique in applied statistics, and because it is critical of the way regression analysis is used in the sciences—specifically, the social and behavioral sciences. Although the book can be read as an introduction to regression analysis, it can also be read as a thorough critique of this class of techniques, or at least of some of the methodological superstructure that has been built on top of it. The subtitle, "A Constructive Critique," is appropriate enough if one interprets it as applying to regression analysis in general; however, the book does some pretty destructive work in the area of regression modeling and regression inference. That is another reason why it is a pleasure to write this preface—I like debunking, and I wholeheartedly agree with Berk that there is plenty to debunk in this area.

Let me add my own perspective, which is not very different from that of Berk, but perhaps emphasizes other aspects of the methodological situation. Regression analysis is by far the most frequently used data analysis technique. It dominates data analysis in the social, behavioral, educational, environmental, and biomedical sciences, and it figures prominently in policy studies, court cases, and various types of interventions. It is a multifunctional technique used in many different situations and for many different purposes. Let us try to disentangle some of its uses.

Description

In the first place, regression analysis is used for description. As explained extensively in this book, regression analysis is used to describe the distribution of a variable under a number of different conditions. These conditions are usually defined as combinations of the values of a number of other variables, and we often say we are studying the conditional distribution of an outcome variable given the values of a number of regressors. Thus, for instance, we look at the distribution of school achievement for students with various combinations of gender, race, and income. Specifically, we look at the the eight distributions of SAT scores for students who are Male/Female, Black/White, and Rich/Poor, in all possible combinations. Regression analysis is a data analysis technique to present the differences in these conditional distributions in a clear and convincing way.

This definition is very general. In our example, we could, for instance, present eight "parallel" histograms or boxplots, and we have an example of regression analysis. But this works only in the example, because we do not have too many "cells" in our "design." We have only eight possible combinations and, presumably, enough observations in each of the eight cells to draw the histograms or boxplots. But what happens if we have only a small number of observations, for instance, only 50? On the average, there will be about six observations in each cell, not enough for a decent histogram. What we will tend to do, in that case, is to apply smoothing. Our regression analysis could take the form of plotting eight parallel normal densities, with different means and variances. This is a smoothed version of the parallel histograms, and it provides us with a cleaner picture. It also gives us the opportunity to summarize our data analysis in 16 numbers (eight means, eight variances), which is a pretty concise data reduction summary.

The problem with this form of smoothing the histograms is clear. The device of using the different normals may or may not be appropriate in a particular empirical situation. In this context, it is never false, because it is just a graphical or analytical device, but it may be wasteful because it throws away much interesting information, or misleading because it distorts information. Maybe the conditional distributions are skewed, for instance, or maybe they have very heavy tails.

We get into more serious problems if the number of regressors, and thus the number of cells, increases. Ten variables, with five values each, produce about 10 million cells, and we will not have enough observations to fill the cells. Most of them will be empty; the others will have one or two observations. We can no longer compute cell variances, and thus we have to resort to more aggressive smoothing. We use normal densities, which all have the same variance and are merely shifted along the real axis. And even that may not be enough, because we may not be able to compute cell means reliably. Additional smoothing is introduced by requiring our cell means to be linear combinations of our five variables, and thus we reduce the number of parameters in the graphical representation from 10 million means (and a variance) to five regression coefficients (and a variance). Of course, we are not actually going to graph the 10 million normal densities; we just summarize the data analysis using the six parameters. This is a gigantic amount of data reduction, with plenty of possibilities to distort and/or to smooth away interesting aspects of the data.

As Berk explains in his book, using regression analysis for description cannot really be criticized in general methodological terms. It can definitely be criticized in any specific situation, because the actual device that is chosen may be misleading or wasteful, or it may oversmooth or undersmooth. But comparing conditional or cell distributions is a basic technique in many of the sciences, and in the case of small samples or many cells, we have to use data reduction or smoothing devices of some sort. What we criticize in this context is a lack of craftsmanship, or, in some cases, even a fraudulent use of the available tools.

Prediction

Regression analysis is also used for prediction. Imagine the following situation. Parents want to enroll their child in one of a number of high schools, and they want to do this in such a way that the child is most likely to be admitted to a particular university after 6 years. They go to a counselor, and they give the counselor all kinds of information about the child. The counselor plugs these data, together with data about the high schools, into a regression equation she keeps in a drawer, and the regression equation comes up with estimates of admission probabilities. The counselor then suggests that the parents choose the high school that produces the highest admission probability and collects the counseling fee. Similar scenarios can be constructed for stockbrokers, economic macro-model predictors, clinical psychologists, and so on.

It seems clear that using regression analysis to construct prediction devices again cannot be criticized in general methodological terms. They either work, or they do not. If they do not work, the counselor will go out of business, and a competitor with a better regression equation takes over. You can criticize a device by inventing a better one, but you cannot say the equation in the counselor's drawer is "false." That does not make sense.

There are more complicated forms of prediction, but basically, the same methodological considerations apply. If we have 10 million cells, and a smoothed description, then we can give values to the empty cells. Although we have no observations in the empty cells, we can still use our regression coefficients to make the linear combination of the variable values correspond with the cell. We can predict the value of an observation in that cell, and then go out into the world, collect such an observation, and compare it with our prediction. Or, someone else may come up with such an observation. If our interpolation is wrong, we have to adjust our smoothing device, because otherwise, we are clearly at a competitive disadvantage.

In linear regression models, prediction also occurs in other forms. If we have used gender, race, and income as our predictors, and we have computed regression coefficients, then we can say that "increasing family income by $100 will result in so-and-so many additional points on the SAT." This refers to a possible experiment, and it predicts the outcome of that experiment. It is useful insofar as such an experiment is feasible and will actually be undertaken. If it is just a hypothetical experiment, then predicting its outcome is not very interesting. We could all sit at our desks and perform hypothetical experiments in our heads all day, and science would not advance one iota. Berk shows in this book that these types of predictions, often presented in the form of explanations, are very common in the social sciences—and quite useless. The corresponding experiments can never be carried out, and thus the predictions are not really predictions. They are just another form of "idling of the machine," in this case, the social science regression machine, with all the fancy LISREL bells and whistles huffing and puffing.

Inference

Regression analysis is also used as a statistical technique to make inferences from a sample to a population from which the sample is drawn. As Berk explains, this particular approach gets us into trouble right away in many situations. We are dealing with a sampling model, and with a regression model on top of that. Often, the sampling model cannot be plausibly defended. There is no sample, or the sample is not random, or the whole notion of a sample does not make sense.

Even if the notion does make sense, the assumption that we are dealing with a simple random sample cannot be falsified in any conceivable way. We are specifying, at least if we are frequentists, what would happen if we repeated our experiment or our data-gathering procedure a large number of times. But we have no way to actually replicate, so the sampling model, or the replication framework, is just a leap of faith. And even if we would perform all these hypothetical replications (e.g., in a thought experiment), it would be abundantly clear that the linear model that sits on top of the sampling model would be false. One could argue that maybe it would be only a little bit false, and still useful, but because we are talking about hypothetical replications in our head anyway, that sort of discussion is somewhat silly.

The standard statistical way of doing inference is to assume that our observations are realizations of random variables. This means that we make up a framework of hypothetical replications, and all of our subsequent statistical statements are about this hypothetical framework. To use Bishop Berkeley's apt phrase, we are talking continuously about "ghosts of departed quantities." As long as we are tossing coins, or drawing random samples from well-defined, finite populations, at least we have a plausible replication framework. But these situations are rare, and it is far more common to have an implausible linear model on top of an equally implausible sampling model. Berk quotes

Box, who said that all models are false, but some models are useful. Many statisticians are now familiar with this quote, but they still happily go about their business, which is to make various statements about random variables that are all conditional on the assumption that the model describing them is true. In the meantime, they have thoroughly lost the connection with the analysis of the actual data. I think the only way out of this dilemma is a radical break with the idea that statistics is about models. Statistics is about techniques for describing data. In many cases, it is useful to study the properties of techniques by applying them to models formulated in terms of hypothetical random variables, but this is just one way of validating the techniques, one form of quality control. Sometimes, models are even useful to suggest techniques, by applying some general principle such as maximum likelihood or posterior mode, but such a technique still must be tested out and validated in actual data analysis situations.

In short, these considerations of regression analysis arrive at basically the same conclusion as this very provocative book. Regression analysis is an eminently useful, and quite indispensable, statistical technique that can be used for both description of a large variety of data sets and prediction of outcomes in many situations. As with all statistical techniques, its inferential aspects are problematical, even in simple situations. And as Berk's book illustrates in great detail in the later chapters, these fundamental problems cannot be solved by using more complicated models that introduce hosts of additional parameters to "save the phenomena."

It was a pleasure for me to read this book. I see it as a critique of quantitative social science, which often takes the unholy route of forcing the data to serve an obviously fanciful model, but also, more generally, as a critique of all of those statistical methods and publications that concentrate on the statistical model and use the data merely as an afterthought. It is good to have this book in our series.

—Jan de Leeuw

Preface

I am a part of the generation of social scientists for whom multivariate statistics became a routine research tool. Dramatic advances in statistical theory, computer power, and user-friendly software, coupled with the growing availability of large data sets, opened up a new world of research possibilities. Like so many social scientists, I was thrilled by the prospects; virtually all scientific and policy questions would be meaningfully addressed. The only real constraints were resources.

I was encouraged by the post-World War II generation of social scientists whose energy and scientific optimism were an inspiration: Don Campbell, Dudley Duncan, Jim Coleman, Jim Short, Al Reiss, Pete Rossi, and many others. But as the years passed, I began to hear grumblings that the reach of quantitative social science was far exceeding its grasp. For too many researchers, scientific optimism had become scientific arrogance, and innovative tools were being applied thoughtlessly. In personal conversations with a number of senior researchers, growing disillusionment was candidly expressed. There were even some serious second thoughts about much earlier work.

Nowhere were the grumblings louder than when social science was applied to matters of social policy. I recall a conversation with Don Campbell in which he openly wished that he had never written "Campbell and Stanley" (1963). The intent of the justly famous book, *Experimental and Quasi-Experimental Designs for Research,* was to contrast randomized experiments to quasi-experimental approximations and to strongly discourage the latter. Yet the apparent impact of the book was to legitimize a host of quasi-experimental designs for a wide variety of applied social science research. After I got to know Dudley Duncan late in his career, he said that he often thought that his influential book on path analysis, *Introduction to Structural Equation Models,* was a big mistake. Researchers had come away from the book believing that fundamental policy questions about social inequality could be quickly and easily answered with path analysis. But by far the most influential was Pete Rossi. Over the years, we worked together on many applied research studies closely linked to policy. He was (and remains) extremely demanding of his applied research and the applied research of others. And as a New Yorker, he was a contrarian by nature. A lot of Pete's style was infectious.

Some of the grumblings eventually found their way into print. Dudley Duncan's *Notes on Social Measurement* (1984) was especially compelling.

Lieberson's *Making It Count* (1985) was on target for many of the larger issues. Illustrations of more focused but equally skeptical writing include Oakes's book on statistical tests (1986), Ed Leamer's powerful condemnation of causal modeling in economics (1978), and critical papers on causal inference by several very visible statisticians (e.g., Holland, 1986; Rubin, 1986; Freedman, 1991).

The language in which concerns were expressed was often quite pointed. Widely noted, for instance, was George Box's statement that "all models are wrong" (1976:792). Moreover,

> since all models are wrong, the scientist cannot obtain a "correct" one by excessive elaboration. On the contrary, following William of Occam he should seek an economical description of natural phenomena. Just as the ability to devise simple but evocative models is the signature of the great scientist, so overelaboration and overparameterization [are] often the mark of mediocrity.

Only a bit less sweeping were Leslie Kish's views on significance tests (1987:19):

> Tests of statistical significance are particularly ineffective as they are commonly used in social research: to test the null hypothesis of zero differences, or null relationships. Such hypotheses are trivial reflections of the actual aims of social research.

Finding myself increasingly drawn into the skeptics' camp, I began expressing my doubts in print (e.g., Berk, 1977, 1988; Berk et al., 1995). I also began to reexamine a lot of my earlier work. But as an applied researcher, I also tried very hard to be constructive: How could empirical work useful for policy be done better? In the 1990s, I moved full-time into the Department of Statistics at UCLA while at the same time including among my research activities an increasing fraction of projects in the environmental sciences. The result was exposure to a much wider range of statistical and scientific thinking than I had seen in the social sciences. This book is part of the process by which these broadening experiences are being integrated. I am trying to bring together in one place not just the contrarian views to which I am drawn but constructive suggestions about how improvements could be made.

Science and policy making are collective enterprises. Insofar as this book contributes to either, I am indebted to several wonderful colleagues with whom I have had many animated discussions over the past few years: Jan de Leeuw, Don Ylvisaker, Rob Weiss, Rob Gould, and especially David Freedman. David Freedman, Jan de Leeuw, Coen Bernaards, and Herb Smith provided very helpful written comments on this manuscript. I also offer thanks to the policymakers with whom I have worked for more than 30 years. They are a mixed bag to be sure, but the many good ones convinced me that it was possible to do sound applied research that really mattered. Finally, there is Peter Rossi. He was with me when this long trip began and has remained a steadfast friend and honest critic. To him I am especially indebted.

1 Prologue: Regression Analysis as Problematic

Regression analysis is ubiquitous in the development and evaluation of public policy and in production of the research on which it is sometimes based. It is a key part of the curriculum in all policy-relevant social and natural sciences. There are even primers on regression analysis for policymakers who do not have the time or inclination to study the technique in depth (e.g., Kaye and Freedman, 2000).

Yet there have long been skeptics. Perhaps most commonly, particular studies are examined and the various errors described. An excellent early example is a National Research Council report on sentencing research (Blumstein et al., 1983). A large criminal justice literature dominated by regression analysis was reviewed and found wanting.

There have also been critics who concentrate on particular technical difficulties in the existing approaches, often offering suggestions for major improvements. Recent work by Manski (1990, 1994) and others on bounding estimates of causal impact are one example.

Far more rare is genuine heresy, questioning the entire regression enterprise or the entire enterprise when used to address certain kinds of empirical phenomena. The recent controversy, launched primarily by a small group of statisticians, over causal inferences drawn from regression analysis is perhaps the best known instance (Freedman, 1985, 1991; Holland, 1986; Rubin, 1986; Berk, 1988).

This book is intended to fall into the third camp. The basic theme is this: If one looks carefully at regression analysis and the empirical questions it is supposed to answer, the data too often are dominated by information of doubtful quality brought to the analysis from outside. One key illustration is statistical inference, commonly used to attach confidence intervals to point estimates or to conduct formal hypothesis tests. Another is causal inference, commonly used to infer cause-and-effect relationships from observational data. Both depend fundamentally on how the data used in the regression analysis were generated: How did nature and the investigator together produce the data then subjected to a regression analysis? Was there a real intervention? Can the data be properly viewed as a random sample from a real population? How were key variables measured? There is precious little in the data themselves that bear on such matters. One must bring to the regression analysis an enormous amount of information about data, and this information will, in practice, do some very heavy lifting.

Unfortunately, even when the data generation process is well understood, it often will not provide a reasonable foundation for the conclusions the investigator wants to draw. There may be no defensible way to get from the data on hand to where the investigator wants to go. Worse, there often will be no clear understandings about how the data came to be. A common practice then is to construct some convenient account giving the investigator a free hand. But if the inputs are a matter of convenience, so are the outputs. Another approach is to note those features of the data generation process that are important and then simply list the assumptions that will allow the analysis to proceed. Such "assume-and-proceed" statistics allow the investigator to meet the obligation of full disclosure as if that were sufficient to justify completely all that follows. Finally, there are a great many regression analyses that reflect only the dimmest understandings about what can be learned from the data alone. Anything goes as long as SPSS or SAS can be made to run.

Some readers are no doubt already wondering whether the pages ahead just contain another long harangue about assumptions. Whether this book is a long harangue I leave to others to decide. But many of the key assumptions discussed are not widely understood, if the existing applications literature is any guide. Or, if they are understood, they are commonly ignored. More important, this book is less about formal assumptions and their consequences and more about what those assumptions imply about how natural and social processes are supposed to work. Statistical assumptions invoked to justify an analysis of real data are not just statistical abstractions but statements about nature. If the assumptions made so that a statistical analysis plays through are factual nonsense, one surely has to wonder about the conclusions that follow. Finally, clear links will be made between these requisite assumptions and how the data were generated. At the very least, this may push applied researchers to say a lot more about the data than a perfunctory $\mathbf{y} \sim \text{NIID}(\mathbf{X}\beta, \sigma^2)$.

A more interesting reaction to the book's central agenda is to note that all of the assumptions about the data are always approximations and all regression analyses will be imperfect. The yardstick is not perfection but usefulness. We will return to this issue in some depth later, but suffice it to say that the impossibility of perfection does not mean that anything goes. And if "usefulness" is to be the yardstick, usefulness cannot just be asserted; it has to be demonstrated. For example, just because a paper using regression analysis is published in a peer-reviewed journal does not mean that a policy (or scientific) discourse has been advanced.

In the chapters to follow, the goal is to unpack what goes into a proper regression analysis. Some of this is well understood and well explained in any number of textbooks. But even the best treatments are often incomplete, some for lack of space or because other issues are more salient. We will see that when the data are generated in a manner required for the investigator's analytical goals, regression analysis can be an instructive tool. If not, the results can be terribly misleading. In the end, we will see that regression has too often been applied to answer questions for which it was ill equipped. Misinformed science and policy are the inevitable result. We will also see that the solution is either to pose questions that can be usefully answered with regression analysis using the data on hand or, when possible, to collect the data needed. This will often mean lowering aspirations or putting in a lot more effort at the front end.

The aim is not to write a textbook on regression. There are already many, some quite good. This book assumes that the reader has already been through at least one such book. Readers are invited in the pages ahead to reconsider what they know about regression analysis when it is applied to real data sets. In some cases, this will require, in the words of David Freedman (2001:1), "the suspension of belief." Sometimes, the material will need to be approached with earlier understandings about regression analysis at least temporarily on hold.

Finally, the material to be covered draws heavily on real policy applications. However, because the point is to raise statistical issues, most of the detail that speaks to other concerns is not included. Readers who share those concerns will need to look elsewhere. Also, in many cases, extensive insider knowledge about the policy applications is required. What commonly is reported in professional journals or official documents is insufficient. As a result, the applications draw very heavily on my own experience. The selection of applications discussed should not distort the general points to be made. They are only meant to be illustrative.

2 A Grounded Introduction to Regression Analysis

2.1 Some Examples of Regression Analysis

The best place to start is with some examples of what the fuss is all about. Following are some illustrations of policy-relevant regression analyses. The rendering of each example is necessarily brief, and many key concepts are not defined. These and other important notions will be addressed extensively in later chapters. Any serious consideration of the strengths and weaknesses of the studies will have to wait. The illustrations are meant solely to launch the discussion.

2.1.1 Abortion and Subsequent Crime

Social policy surrounding abortion has always been controversial and perhaps even more so since *Roe v. Wade* in 1973. Donohue and Levitt (2001) add to the controversy when they examine possible causal relationships between the legalization of abortion and declines in crime nearly two decades later. Two mechanisms are suggested: (a) the size of the population at risk is reduced and (b) unwanted children, who would likely receive inferior care, are not born. The first mechanism lowers the number of potential perpetrators and victims overall. The second lowers the number of children more likely to be associated with serious criminal conduct. Using regression analysis, Donohue and Levitt find the anticipated reduction in crime. One conclusion tossed into the policy area is that at least part of the reductions in street crime, beginning in the early 1990s, resulted from a substantial increase in the number of abortions nearly two decades earlier.

The initial response from the academic community was highly critical. Joyce (2001), using different regression models, failed to find any meaningful statistical relationships between the legalization of abortion and subsequent crime. Lott and Whitley (2001), using still other regression models and somewhat different data, claim that the relationship may well be positive; legalization of abortion causes subsequent increases in crime.

All three studies use the state as the unit of analysis and capitalize on some states legalizing abortion a bit before others. Although *Roe v. Wade* gave women nationwide the right to have an abortion, some states had legalized abortion a few years before the 1973 decision. Consequently, the states that legalized abortion later can serve as a comparison group for the states that legalized abortion earlier. If abortion affects subsequent crime, its effects should be found for the early legalizers and not the late legalizers.

For example, suppose that State A legalized abortion beginning in 1970 and State B legalized abortion in 1973. If there are subsequent crime reductions because of legalized abortion, State A should begin experiencing them 3 years earlier (e.g., 1985 compared with 1988). Thus, during that 3-year window, State B is a control observation for State A. The five states that repealed their antiabortion laws before 1973 (New York, Washington, Alaska, Hawaii, and California) are therefore the experimental group, with all other states as the control group.

For each study, a variety of crime measures served as the response variable, hypothesized to decline in the late 1980s or early 1990s. The key analyses in each article introduce, through regression-based causal modeling, an explicit representation of the essential causal mechanisms; the regression model was a causal model. As a result, a variety of statistical controls are introduced for the many potential confounded variables at the state level. These variables are almost anything that might affect aggregate crime: a range of demographic factors, the economic climate, crime control initiatives, and social service programs or various proxies thereof. In some cases, the regression models employ over 100 parameters. In the end, regression analyses are used to make causal statements and construct statistical tests.

What does the scientific or policy community make of such results? Some might argue that more studies of higher quality are needed before the issues can be resolved. Alternatively, the questions being asked may not be the sort that can be credibly answered with observational data and regression analysis.

2.1.2 Mandatory Basic Education for Welfare Recipients

For more than a decade, federal funds have been available to states to provide basic education, coupled with mandatory employment programs, for welfare recipients. In a recent study, Boudett and Friedlander (1997) asked whether such education is beneficial. Their earlier work, based on the GAIN (Greater

Avenues for Independence) welfare-to-work randomized experiment in California, found that the educational component of the program had no demonstrable impact. That is, when the randomly assigned members of the experimental group were compared with the randomly assigned members of the control group, the average achievement scores for the two groups were effectively the same, and routine significance tests failed to reject the null hypothesis of no treatment effect. Regression analysis was used to arrive at these conclusions, which seemed to be quite compelling on their face.

However, not all members of the experimental group participated in the basic educational component of GAIN. Thus, random assignment was really to "intention to treat." Perhaps the null findings resulted from the inability to deliver the educational intervention to all who were supposed to get it.

In response, Boudett and Friedlander (1997) examine the impact of actual participation. Random assignment no longer applied, so it was necessary to introduce through regression analysis approximately 20 control variables that might influence who participated in the basic education program and later performance on achievement tests. Random assignment to GAIN was used as an instrumental variable in the estimation of the education effects because it was likely to meet the assumptions required (Angrist et al., 1996). Several variants on the basic model were employed as well. In the end, there was a bit stronger indication that basic education programs might raise the achievement scores of welfare recipients. But the improvements were small in practical terms. The results probably did not change any minds about the lack of educational effects.

2.1.3 Gender and Academic Salaries

The regression analyses used in the study of abortion legalization and the impact of basic education for welfare recipients are driven by very high ambitions: to determine the causal impact of abortion legalization or the causal impact of educational programs while taking into account through statistical inference the impact of random sampling error. Similar goals are common in studies of sex discrimination in salary determination (Gray, 1993). But regression analysis can be usefully applied when ambitions are far more modest.

In the fall of 2000, a committee at UCLA composed of faculty and administrators issued an interim report on gender equity at that university (Currie and Kivelson, 2000). In that report, rather complicated regression analyses using current payroll records were presented, showing differences in average salaries for men and women faculty members. The goal was to characterize patterns in those records, which were treated as the population; no use was made of statistical inference. No causal inferences were to be made from the regression analysis itself, and, consequently, there was no attempt to represent explicitly in the regression model the actual causal mechanisms.[1] Excluding the medical and dental schools for lack of good data, on average, male faculty members earned about 15% more than female faculty members. When statistical controls were introduced for seniority and the highest degree earned, the gap dropped to about 11%. When academic rank and department were added to the regression model, the disparity fell to a little over 2%. An inspection of the regression coefficients suggested that the bulk of the income differences between men and women were associated with differences in average ranks. In particular, there were very few women at the highest ranks, where the largest salaries were to be found. This, in turn, led to a number of recommendations for further study of the promotion process and several changes in current policies. And all this was done without using the regression analyses to make causal statements and without formal tests or confidence intervals. The regression analysis served as a data-reduction technique by providing a description of patterns in data on hand.

2.1.4 Climate Change and Water Resources in India

Regression analysis rarely plays a central role in the study of physical and biological phenomena. And the regression analyses used tend to be comparatively simple, even for complicated and politically controversial topics such as global warming.

For example, in a paper on the implications of climate change on water resources in India, Lal (2001) regresses mean annual surface air temperature on year for the period between 1881 and 1997. He uses the regression parameters to describe a positive linear trend of about half a degree Celsius per 100 years. No statistical inferences are made. The goal is solely description. He concludes that there is evidence of a strong warming trend.

2.1.5 Deforestation and Soil Erosion in the Yangtze River Valley

Deforestation is linked to global warming and has a host of other environmental implications. Controlling deforestation has been a critical policy concern for some time, especially in developing nations.

Cheng (1999) uses regression analysis to examine the relationship between annual precipitation and runoff in the Upper Yangtze River Valley. The analyses are undertaken for different decades to study the impact that deforestation might have on soil loss. Deforestation has increased, and Cheng reports that the relationship between precipitation and runoff has strengthened during the past 30 years. But the regression model employed does not represent any causal

[1] This is not to say that causal ideas played no role. The point is that the regression analysis was not based on a "causal model" in the sense that will be considered at length in later chapters.

mechanisms explicitly. Causal inferences are based on information not in the data or the regression model. The regression results are consistent with hydrological theory and empirical field studies indicating that deforestation increases the strength of the relationship between precipitation and runoff. The regression results are a way to describe important physical relationships of which causal links are justified elsewhere.

2.1.6 Epidemics of Hepatitis C

Explicit causal modeling using regression analysis is sometimes done in the natural sciences. Pybus and colleagues (2001) use regression analysis to develop a causal model for the transmission of the hepatitis C virus (HCV). The study capitalizes on the recent insight that the HCV gene sequences (and gene sequences more generally) contain information about earlier population dynamics useful for inferring how a current epidemic might unfold.

The response variable used by Pybus et al. (2001) is the number of infections at a given moment in time. The dynamics require that units of nucleotide substitutions per site be mapped into units of conventional time (e.g., years). Then the causal variable is time itself. A logistic functional form is assumed containing three parameters for which values can be estimated: (a) the growth rate of the disease in a population of people, all of whom are susceptible; (b) the number of infected people at time 0; and (c) a shape parameter for the logistic curve. The model is applied to different HCV strains, and the various time paths of simulated epidemics are displayed. Confidence intervals are provided for the parameter estimates. Among the many conclusions is that different strains of the virus evidence different epidemic potential. The post hoc explanation is that their means of transmission differ. If this explanation is correct, it has important implications for public health officials trying to control the spread of hepatitis C.

2.1.7 Onward and Upward

It should be clear that regression analysis can be used in a variety of fields and that how much information of what kind one wrings from the analysis varies widely. One issue is whether the regression model is a causal model. Another issue is whether statistical inference will be undertaken. These and other matters will eventually be addressed in considerable detail. But before that is done, it is necessary to revisit some fundamentals. These are the fundamentals that can be easily understood but then get lost as the regression vehicle gets loaded down with lots of additional cargo. This is one of the moments when a temporary suspension of belief will be useful. Try to forget what you already know about regression analysis for the rest of this chapter.

2.2 What Is Regression Analysis?

Cook and Weisberg (1999:27) provide an unusually clear definition of regression analysis consistent with standard statistical practice: "[to understand] as far as possible with the available data how the conditional distribution of the response y varies across subpopulations determined by the possible values of the predictor or predictors." That is, one is interested in how the entire distribution of y may vary with values of the predictors. In practice, attention is usually directed toward one or more summary statistics from the conditional distribution, often the mean and the variance, but those are just special cases. In the examples presented in the previous chapter, variation in the mean of each conditional distribution was the primary focus. Donohue and Levitt (2001), for example, were interested in how the mean amount of crime changed after *Roe v. Wade*. However, limiting one's attention to the mean already implies a decision about what matters that can rest heavily on information beyond the data themselves; we are not ready to go there yet.

Note also that there is nothing in the definition about hypothesis tests or confidence intervals. Likewise, cause and effect is not mentioned. Indeed, variation in the predictors stems from looking at different *subsets* of the data. In the definition, there is no talk about interventions, and the predictors are not being manipulated in any way whatsoever. Again using the Donohue and Levitt article (2001) as an example, early adopter states simply are compared with late adopter states.

We turn to some fictitious data to provide a concrete sense of what this all means.

2.2.1 A Simple Illustration

We begin with a set of observational units. These units can be just about anything: people, schools, cities, political parties, businesses, water samples, stands of trees, chemical compounds, earthquake faults, herds of caribou, and so on. They can also be locations in time and/or space that might be found, for instance, in a lake at certain times of the day or a grassland in certain seasons. These observational units have characteristics of interest that are denoted by numbers, although numbers may indicate only a rank or membership in a category.

The numbers are organized so that those characterizing the same feature of the observational units are collected in an array with as many elements as there are observational units. There will often be several such arrays or more. Each array is a variable, and the collection of all arrays is a data set.

Imagine now a data set with three variables: x, z, and y. For each, there are 200 observational units. At this point, the variables and the observational units have no subject matter content. The variable y will be taken as the response,

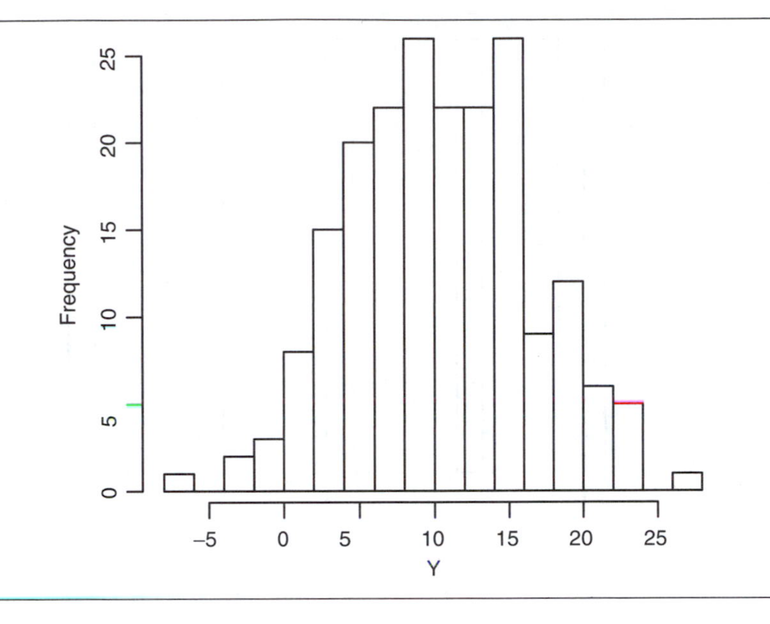

Figure 2.1. Histogram of y

with x and z as predictors. To simplify the exposition, all three will be treated as equal-interval variables. But there is nothing in the definition of regression analysis making this a requirement, and, for example, we could have proceeded with x, z, and y as categorical variables.

Consider first the histogram for y shown in Figure 2.1. There are 20 bins, which in this case means that there is not much collapsing of the y values. As a result, very little information is lost in the graph. One can see the range of values (about 30), the approximate center of the distribution (about 10), and that the distribution is not particularly skewed (but certainly not even close to normal). One might also guess that the standard deviation is around 6.

Suppose x is the key predictor. There are 5 discrete values, all with 40 observations. From Figure 2.2, we see that x has a rectangular distribution with a center at 3 (which equals the mean and median) and a range of 4. The standard deviation is around 1.5.

For now, suppose z is a discrete variable like x and is associated with x. The variable z may be confounded with x and y if it is also associated with y. By the usual definition, a confounder must be associated with *both* the response and a given predictor. Thus, if z were associated with only x or y (or neither), it would not be a confounder. This will matter in later chapters.

From Figure 2.3, we see that the range of z is about 14. The center of the distribution is around 3, there is again no strong skewing, and the standard deviation is around 3.

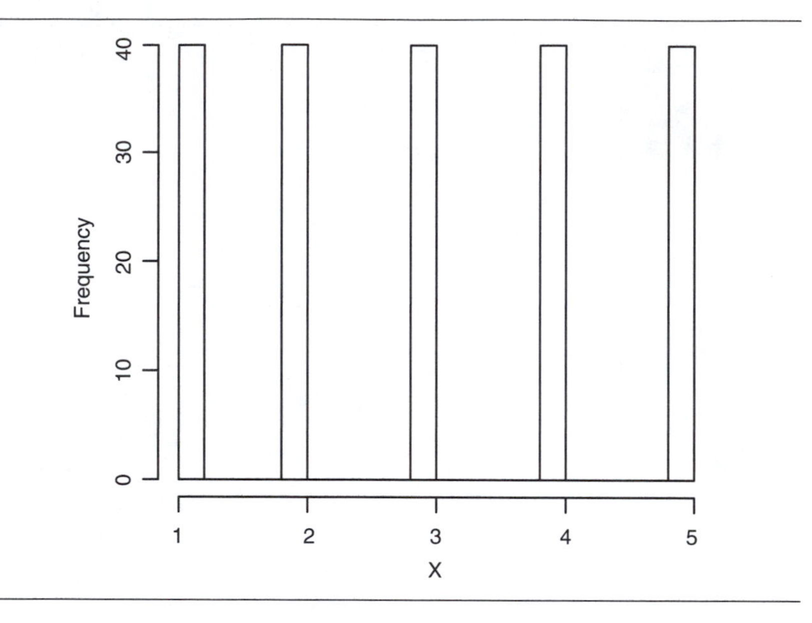

Figure 2.2. Histogram of x

Figure 2.4 shows a scatter plot of y on x. Each vertical slice of the data represents a conditional distribution of y given a particular value of x (i.e., $y|x = \tilde{x}$). By our earlier definition, regression analysis considers *how each of these conditional distributions may differ depending on the value of x chosen.* Here, there are five such distributions to compare.

It is easy to see that the distributions shift upward as one moves from left to right. There is also some evidence for a bit more variability in the conditional distribution of y for $x = 5$. Typically, an investigator focuses on features of the conditional distribution of particular interest, such as the conditional mean of y, $\bar{y}|x = \tilde{x}$. Here, there are five conditional means: 4.6, 7.0, 11.1, 13.5, and 16.2 going from left to right. Clearly, the mean of y is increasing with larger values of x. One might also be interested in the conditional variance of y, $\text{Var}(y|x = \tilde{x})$. For these data, those variances are 16.8, 13.7, 14.4, 16.9, and 25.0 going from left to right. A simple pattern is hard to discern except that the distribution of y when x is 5 has a greater spread than the rest.

The examination of Figure 2.4 constitutes a regression analysis. It is nothing more than the study of how the distribution of y (or certain features of that distribution) varies with different values of x. In the words of the old Peggy Lee song, "That's all there is." There is no talk about correlations, slopes, causes, t-tests, variance explained, model selection, or any of the stuff that dominates

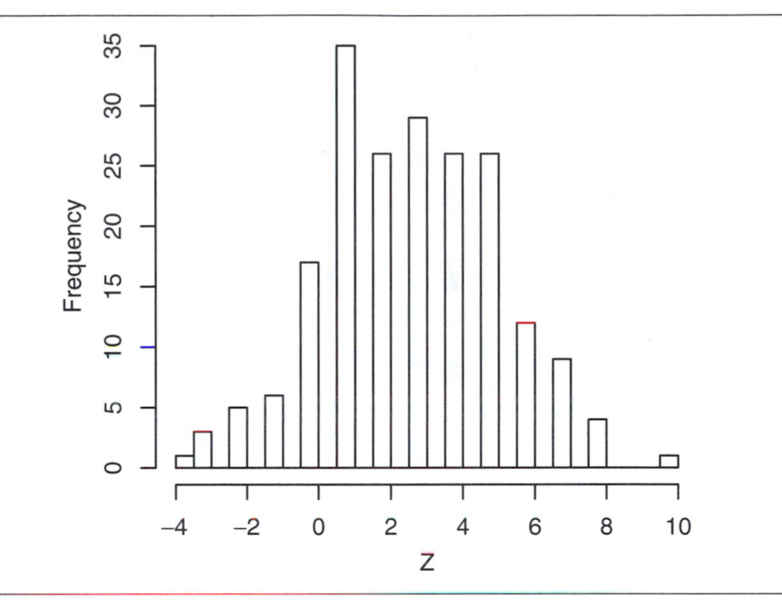

Figure 2.3. Histogram of z

applications of regression analysis to real data. And there is a very good reason: The moment one moves beyond the study of conditional distributions, information must be introduced that is *not* contained in the data themselves. Thus, for example, there is nothing in the data themselves that could ever determine that x is a cause of y. Nor is there anything in the data to indicate whether y should be treated as a random variable or whether the x can be taken at face value without measurement error. The data are, after all, just a collection of numbers. These and other issues all depend on how the data were generated and what is known about those processes. Was there random sampling, for instance. What are the steps by which x was measured? Does x represent an intervention? This is a theme to which we will return many times and in increasing depth.

2.2.2 Controlling for a Third Variable

Another way to think about Figure 2.4 is that each conditional distribution is the distribution of y with x "held constant" at $x = \tilde{x}$. By "held constant," one means that the value of x is fixed at a particular value, in this case, a 1, a 2, a 3, a 4, or a 5. When x is fixed at a particular value, it denotes that all of the cases have that value and only that value for x.

This idea can be applied to a third variable. One can examine the conditional distribution of y for different values of x, conditioning on a third

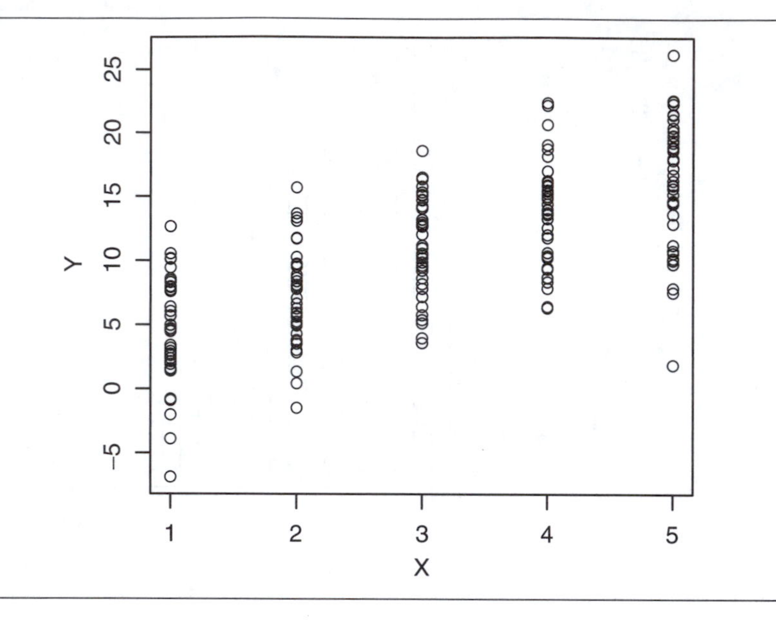

Figure 2.4. Scatter Plot of y on x

variable z. In effect, one is conditioning on both x and z: $y|(x, z)$. Figure 2.5 is a "conditional scatter plot," known as a "coplot," which displays the conditional distribution of y for different values of x, holding z constant at different values. Each scatter plot shows y and x as usual but for the subset of cases with $z = \tilde{z}$. Because there are 14 different values for z, there are 14 scatter plots. Each of these can be examined in the same manner as the single scatter plot in Figure 2.4.

The top panel shows the intervals into which the conditioning variable (here, z) is split. For ease of interpretation, each of these intervals has been set to the single integer value for z, overlaid on each bar. So the first subset of the data is for $z = -4$. This corresponds to the scatter plot in the lowest left corner. For $z = -3$, the corresponding scatter plot is just to the right. One proceeds in this fashion from left to right until the end of the row and then to the far left scatter plot in the row immediately above.

What can be observed? First, there are too few observations in some of the scatter plots to learn much of anything. This is especially true for scatter plots in which the value of z is near either tail of the z distribution. Second, when there is a reasonable number of observations, there is in each scatter plot an apparent upward movement of the distribution of y with larger values of x. Third, the rate of increase looks to be about the same in each plot. Fourth, z has an independent association with y because the data within each plot move up vertically as one moves from plot to plot. Finally, the common rate of increase

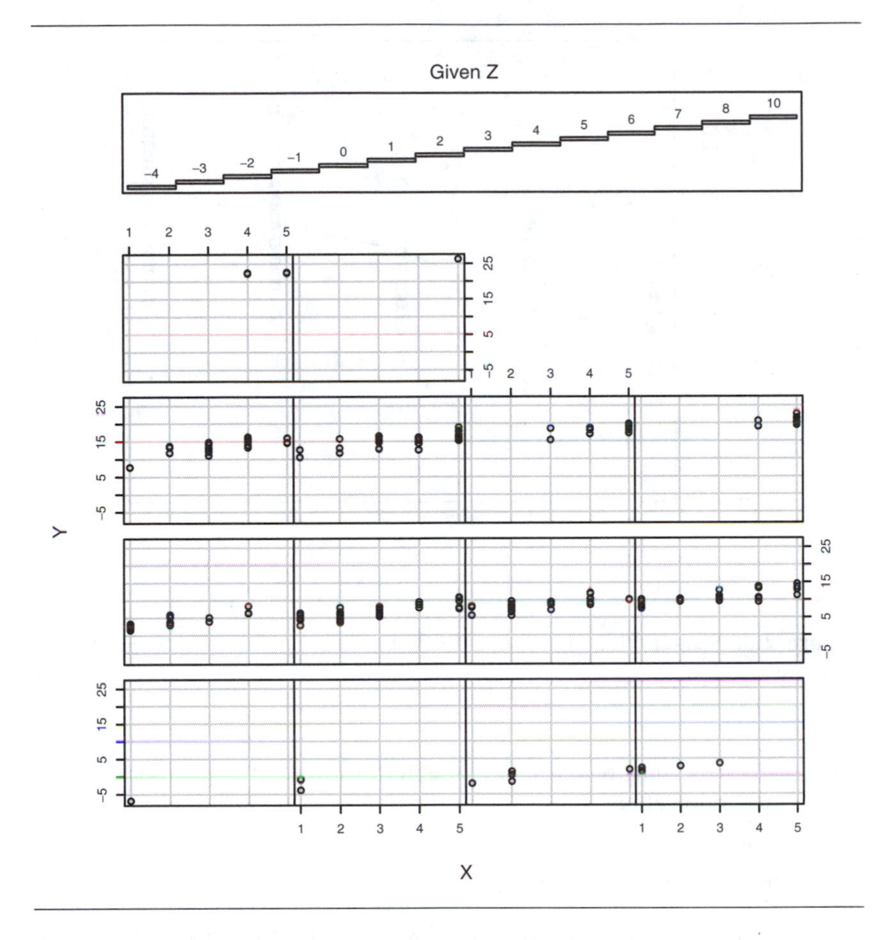

Figure 2.5. Scatter Plot of y on x Conditional Upon z

is less dramatic than when z was not held constant. (Compare Figure 2.5 with Figure 2.4.) In fact, when z is ignored, the mean of y increases about 3 units for every unit increase in x. When z is held constant and there is a sufficient number of observations, that increase drops to about 1 unit. Holding z constant alters the conditional relationship between y and x because z is associated with both x and y and, as such, is a confounder.

What would have happened in Figure 2.5 if the different scatter plots would have shown meaningfully different relationships between y and x? For example, some might show the distribution of y increasing, on the average, with x, and some might show the distribution of y decreasing, on the average, with x. When the conditional distribution between two variables differs

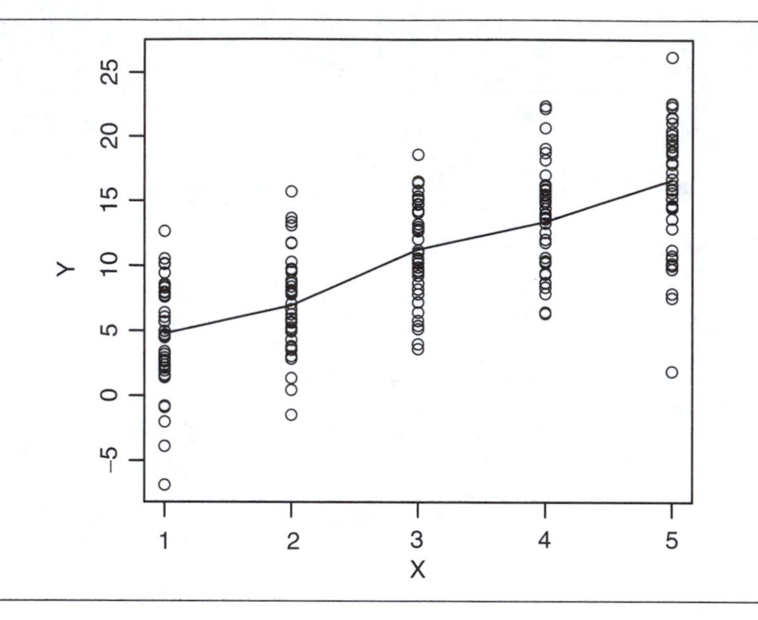

Figure 2.6. Scatter Plot of y on x With Broken Line Through the Means of y

importantly depending on the values of a third variable, it is common to speak about "interaction effects."

2.2.3 Imposing a Smoother

Suppose one were solely interested in how the mean of y varied with different values of x.[2] Then it might be useful to systematically characterize the "path" of these means. Drawing a broken line connecting the means would be one easy way to help visualize how the means vary. Figure 2.6 shows the result.

However, a broken line is not easily described; a smoother line would be more simple. And in this case, a straight line (i.e., the smoothest smoother) might still capture the essential features of the path of the means. Figure 2.7 shows an overlay of a straight line. Clearly, some information has been lost,

[2]There is nothing special about this interest. One might have chosen a different measure of central tendency (e.g., the median) or some other location in the conditional distribution of y, such as the 90th percentile. Or one might be interested in the variance of the conditional distribution of y or some other measure of spread. But it is common in policy applications to focus on the mean, and using the mean as the central tendency measure has some convenient statistical consequences we shall address later.

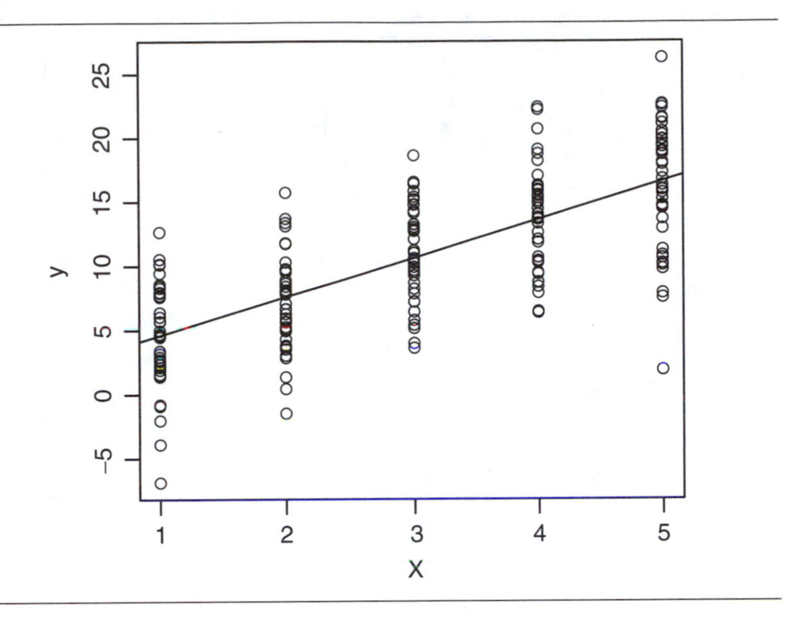

Figure 2.7. Scatter Plot of y on x With Linear Overlay

but if one is only interested in a linear trend, that information is probably not important.

With the use of a straight line to characterize the path of the means, one is imposing a particular representation on the data. There is nothing in the data requiring a linear summary; indeed, the broken line in Figure 2.6 captures the path of the means perfectly. Moreover, there is a limitless number of straight lines one could have imposed on the data. To overlay a particular line representing the path of the means, there needs to be a rationale for picking a single line. This too must come from outside of the data. One needs a way for deciding which particular line of the limitless possibilities is the "best" line for one's purposes. There are several different definitions of "best" that are used in practice, which will be considered later.[3]

Figure 2.8 shows a case where a particular straight line chosen would seem to throw out too much information; the straight line imposed on the data does not seem to satisfactorily capture the central tendencies of $y|x$. And even a brief inspection of the figure suggests that a curved line would probably do much better. But exactly what kind of curved line, and precisely where on the scatter plot would it be placed? Once again, there is nothing in the data alone that can tell us.

[3]The same issues would arise had we tried to summarize the path of the means for each of the scatter plots contained in the coplot.

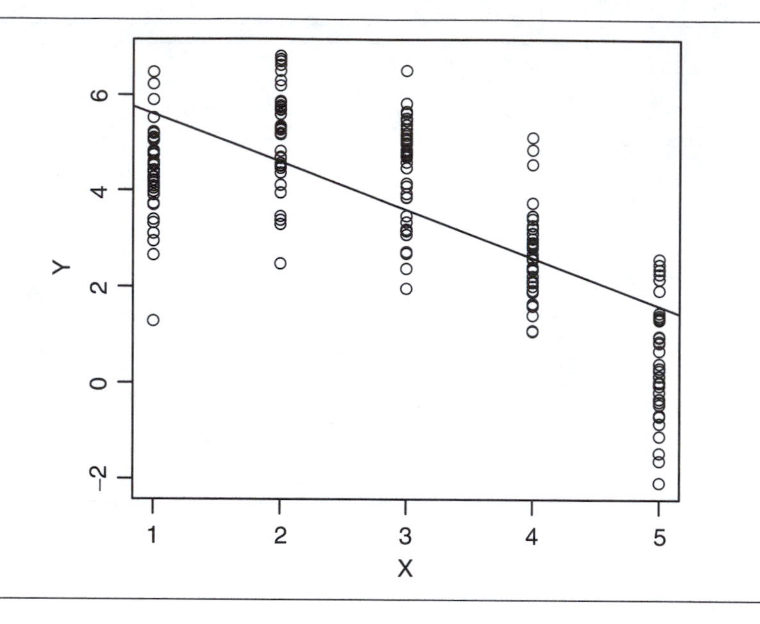

Figure 2.8. Scatter Plot of Another y on x

2.3 Getting From Data to Stories

Although the data used in regression analysis can provide only conditional distributions, researchers routinely draw inferences that go far beyond the information contained in those distributions. The inferences are the basis of a subject matter "story" the researchers tell.

Information that is used to transform conditional distributions into stories comes in two forms. The first form depends on judgment calls by the data analyst, typically driven by the empirical question(s) at issue and which features of the conditional distribution of y are important. What summary statistics should be used to represent them? What is the balance between detail and ease of analysis? What role should graphics play? And so on. Such discretionary decisions are inevitable because judgment calls are a necessary part of doing good empirical work (Berk, 1977). They are often a key point at which creativity and intuition are introduced. Although these types of discretionary decisions should always be examined, and although they will be addressed in the pages ahead, they will not be a central concern.

A second kind of information will be the primary focus: information introduced from outside of the data that commits the researcher to a particular vision of how the natural and social world works. Often, this information will be an account, sometimes by implication only, about *how the data were generated.*

Thus, one important issue is whether the data were generated by probability sampling or, as we will see later, by a proxy or even a substitute for it. Alternatively, the data may be a "convenience sample" or an entire population. The differences between data that are generated through probability sampling, nonprobability procedures, or as a population will figure centrally in later discussions of statistical inference. And what the researcher decides, often by default, becomes a statement about how the world works.

A second important issue is whether there is an intervention, ideally over which the researcher has had some real control. Although this will be considered at length eventually, if there is no such intervention, the data represent an "observational study."

If there has been an intervention, another central matter is whether there has also been random assignment to treatments. If observational units are assigned to treatments by random assignment, the data were generated as a "true experiment." If not, one has a "quasi-experiment." The existence and nature of an intervention will have critical implications for causal inference and, at the same time, will require another commitment to how the world works.

Consider again the example of the impact of legalizing abortion on subsequent crime. For that study, y is the amount of crime; x is the legalization of abortion (represented as a binary variable); and z can be thought of as all of the control variables, such as measures of the local labor market, crime control efforts, and the state-level demographic mix. The information in the data essential for regression analysis is a set of conditional distributions much like Figure 2.5. That is, one can examine how the distribution for the amount of crime varies by whether a state has or has not legalized abortion, conditioning on whatever else seems relevant. There is nothing in the data themselves about whether the legalization of abortion can affect the amount of crime. There is nothing in the data themselves about what the set of states represents or how the states were chosen. Yet these matters must be resolved for the analysis to move beyond description of the data on hand. And with the resolution necessarily comes statements that must be taken as factual.

If the goal is to do more than describe the data on hand, information must be introduced that cannot be contained in the data themselves. Such information is not a mere technical convenience but a statement about processes operating in the real world. To answer the empirical questions posed by the data analyst, other empirical questions must be sensibly answered first. Yet in the pages ahead, a case will be made that these questions, upon which the data analysis fundamentally depends, are typically given short shrift. And if the premises upon which the analysis rests are, at best, cartoons, how seriously should results of the analysis be taken? The bottom line is simple: If so much depends on the information brought in from outside of the data, that information had better be pretty damn good.

3 Simple Linear Regression

3.1 Introduction

The goal of this chapter is to examine how one gets from a two-variable scatter plot to two-variable (simple) linear regression. As before, interpretative issues will be emphasized: how one uses regression analysis to make sense of a data set. This chapter, along with the next two, will not move beyond two variables. Remaining within the simple regression framework will simplify the exposition, and most of the important lessons learned will generalize to the regression analyses using more than one predictor.

As before, we begin with a data set in which the aim is to describe how the conditional distribution of some variable y varies depending on the values of another variable x. The roles of "predictor" and "response" are determined by the scientific or policy question at hand and imply nothing necessarily about cause and effect.

To help begin the discussion, consider the following example. In many major cities in the United States, the ozone in smog can have serious health consequences for young children, the elderly, and people with existing respiratory problems. In such cities, it is common to call "smog alerts" when high ozone concentrations are anticipated. During these alerts, people at risk are advised to limit their physical activities and stay indoors.

It has long been recognized that ozone concentrations tend to build up as the temperature increases throughout the late morning and early afternoon. Thus, public health officials in a particular city might be interested in the local relationship between temperature and ozone concentrations, especially during the summer months.

For a particular summer, city air-quality officials record the daily high temperature and ozone concentrations in the center of the city. They decide in their analysis to focus on how the mean of the ozone concentrations varies with temperature. Such information could help them understand when the health risks from ozone are likely to be the greatest and might even be useful for forecasting insofar as daytime temperatures could be projected reasonably well even a few hours in advance.

So far, there is nothing new. There is a need for a regression analysis, which has already been discussed. But suppose—for simplicity of interpretation or because of theoretical understandings about how ozone concentrations and temperature are related—there is a desire to characterize with a straight line how mean ozone concentrations are related to temperature. What then? How does one impose a linear function on the data?

3.2 Describing a Conditional Relationship With a Straight Line

Consider the following identity in which $\bar{y}$ represents the mean of y.[1]

Let

$$y|x = \bar{y}|x + (y|x - \bar{y}|x) = \bar{y}|x + e|x, \tag{3.1}$$

where the last term is an "error" only in the arithmetic sense. The error is what is left over after the conditional mean of y is subtracted from the observed y. In a data set, each value of y, given a value for x, equals a sum of a conditional mean and a conditional deviation from that mean. This is true by definition. Note that the errors around each conditional mean of y have a mean of zero because they are deviations around a mean (such deviations always sum to zero). This is a more important point than it might seem because if, for any reason, $\bar{e}|x \neq 0$, there can be very important consequences, as we shall see shortly.

[1]The data are at this point being taken at face value. They are neither a sample nor a population because such a designation requires information about how the data were generated. We will get to such issues later. As a result, the expectation operator for a sample does not make formal sense, and a symbol for a population parameter does not make sense either.

Although $\bar{e}|x = 0$, at this point we allow for nonconstant variance in which $\text{Var}(e|x) = \text{Var}(y|x)$. That is, variation around the conditional means, given x, does not have to have the same spread for all values of x.

Suppose y represents ozone concentrations and x represents temperature. One could stop the technical discussion here and proceed with the sorts of analyses of conditional means we undertook in the previous chapter. One might well study a scatter plot with temperature on the horizontal axis and ozone concentrations on the vertical axis. One would be doing a perfectly legitimate regression analysis.

But suppose there were a desire to summarize the path of the means with a straight line. Such a summary might help convey easily the relationship between temperature and ozone; the straight line is a heuristic device, nothing more.

More formally, we let

$$\bar{y}|x = \eta_0 + \eta_1 x, \tag{3.2}$$

where η_0 represents the intercept and η_1 represents the slope of a straight line. The mean of y is a linear function of x. This implies that

$$y|x = \eta_0 + \eta_1 x + e|x. \tag{3.3}$$

If it is *really* true that the means of y are a linear function of x, then as before, $\bar{e}|x = 0$. This is because the line imposed runs right through each of the conditional means of y. In a very important sense, nothing has been lost as a result of characterizing with a straight line how the means of y depend on x. And a lot of simplicity has been gained. Once you know that line, you pretty much know the story.

As long as the goal is solely to construct a linear description of the path of the means of y, whether the mean $\bar{e}|x = 0$ may not matter much; given a prior commitment to the linear form, whether the conditional mean of the errors is zero is essentially irrelevant. Should the conditional mean of the errors not be zero, there is information in the path of the means that is not being exploited. The description is in some sense incomplete. But presumably, the researcher has decided already that a linear description is sufficient for the purposes at hand.

Figure 3.1 shows for a (fictitious) data set a linear summary of the relationship between ozone concentrations and temperature. We will see later that this is the usual least squares line, but for the current discussion, any straight line will do that characterizes the path of the means reasonably well.

The intercept η_0 is the mean of y when the value of x equals zero. This value is needed to locate the straight line vertically on the scatter plot, but it may or may not make any subject matter sense. For example, in the ozone illustration, η_0 makes no subject matter sense because it is a negative number. (Ozone concentrations cannot be negative.) The linear relationship is being extrapolated well beyond where there are any observations. If there were observations for

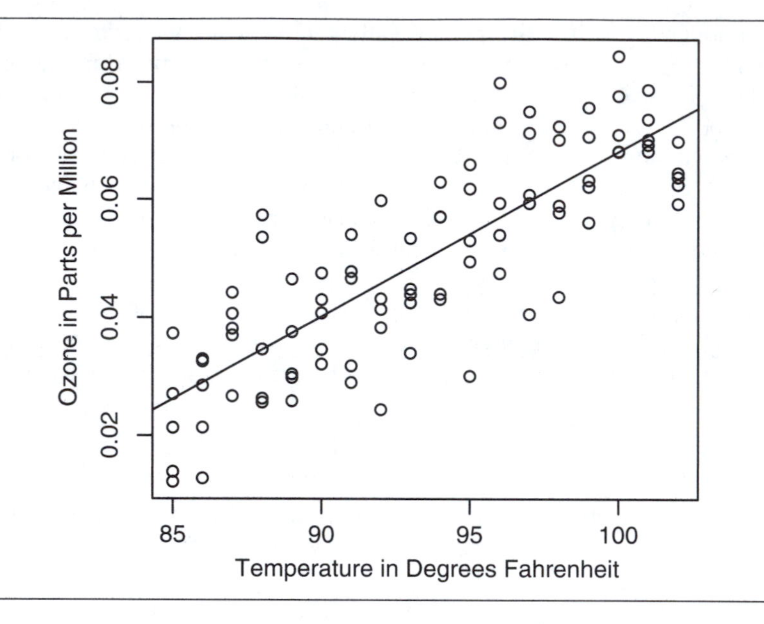

Figure 3.1. Regression of Ozone on Daily High Temperature

temperature values much lower than the ones recorded, it is certain that either a less step linear summary would represent the data more appropriately, or, more likely, the linear relationship would be superseded by a curved relationship.

The slope η_1 denotes the change in the mean of y for a 1 unit change in x. Here, that is about 0.004; for every additional degree of temperature, the average ozone concentration increases 0.004 parts per million. But be clear that no cause and effect is necessarily implied. The slope is merely a convenient summary of how the conditional mean of y varies with x, nothing more.[2]

3.3 Defining the "Best" Line

There is a limitless number of straight lines one might impose to capture the path of the means. How is a single line selected?

[2]Ozone concentrations are affected in a complicated and nonlinear fashion by many factors, such as the concentration of ozone precursors (e.g., volatile hydrocarbons, NO_x), sunlight, and the direction and strength of prevailing winds.

Recall that, by definition, for a given data set

$$y|x = \bar{y}|x + e|x. \tag{3.4}$$

Also recall that the mean is the central tendency measure for which the sum of the squared deviations around the mean is as small as possible. Another measure of central tendency would produce a larger sum of squared deviations (unless it happened to equal the mean). The mean, therefore, is a "least squares" summary statistic and, under the least squares criterion, is the central tendency statistic that fits the data best. It follows that each conditional mean also has this property.

Then if the goal of a linear overlay is to characterize well the path of the means, it might well make sense to apply the least squares criterion again. That is, one would want to find values for η_0 and η_1 so that a least squares criterion was met.

Looking again at the linear summary

$$y|x = \eta_0 + \eta_1 x + e|x, \tag{3.5}$$

the goal would be to minimize the sum of the squared deviations around the line (represented by e), which are akin to the deviations around each mean. And at this point, with description as the goal, no additional assumptions are required.

More formally, we begin with an objective function to specify what exactly we want to minimize. For the least squares criterion, we use

$$RSS(h_0, h_1) = \sum_{i=1}^{n} (y_i - [h_0 + h_1 x_i])^2, \tag{3.6}$$

where h_0 and h_1 are two candidate values for η_0 and η_1, respectively, and *RSS* stands for the residual sum of squares. Minimizing the residual sum of squares leads to the conventional least squares formulas for $\hat{\eta}_0$ and $\hat{\eta}_1$ that, in turn, define the least squares line. At this point, the notation $\hat{(.)}$ merely denotes that the statistic in question characterizes some feature of a data set based on a least squares objective function. It has absolutely nothing to do with estimates of population parameters.

For all practical purposes, the least squares formulas can always be applied. The question is whether the least squares criterion is responsive to the investigator's goals. Just as for the mean itself, the least squares objective function is quadratic. This implies that deviations farther from the line are given especially heavy weight by the squaring process compared with a linear criterion. One important consequence is that a few very atypical observations can have a dramatic effect on where the least squares line is placed.

Recall that the median is the value that minimizes the sum of the absolute values of the deviations. Its objective function is piecewise linear rather than quadratic. This leads to another kind of regression summary in which the goal is to represent the path of the conditional medians rather than the path of conditional means. And just as the median is resistant to outliers, median regression is resistant to the impact of large deviations. We will return to this issue later when "influence" is discussed. For now, however, it may suffice to note that median regression (also called "L1" regression) has never caught on with applied researchers.[3]

A second consequence of the least squares criterion is that deviations above the least squares line are treated the same as deviations below the least squares line. The objective function is symmetric. There will sometimes be policy applications in which this symmetry is undesirable. If one thinks about the large deviations around the line as representing observations that are not well characterized by the least squares line, and if, in a given application, the costs of the errors are larger if they are positive rather than negative (or vice versa), the least squares symmetry may be misleading.

For example, in California (and more generally in the United States), soon after male inmates are officially admitted to prison, they are housed in a facility with a particular security level. The higher the security level, the more restrictive the setting. But higher security levels are more costly. The price per cell of a new high-security facility can exceed $150,000. The yearly expense of keeping an inmate in a high-security setting can exceed $25,000. Minimum-security facilities are sometimes an order of magnitude less expensive.

Thus, higher security housing needs to be rationed carefully. That rationing depends heavily on estimates of the risks for prison functioning posed by inmates. Among the risks of greatest concern are drug trafficking and various forms of violence directed at other inmates or prison staff. But insubordination in any number of guises or a more general reluctance to follow prison routines and procedures can be extremely disruptive.

Inmate placements are substantially determined by classification scores computed from background information (e.g., age, length of sentence, prior record). A classification score is supposed to indicate the likelihood of inmate misconduct.

The scoring system currently applied in California was developed using the results of several conventional regression analyses of data collected on inmates in the recent past. Symmetric objective functions were implicitly assumed. However, one might prefer a classification score that took more seriously the possibility of underestimating an inmate's risk rather than overestimating it. Failing to anticipate trouble might be more important than imposing unnecessary constraints on a prisoner's activities (or the reverse).

In practice, however, such concerns rarely seem to surface in policy-related research. Symmetric objective functions are the order of the day in part because

---

[3]Median regression is a special case of quantile regression in which the goal is to summarize the path of any particular quantile. The median is the 50th quantile.

they are more manageable for theoretical development and in part because they are the basis for most of the readily available software.

3.4 Some Useful Formulas

The least squares formulas for the regression line take the following form:

$$\hat{\eta}_1 = \frac{SXY}{SXX} = r(x, y)\frac{\mathrm{SD}(y)}{\mathrm{SD}(x)} = \sum_{i=1}^{n}\left(\frac{x_i - \bar{x}}{SXX}\right) y_i. \tag{3.7}$$

SXY is the sum of cross products for x and y, SXX is the sum of squares for x, $r(x, y)$ is the correlation between x and y, $\bar{x}$ is the mean of x, and SD(.) represents the standard deviation. One can see that the formula for the slope is a linear function of y. (If we condition on x, functions of x are constants.) The importance of this linearity will be considered in the next chapter.[4] The formula for the intercept is

$$\hat{\eta}_0 = \bar{y} - \hat{\eta}_1\bar{x}. \tag{3.8}$$

One implication of Equations 3.7 and 3.8 is that the regression line (fitted values) always goes through $\bar{y}$ and $\bar{x}$.

There is a simple way to get the RSS that shows why the RSS must be less than or equal to the sum of squares of y, SYY:

$$RSS = \sum_{i=1}^{n} \hat{e}_i^2 = SYY(1 - r^2(x, y)), \tag{3.9}$$

where $r^2(x, y)$ is the squared Pearson correlation between x and y. Thus, unless the path of the means is flat, one can fit the conditional distribution of y better using what is known about its dependence on x than if that dependence is ignored.

A popular measure of fit is

$$r^2(x, y) = 1 - \frac{RSS}{SYY} = \frac{SYY - RSS}{SYY}, \tag{3.10}$$

which represents the proportion of variance "explained." Sometimes, SYY–RSS is called the "regression sum of squares." And if one divides this by the degrees of freedom $(n - 2)$, it is sometimes called the "explained variance."

One must not lose sight of the interpretive differences between $\hat{\eta}_1$ and $r^2(x, y)$. The former represents how much the mean of y varies with a unit change in x.

[4]Treating $\bar{y}|x$ as a linear function of x, as one does in simple linear regression, is another matter.

The latter represents how tightly the observations fit around the regression line. These are very different features of the least squares line. Moreover, the absolute value of $\hat{\eta}_1$ can be large even if $r^2(x, y)$ is small, and vice versa. In this context, it can be very important for data analysts to avoid imprecise language when talking about either $\hat{\eta}_1$ or $r^2(x, y)$. For example, it can be confusing when data analysts refer to the proportion of variance explained as "strength of the relationship between y and x," or worse, imply that a high value of $r^2(x, y)$ means that the relationship between y and x is understood in a scientific sense. Likewise, $\hat{\eta}_1$ by itself does not represent a causal effect. It captures variation in the mean of y for different values of x. Why the mean of y varies in this manner is another issue.

3.5 Standardized Slopes

In certain disciplines, it is common to "standardize" the value of $\hat{\eta}_1$. Two forms are popular: the "elasticity" and the "beta coefficient." The elasticity is defined as the percentage by which the mean of y varies for a 1% change in x. The elasticity may be approximated as follows:

$$\hat{\epsilon} = \frac{\partial y/\bar{y}}{\partial x/\bar{x}} \simeq \hat{\eta}_1 \times \frac{\bar{x}}{\bar{y}}, \tag{3.11}$$

where $\bar{x}$ and $\bar{y}$ are the unconditional means of x and y, respectively. It can also be approximated for small changes in x by taking the log of x and y and then applying the computational equation for the slope to the logged data.

The beta coefficient is defined as how many standard deviations y varies on the average for a 1 SD change in x. The formula is

$$\hat{\beta} = \hat{\eta}_1 \times \frac{\mathrm{SD}(x)}{\mathrm{SD}(y)}, \tag{3.12}$$

where $\mathrm{SD}(x)$ and $\mathrm{SD}(y)$ refer to the standard deviation of x and y, respectively. Alternatively, it can be calculated by transforming x and y into z scores and then applying the computational equation for the slope to the transformed data. In this form, readers may recognize that the beta coefficient for the simple linear regression is nothing more than the Pearson correlation coefficient. Sometimes, Equation 3.12 is altered so that only the predictor is transformed. The term $\mathrm{SD}(y)$ is deleted. Then, the beta coefficient indicates how the mean of y varies for a 1 SD change in x.

In economics, elasticity is a widely used concept that has formal theoretical foundations. For economists, therefore, there will often be applications in which interest focuses more on an elasticity than on a regression coefficient. Standardization per se is not the point.

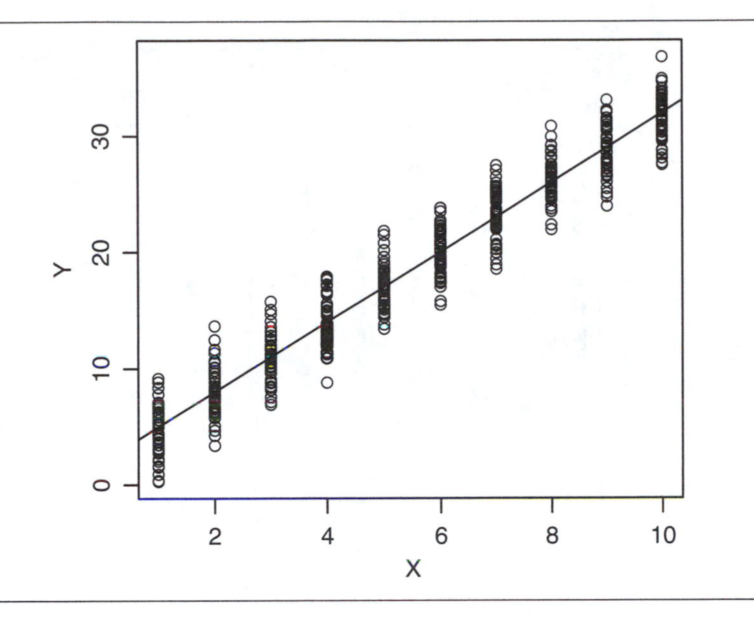

Figure 3.2. Regression With a Good Fit: Intercept = 2, Slope = 3, Beta = 0.97

But for both the elasticity and the beta coefficient, standardization can be a goal. If the units in which y and/or x as recorded have little intuitive meaning, some data analysts feel that they can better understand the size and meaning of the slope if it can be interpreted in either percentage units or standard deviation units. For example, x may be scores on a scale of stressful life events and y may be scores on a scale of symptoms associated with anxiety disorders. Then, it might be difficult to link either variable to some sense of how much variation is important. If y varies 3 units with a 1-unit change in x, does that represent an important difference in psychopathology? One proposed solution is to transform the variables into unit-free scales that are easier to interpret. However, when standardized coefficients are used, the associated text must be very carefully written.

Consider Figures 3.2 and 3.3. In both plots, one can see that the regression lines are similar. In fact, they both have an intercept of 2 and slope of 3; they are identical. But the beta coefficient for Figure 3.2 is 0.97, and the beta coefficient for Figure 3.3 is about one third the size (0.37). In this constructed example, the difference in the standardized coefficient results solely from the larger standard deviation for y in Figure 3.3.[5] Although the path of the means in the original units is exactly the same in both figures,[6] the standardized coefficients indicate

[5]In practice, the standard deviation of both x and y can affect the beta coefficient.

[6]Keep in mind that the vertical scales are different because, for Figure 3.3, y is more variable.

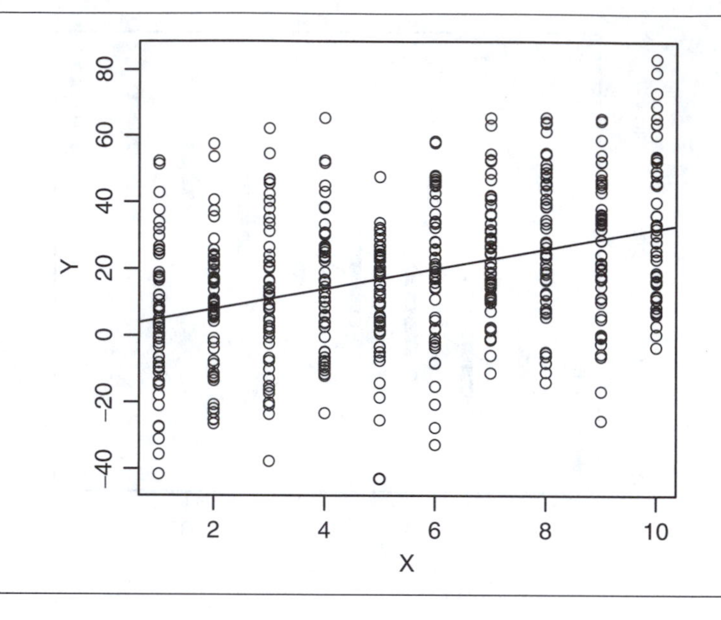

Figure 3.3. Regression With Bad Fit: Intercept = 2, Slope = 3, Beta = 0.37

that, in standard deviation units, the path of the means is about three times steeper in Figure 3.2 than in Figure 3.3. There is no contradiction as long as one keeps the units clear. But it is easy to make interpretative errors in practice. Consider the following example.

These days, standardized tests used to help determine admissions to college are under attack for a variety of reasons. One of the concerns about using SAT scores as a key factor in admissions to college is that SAT "prep" courses charge tuition and are therefore beyond the means of many low-income children. As a result, low-income children are disadvantaged. But a prior question is how effective these courses really are.

Suppose one wanted to compare a particular course to help high school students perform well on their SATs to no formal course whatsoever. For the students taking the course, x is the number of class sessions. For students not taking the course, x is the number of self-study sessions using free materials that may be obtained from the Educational Testing Service (ETS) Web site. Let y be the change in score between the practice SAT given sophomore year and the real SAT given junior year; y is a change score.

For which method is the relationship between the change score and number of sessions stronger? In units of SAT points and number of sessions, suppose both methods on the average have the same rate of return: three points per session. But if the rate of return is calculated in standard scores using the beta coefficient, the rate of return could be four times higher for one method than the other. Yet this difference results solely from smaller variation in gain scores for the method with the greater beta coefficient. The beta coefficient here confounds two very different features of the data analysis: the slope (in its original units) and the standard deviation of the response. Why not keep them separate?

We shall see later, when more than one predictor is considered, that standardized coefficients are sometimes advocated as a way to permit useful comparisons between the regression coefficients of predictors measured on different scales (e.g., in a study of heart disease, age in years and body weight in pounds). By putting all slopes in the same standardized units, one is supposed to be able to determine which predictors are "stronger" than others. We shall learn later that, on closer inspection, this argument is typically unpersuasive.

3.6 Using Transformations for a Nonlinear Fit

The "linear" in simple linear regression refers to the way in which x is transformed into $\hat{y}$:

$$\hat{y} = \hat{\eta}_0 + \hat{\eta}_1 x, \tag{3.13}$$

where $\hat{y}$ is the fitted values and therefore the regression line. Note that x is multiplied by a constant ($\hat{\eta}_1$), and to this product, a constant ($\hat{\eta}_0$) is added. Multiplication by a constant and/or adding a constant defines a linear transformation. Thus, $\hat{y}$ is a linear transformation of x. This is one sense in which simple linear regression is linear.

A key feature of simple linear regression is that x and/or y may be transformed in a nonlinear fashion (e.g, taking the logarithm), and simple linear regression is *still* linear in the sense of Equation 3.13. The difference is that x is now replaced in Equation 3.13 by the transformed x; the linear relationship is between y and the transformed x, not the original x. To reconstruct the relationship between y and the original x, one simply proceeds in two steps: from x to the transformed x and from the transformed x to y. One can employ nonlinear relationships between x and y with simple linear regression if that is useful for descriptive purposes. If a nonlinear description is more instructive than a linear one, linear regression can still be applied.[7]

Consider the following illustration. The very high rates at which inmates return to prison for new offenses or parole violations have been a policy concern for generations. Recidivism rates are typically well over 50%.

Suppose one followed a cohort of released prison inmates on parole for two years after their release from prison. At the very beginning of the study, all

[7]Linear transformations of x and/or y leave the form of the relationship between x and y unchanged except for scale. For example, if y is multiplied by 5, slope and intercept are 5 times larger. If x is multiplied by 5, the slope is 5 times smaller but the intercept is unchanged. In either case, if the original relationship is linear, the relationship is still linear.

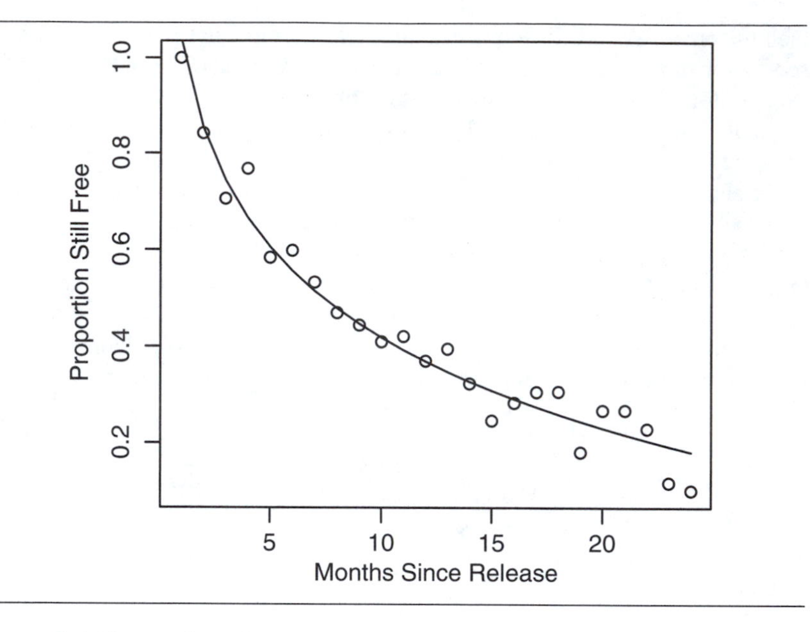

Figure 3.4. Regression of Proportion Remaining on Months Since Release

inmates would be free. But the proportion free would almost certainly decline over time.

Figure 3.4 shows for imaginary data the relationship between the proportion remaining free and months since release from prison.[8] Clearly, the relationship is nonlinear. The proportion that remains free declines but at a declining rate; the negative slope becomes less steep over time. Yet the line superimposed on the scatter plot was constructed in a linear fashion from the fitted values of the following equation:

$$\hat{y} = 1.0 - 0.25 \times \ln(x). \tag{3.14}$$

Equation 3.14 linearly transforms the *logarithm* of x into $\hat{y}$ so that the relationship between x in its *original* units and y is nonlinear. In Figure 3.5, the predictor is the logarithm of x, and the scatter plot clearly shows a linear relationship.

In summary, linear regression can be used to describe a wide variety of nonlinear relations between x and y. The idea is to apply nonlinear transformations to x and/or y and then construct the least squares line using the

[8]These data are manufactured but are qualitatively consistent with what is known about recidivism over time.

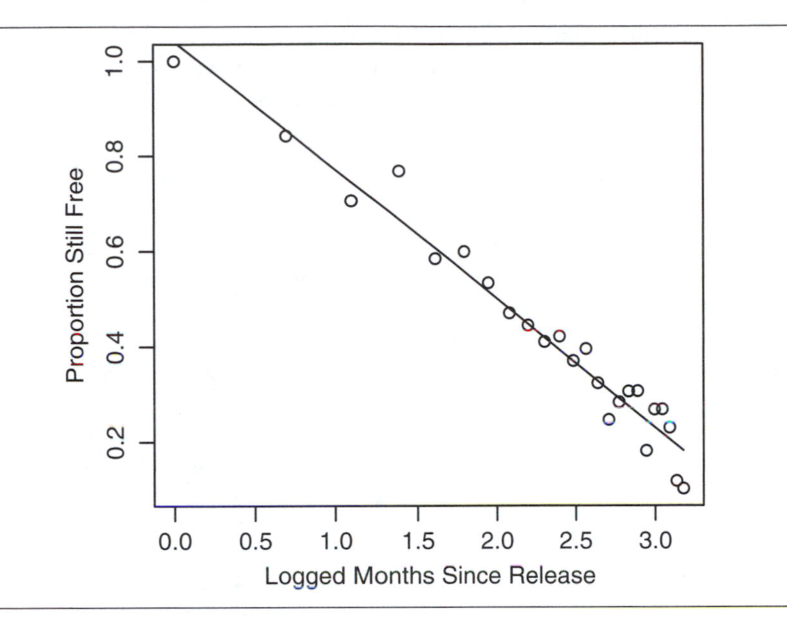

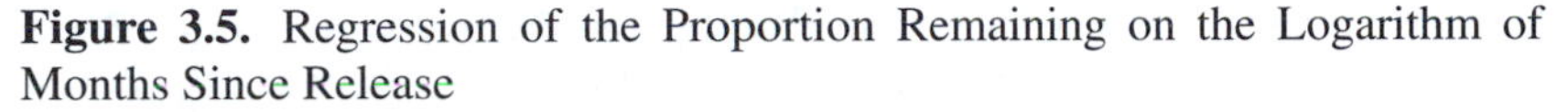

Figure 3.5. Regression of the Proportion Remaining on the Logarithm of Months Since Release

transformed variables. In the transformed variables, the fit is linear. Thus, in these scales, all of the handy features of linear regression play through. Still, in the original variables, the fit is nonlinear.

In practice, one would proceed something as follows:

1. Construct the scatter plot for x and y in their natural units.
2. If information external to the data (e.g., scientific theory) and/or the scatter plot indicates a substantial nonlinear relationship, transform x and/or y so that a useful nonlinear characterization of the path of the means results.
3. Apply linear regression to the transformed data.
4. Interpret the results back in the original (untransformed) units.

Sometimes there will be subject matter information strongly indicating the need for a nonlinear transformation and even what that transformation should be. In economics, for example, there are often theoretical reasons for transforming the response and/or the predictor into logarithms. When such theory exists, it can be an excellent justification for applying transformations. Very often, however, no such theory exists, or if it does, the data do not conform to it. Then, it is necessary to proceed far more inductively.

It is always important to begin by looking carefully at the scatter plot, which will often suggest plausible relationships. As a next step, it can be handy to explore a number of "scaled power transformations," which take the form of

$$\upsilon^{(\lambda)} = \begin{cases} (\upsilon^{\lambda} - 1)/\lambda & \text{if } \lambda \neq 0 \\ \ln(\upsilon) & \text{if } \lambda = 0, \end{cases} \tag{3.15}$$

where ln(.) refers to the natural logarithm and υ is a place holder for any variable. Generally, one focuses on either the response variable or the predictor and experiments with different values of λ until a useful fit of the scatter plot is found. The variable chosen is usually driven by subject matter concerns. Candidate values for λ can be selected by visual inspection of the scatter plot with the fit superimposed.

Consider again the example of inmates released on parole. It is clear from Figure 3.4 that some fractional λ value of the months since release will produce a better fit than a straight line. Experimenting with the sequence $\lambda = 0.8, 0.6, 0.4, 0.2, 0.0$ indicates that the fit improves at each step, although to the eye, there is not much difference between 0.2 and 0.0.[9] So, how does one choose the "best" value of λ? Sometimes, there will be good scientific reasons for a choice. Often, however, the choice will be substantially affected by how easily the results can be interpreted. The log transformation (i.e., $\lambda = 0.0$) is probably a better choice here because log transformations are generally easier to interpret than fractional powers. Expanding on a point made earlier when elasticities were discussed, economists have long exploited the fact that

$$\ln(\upsilon_i) - \ln(\upsilon_j) = \ln\left(\frac{\upsilon_i}{\upsilon_j}\right) \simeq \frac{(\upsilon_i - \upsilon_j)}{\upsilon_i} \tag{3.16}$$

for small differences between υ_i and υ_j. For small differences in the value of some variable υ for case i and case j, the difference in the logarithm of the values is approximately the same as the proportional difference (e.g., $\ln(8) - \ln(7) \simeq 0.13 \simeq (8 - 7)/7$).[10]

There may be trade-offs between transformations that fit the data well and transformations that can be more easily interpreted. The transformation that leads to the best fit may not be the transformation most easily understood. Unless the regression analysis is an exercise without subject matter content, it will usually be preferable to select from a set of transformations, all leading

[9] With an interactive statistical programming language like R, Xlispstat, or S+, it is easy to experiment with different values of λ and plot each set of results.

[10] Note that $\ln(x_i/x_j) = -\ln(x_j \neq x_i)$ but that $(x_i - x_j)/x_i \neq -(x_j - x_i)/x_j$. In the log form, a given change up the scale and down the scale produces the same result except for the sign. In the proportional change form, this is not true because the denominators differ. But when the change is small, the difference between the two will be small because the difference between the denominators in the proportional change form is small.

to reasonably good fits, the one that provides the most useful subject matter interpretation, even if that fit is not formally the best. The following example illustrates this point.

Runoff from storm drains is a major source of water pollution in metropolitan areas around the country. Rains and water used for irrigating lawns and gardens carry all manner of chemical compounds into storm drains that, in turn, empty into streams, rivers, lakes, and the near-shore ocean. A key issue in research on runoff is how much water arrives how fast at its final destination.

The theoretical equations used to study urban runoff commonly use the square of the diameter of the storm drain to predict the velocity of the water coming down the pipe (along with other factors). If one fit implied a λ of 2.2 and another, slightly worse fit implied a λ of 2.0, the latter might well be preferable. A λ of 2.0 might make good scientific sense but a λ of 2.2 might not. Indeed, a working hydrologist might decide to treat a computed λ of 2.2 as if it were really 2.0 anyway. Once again, external information brought to the analysis can be critical.

It is also possible to include λ as one of the values to compute in the least squares procedure. We shall return to this issue later when we consider more than one predictor. But one must be very careful of such blind procedures for the reasons just considered. The value of λ chosen in the process of minimizing the sum of the squared residuals (or maximizing a likelihood function) may not make much subject matter sense. A value of λ when the sum of squared residuals is not quite minimized may do nicely.

Finally, there can be other reasons to transform variables in addition to improving the fit (Atkinson, 1985). We will consider some of those later as well.

3.7 What About the Variance Function?

To this point, our emphasis has been on the path of the means: the mean of y conditional on values of x. Because most policy applications concentrate on the mean or some other measure of location, we have as well. However, it can make good sense in some policy applications to also examine how the variance of y depends on values of x.

For example, one of the issues in the delivery of medical care by HMOs is how much patients pay for medical services not provided as part of their routine coverage. If one were interested in the relationship between household income and the amount of money households spend on health care beyond that covered by their HMO, both the mean and variance function might be of interest. More wealthy families might spend more on out-of-pocket health care on the average, and more wealthy families might have more variability in their discretionary health care expenditures. With a greater capacity to spend on health care would come more flexibility in whether to seek noncovered procedures.

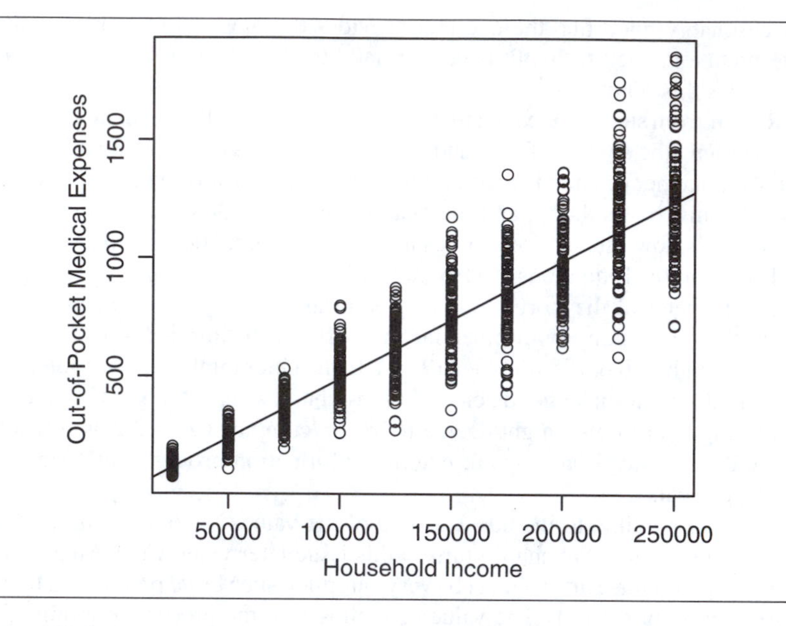

Figure 3.6. Scatter Plot of Medical Expenses Not Covered by Insurance Against Household Income With Least Squares Line Overlaid (Both Variables in Dollars per Year)

In order to get enough higher-income households to explore properly this relationship, imagine a data set in which households at particular income levels were sampled, with higher-income households oversampled. Figure 3.6 shows for these fictional data a scatter plot of out-of-pocket health care expenditures and household income with a least squares line superimposed. Both variables are in dollars for a given year. Clearly, both the mean and variance of medical expenses not covered by an HMO tend to increase with household income. And as a descriptive matter, both are of interest.

Briefly, there are a number of ways to examine more directly the variance function. One obvious way is to compute the variance of y conditional on each value of x. Comparisons can then directly be made between these conditional variances.

If a regression line has been computed to represent the path of the means, it is typically the variance around the fit that will be of interest. The path of the means has become a stand-in for the means themselves. Then perhaps the easiest and most commonly used approach is to plot the residuals of the fit against x. If some vertical slices of the residuals are substantially more variable than others, there may be a strong indication that the variance function is not constant. And from the plot, patterns in the nonconstant variances can be interpreted. In the

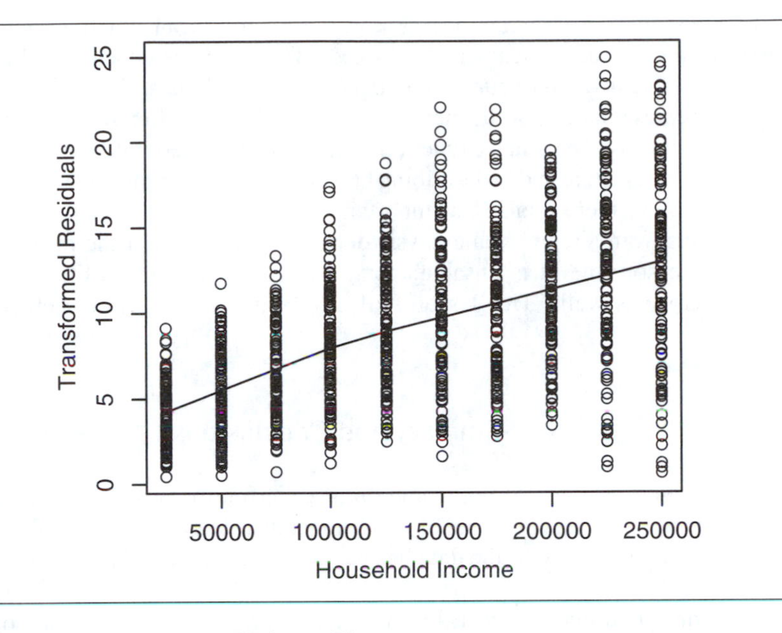

Figure 3.7. Nonconstant Variance Plot

health expenditures illustration, one would expect to see more variability in the residuals for higher-income households.

Another simple strategy is to fit a smoother as usual to the original scatter plot and, in addition, a second set of smoothers that characterize the path of $+1$ and -1 SD from the fit. As the SD varies conditional on x, so would the smoother. If these two paths are not about the same distance apart for all values of x, there is evidence of nonconstant variance. For the health expenditures, the distance between the pairs of standard deviation fits would increase with increases in household income.

It can also be useful to plot a transformation of the residuals against x and overlay a smoother. The square root of the absolute values of the residuals can be a useful option (Cook and Weisberg, 1999:347). If the path through the transformed residuals is not approximately flat (i.e., parallel to the horizontal axis), this, too, is evidence of nonconstant variance. Thinking again about the health expenditures example, the smoothed fit would increase with increases in household income. Figure 3.7 shows the result. The variance of the transformed residuals is clearly increasing, but not at a constant rate. The rate of increase decreases a bit for high-income values. In short, if there is interest in the variance function, there are many ways to study it. We will return to these issues in a later chapter.

Making sense of apparent nonconstant variance is often difficult. Once a smoother (including the least squares line) for the mean function is overlaid and interest turns to the variance around the fit, the mean function and the variance function are fundamentally linked. The residuals depend on the fit, and the empirical variance function depends on the residuals. As a result, two different representations of the mean function can lead to different conclusions about the nature of the variance function. Although this is certainly an important concern if one is interested in describing how the variance around the fit depends on values of x, there is also an important general lesson. Virtually all that one extracts from a regression analysis depends on the path of the means. If, for some reason, the fit is unsatisfactory, all of what follows is likely to be unsatisfactory as well. This lesson will have some real bite in the chapters ahead.

3.8 Summary and Conclusions

The imposition of a least squares line on a scatter plot may seem like a very small step beyond studying a set of conditional distributions directly. But the process of going outside of the data has begun in earnest. One has:

1. made a commitment to a linear relationship between the means of y and x;
2. determined which transformations (or no transformations) of the data are appropriate;
3. determined the fit by minimizing a symmetric, quadratic function of the residuals; and
4. perhaps standardized the slope of the fitted line.

Viewed as a set of procedures to facilitate a description of the relationship between y and x, there may be nothing about which to become very concerned. The data analyst has simply made a number of judgment calls. And some judgment calls are unavoidable. Moreover, because the regression analysis is still very close to the data, another researcher could evaluate what was done and, if desirable, make different discretionary decisions. However, if the decisions are unexamined or, worse, interpreted as formally mandatory, one has started down the slippery slope toward statistical ritual. And we will see soon how such rituals can lead researchers away from the empirical world they are seeking to understand. Indeed, the rituals can implicitly commit investigators to a rendering of the world that may make little sense.

4 Statistical Inference for Simple Linear Regression

4.1 The Role of Sampling

In this chapter, we consider statistical inference for simple linear regression. As such, statistical inference is usually undertaken as an extension of a descriptive exercise; statistical inference is applied to the results of a descriptive regression analysis. Nevertheless, the transition from description of the conditional distribution of y to inferences about that distribution beyond those data is very significant. To get the job done right requires that one introduce substantial and credible information from outside of the data themselves about how the data were generated. As before, the key lessons learned will generalize to situations in which there is more than one predictor.

4.1.1 Random Sampling

The central question addressed in this chapter is simply stated: When probabilities in simple linear regression are associated with conventional confidence intervals and tests of statistical significance, to what do those probabilities refer? Probability of what exactly? We will see that, under some circumstances, the answer is reasonably clear and the underlying mathematics play through. In other circumstances, the answer is obscure and the underlying mathematics are problematic. Random sampling will often place the researcher in the first set of circumstances, so a good place to begin a discussion about statistical inference for the simple linear model is with data generated by random sampling.

Suppose one were interested in drawing inferences about the results of a regression analysis to data beyond the data on hand. In the ozone example, that might be to summers in general, not just the summer for which the data were collected. One might also be interested in inferences to the set of major cities around the world, perhaps defined by a population greater than 5 million people. For variables such as temperature and ozone concentrations, it is common to find daily data dating back two decades, or even more, for many major metropolitan areas.

If it were practical, the easy solution would be to gather all such data. Then, one could simply repeat the descriptive regression analyses just described. But frequently, there will be serious resource constraints. Data collection can be very costly. A common response is to select a sample of the data instead. The goal is to learn useful things about the full set of data from the subset studied. This process is called statistical inference.

However, sampling raises two well-known problems: (a) potential biases in the sample and (b) the uncertainty necessarily introduced. Here, both will be addressed within frequentist probability traditions. Frequentist probability has dominated the regression literature in most disciplines over many decades and is still the kind of probability typically taught to students in those fields. The alternative of Bayesian approaches, although very popular in statistics, has yet to really catch on elsewhere (Berk et al., 1995). Suffice it to say that Bayesian statistical inference provides a very different answer to the question of probability of what, which so far has not captured the fancy of policy researchers or policymakers.

Recall the basic frequentist thought experiment. There is a well-defined population from which a limitless number of random samples with replacement are drawn. In the population, each observational unit has a known probability of selection. The units in a given sample are selected independently of one another. Thus, the samples are independent as well. And the samples will typically differ one from another in the observational units that are selected.

For each sample, the desired sample statistics are computed. Because the units in each sample are not the same, the summary statistics for each sample will likely differ as well. In the case of regression analysis, we will see that there are, in principle, a limitless number of computed values for the intercept and slope. There is, then, a joint "sampling distribution" of values for the intercept and slope, from which conventional statistical inference can be undertaken, often with the help of confidence intervals and formal statistical tests.

In many practical situations, a thought experiment using sampling *without* replacement from a very large population and producing a large (but not limitless) number of samples will lead to essentially the same result, if each sample is small relative to the size of the population. Sampling without replacement is called "simple random sampling." Each unit has the same probability of being selected into the sample, and each possible sample has the same probability of being selected (Thompson, 2002:20-22).

In regression analysis, there are two basic ways to consider random sampling. In the first case, observational units are selected without respect to their values for x. As each observational unit is chosen, there is an associated value for y and x. Both y and x are free to vary depending on which units are included in the sample.

In the second case, because regression analysis conditions on x, one can employ stratified random sampling. The observational units in the population are organized into "strata" defined by the x values. Then, only for the x values of interest, a random sample of observational units is chosen. There is simple random sampling within specified strata. In the ozone example, the stratifying variable would be temperature. If one were really committed to the linear summary, it might make sense to only sample days that had the very lowest temperatures and the very highest temperatures. The reasons for such a design will be apparent later in this chapter.[1]

In practice, sampling is often more complicated. For example, most national surveys use some form of multistage cluster sampling. But for our purposes here, such variations on random sampling are details. The message from the thought experiment is essentially the same.[2]

If one is prepared to interpret one's regression results conditional on the particular values of x in the sample, simple random sampling and stratified random samples lead to no important differences. In the ozone example, one's empirical conclusions would formally apply only to situations with the same set of temperature values. For instance, if ozone concentrations were observed at 50, 70, 90, and 100 degrees Fahrenheit, the results would only apply to settings in which those same temperatures were found. In short, all is well if either the values of x are fixed in the sampling design (i.e., in stratified sampling) or are treated as fixed once they materialize in a simple random sample.

With the proper thought experiment in place, the standard definition of bias follows. Recall that if the mean of the computed intercepts over the hypothetical samples is the same as the (unknown) intercept in the population, and if the mean of the computed slopes over the hypothetical samples is the same as the (unknown) slope in the population, the summary statistics for the intercept and

---

[1] If the proportion of sampled cases in each stratum is not the same as the proportion of population cases in each stratum, one has disproportional stratified sampling. Proper analysis may then require weighting the data back to the appropriate population proportions. Generally, this will be unnecessary for a regression analysis if the predictor is also the variable defining the strata. But the marginal distribution of y could be misleading.

[2] However, the regression calculations can differ in important ways. We shall briefly consider this later.

slope computed from any given sample are said to be unbiased. Otherwise, the estimates of the slope and intercept are biased.[3]

Matters are rather more complicated if one wants to treat x as stochastic. The difficulties that can follow will be addressed later. We will proceed for now as if x is fixed or is treated as such. In fact, this comports well with common practice.[4]

In reality, of course, one rarely has more than a single random sample. But one can still draw conclusions about the population from that sample, and all of the probabilities produced for statistical tests or confidence intervals are interpreted in the context of the frequentist thought experiment. It is the thought experiment that gives meaning to probabilities; it allows one to answer the question "probability of what?"

The concept of simple random sampling can also be applied to randomized experiments in which observational units are assigned at random to different treatments or to a treatment and control condition. The population is the full set of observational units that could be included in the study. Subsets of the units are sampled at random without replacement and are assigned. Because each sample is likely to be a relatively large fraction of the population, there can be palpable dependence in the selection process. However, the chance process generating the data is well understood and statistically tractable. As a result, there are exact ways to calculate the impact of the uncertainty and often very good practical approximations of those results. The question of precisely what is usefully estimated will be considered later when causal inference is discussed.

Now a key point: If the data on hand were actually generated by random sampling, the logic and the mathematics of statistical inference play through, at least in principle. If not, there can be serious interpretative problems. There may be no clear answer to the question "probability of what?" In response, applied researchers have employed one of four strategies.

4.1.2 Strategy I: Treating the Data as Population

If the data are a population, there is no sampling, no uncertainty because of sampling, and no need for statistical inference. Indeed, statistical inference makes no sense. The only game is describing patterns in the data on hand.

Often, this can be very useful. In the state of California, there was a recent dispute between local school districts and the state agency that distributes funds for expansion and renovation of existing schools. Statewide regulations required that funds for expansion and renovation be determined by the projected growth

[3]Note that there are two possible sources of bias: how the sample was selected and how the sample statistics were computed. For now, we are focusing on sampling bias only. Then, if the estimates are unbiased, the result is sometimes called "design unbiased" (Thompson, 2002:107).

[4]For example, the standard errors estimated by the most popular computer packages assume fixed predictors.

of a district's school population. Projections of growth were taken as evidence of need.

Administrators in low-income school districts believed that officials in suburban and rural school districts were better able to rapidly construct forecasts showing substantial growth because their growth was into undeveloped land. The steps by which development could occur were less constrained than in urban areas, where vacant land was difficult to find and any growth was affected by zoning regulations and environmental impact assessments. As a result, it took longer for urban school districts to file the necessary documents with the state. The suburban and rural schools were getting to the fixed pot of money first.

From the point of view of urban school administrators, the system was unfair. Low-income areas had schools that were more run-down to begin with, and there was far less local money to make improvements. It was the districts that needed the money least that were getting the lion's share.

Figure 4.1 addresses these claims. The observational units are school districts that received money for new construction or expansion. On the vertical axis is the number of dollars per new pupil. The number of new pupils was supposed to determine the need for state money, and by working with dollars per new pupil, an adjustment for this factor is made. On the horizontal axis is the percentage of children getting free meals in school, a measure of local poverty. Overlaid is a straight line summarizing the path of the means. Note that the y is skewed to the right and that x can take on a large number of values. Without the overlaid straight line, it would be difficult to determine the path of the means.[5]

From Figure 4.1, there appears to be almost no relationship between local poverty and the per-pupil dollar allocations. If anything, the relationship is positive. There seems to be little in the data to support the claims made by administrators from lower-income school districts that, when money is allocated, low-income districts are less well treated. However, there is a great deal of variability in per-pupil allocations. The response is already adjusted for the number of new pupils, and yet there is a large spread. Clearly, there are other factors at work despite the regulations specifying that growth in the number of school children should be the determining factor. Something else is going on beyond what the regulations allow.[6]

The central point, however, is that a descriptive analysis of a given data set treated as a population was responsive to the policy questions being raised. The data were not a sample of anything relevant and certainly not a random sample.

---

[5]The few very large per-pupil dollar allocations reflect the construction of new school buildings in school districts with very few new students (e.g., less than 50).

[6]The real issue turned out to be "capriciousness" caused by the way applications for funding were filled out and evaluated. In brief, the applications were complicated and lengthy so that school districts varied in the information included and how accurate that information was. There was also considerable room for lobbying by elected officials so that need did not necessarily translate very directly into dollars.

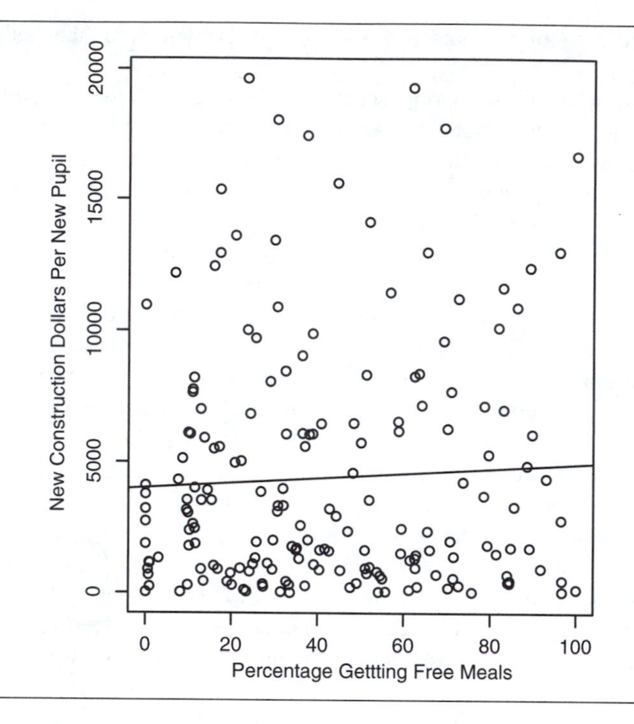

Figure 4.1. Scatter Plot of Construction Dollars Per Pupil on Percentage of Students Getting Free Meals

It is easy to think of many other illustrations: IRS audits of business establishments, personnel records for a firm charged with discrimination in hiring or promotion, and claims to an insurance company after a particular hurricane. All such examples share a concern solely about the data on hand with no need whatsoever to make inferences beyond them.

4.1.3 Strategy II: Treating the Data *as If* They Were Generated by Random Sampling From a Population

If one needs random sampling to make sense of statistical inference, a common strategy is to argue that nature produced the data in a manner that closely approximates random sampling from a real population. Usually, this argument will be difficult to make in a convincing manner. One needs very good theory and/or very good data to make the case.

For example, one might take water samples from a local beach every Wednesday around noon over a summer. The goal might be to measure the concentration of toxic chemicals as a function of storm drain outflow so that inferences can be made to the population of all possible times and days during that summer at that particular beach. If the concentrations are independent of time of day and day of the week, and if the 7-day elapsed time between measures is long enough to erase any "memory" in the system (making the observations independent over time), one could argue that the observations are effectively a random sample from the population of interest. Because all three assumptions could, in principle, be addressed with data, one could imagine bringing substantial evidence to bear.

The case for random sampling would depend on marshaling real data. The sampling assumptions would need to be seriously studied as an empirical matter. Too often, in practice, the reality of the sampling assumptions is unconsidered. In this instance, the researcher would be implicitly asserting that the transport of pollutants from storm drains into the ocean is unrelated to time. And insofar as this is false, there is the real prospect of biases in the way the population is characterized and in how the uncertainty is represented.

A common alternative is to treat, implicitly, the statistical inference as conditional on the random sampling assumptions being approximately true. That is, the investigator clearly states that random sampling is being assumed and stops. Implied is that the regression results depend on the random sampling assumption being a good proxy for the truth. But in fact, there is no way to determine which of the regression results to believe unless the sampling assumptions are explicitly evaluated. The appearance of full disclosure is, in this case, a ruse.

It is very difficult to find convincing instances of "as if" random sampling in policy-related research. Typically, the data sets are "convenience samples." A well-defined population may exist, but the means by which the data are generated are nothing like random sampling: patients at a given health clinic, students who have their parents' permission to take part in a survey study on safe sex, countries that sign a treaty to limit the production of chlorofluorocarbons, business firms that honor a request for information on their profits, or unemployed individuals who are recruited through local unemployment offices.

Perhaps the most dramatic examples come from evaluations of social interventions: new teaching paradigms for children learning to read, housing vouchers for low-income renters, counseling for perpetrators of domestic violence, or special diets for individuals with high blood pressure. For all such efforts, the risk is that the individuals who participate self-select or are selected by program administrators. In each of these instances, making the case that nature randomly sampled from a well-defined population would be extremely difficult. If one proceeded nevertheless as if the data were produced by random sampling, two sorts of errors would likely follow.

First, regression estimates from the data could be misleading as "proxies" for population values. From a scatter plot of the population, some regions are sampled more heavily than others, and some regions are perhaps neglected altogether. The resulting scatter plot for the sample will look very different from the scatter plot for the population. Summary statistics calculated from the sample data may then be very different as well.

For example, in an evaluation of a prison job-training program, inmates who might have stayed in the program simply marking time might not be sampled. Program administrators would perhaps screen them out. Then, in principle, inmates who would have remained in the program for many months (i.e., large values for x) and who would have had little or no earnings after release from prison (i.e., small values for y) would be underrepresented in the data set; the program might appear to be more effective than it really is. The most glaring program failures would be underrepresented.

But sometimes, the distortions can be subtle. Consider an example of the relationship between scores on the Scholastic Aptitude Test (SAT) and later grade point averages (GPAs) in college. In the fall of 2001, the University of California released a report claiming to show that the aptitude part of the SAT (known as SAT I) did not help to predict college GPA once high school GPA and the achievement part of the SAT (known as SAT II) were taken into account (Geiser and Studley, 2001). These findings helped further the argument that the aptitude part of the SAT could be dispensed with and were folded into the controversy over affirmative action in college admissions. If SAT I scores did not predict all that well, and if they were "culturally biased" (another issue), perhaps they should not be part of the admissions decision.

The University of California report raises a number of statistical issues. But for now, consider the impact of sampling on the results from simple linear regression. The discussion will be simplified accordingly. There will be no consideration, for example, of the conditional relationship between SAT I and college GPA, adjusting for other predictors.

Suppose there is a large state university with 12,000 applications for the freshman class. SAT I scores figure heavily in admissions, but questions have been raised about how strongly the SAT I is related to later performance in college. A random sample of 1,000 applicants is taken. For those 1,000 applicants, an effort is made to record each SAT I score along with each student's freshman GPA.[7] The latter requires considerable labor because many of the applicants enrolled in other schools, and transcripts have to be obtained from those schools. Assume for the moment that, for the full set of 1,000, SAT I scores and freshman grade point averages were obtained.

Figure 4.2 shows the scatter plot. SAT I score is on the horizontal axis and GPA is on the vertical axis. The least squares line is superimposed.

It is clear that the relationship is positive. The difference in the average GPA for students who score around 500 SAT points and students who score around 1,500 SAT points is nearly 1 GPA point on the average.

The standard deviation of the residuals is about 0.4, indicating that the average variation around the fit is about half a GPA point, and about 31% of the variance

[7] According to the University of California study, freshman GPA is commonly taken as the key indicator of college performance when the value of SAT scores is addressed.

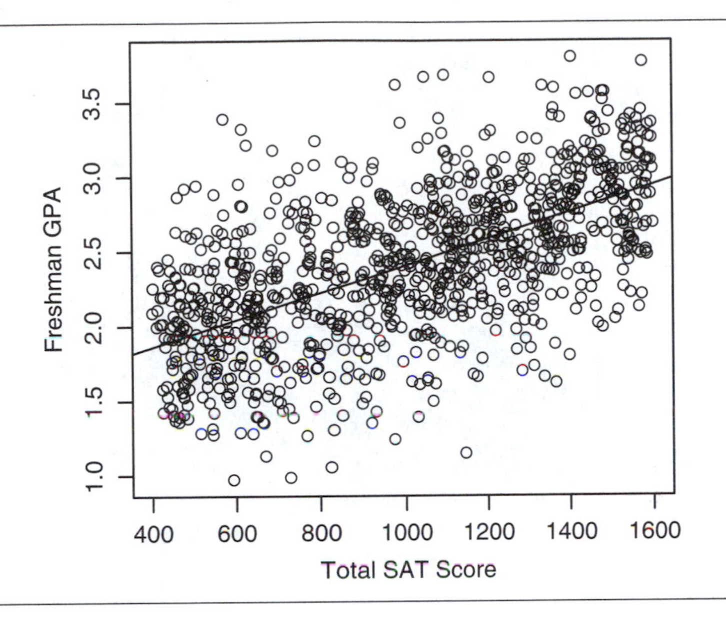

Figure 4.2. Scatter Plot of Freshman GPA and Total SAT I Score for All Applicants

in GPA is explained by SAT score. There are, apparently, a number of other factors at work.[8]

Realistically, not all of the 1,000 original applicants would finish their freshman year. Suppose that, for each of the colleges attended, a GPA of at least 2.0 was required. Hence, for students with less than a 2.0, there would be no freshman GPA to observe. Figure 4.3 shows the result. Figure 4.3 is basically the same as Figure 4.2, but all observations with a GPA below 2.0 have been removed and the plot rescaled. Although the positive relationship remains, it has been substantially altered.

The difference in average GPA between a student with an SAT I score of around 500 and a student with an SAT I score of around 1,500 is about half a GPA point. The slope has been reduced by about 50%. And even though the standard deviation around the regression fit is approximately the same, the variance in GPA explained by SAT I score has dropped to nearly 0.20, also a decline of around 50%. All this comes about because the missing GPA data

[8]Had data been collected in the population of 12,000 applicants, the results would have been effectively the same. The sample size is large enough for the approximation to be sufficiently accurate.

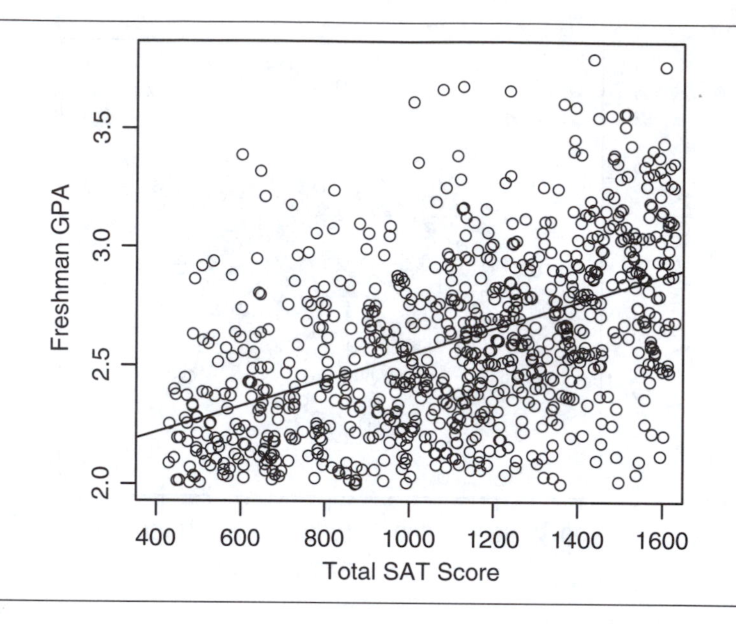

Figure 4.3. Scatter Plot of Freshman GPA and Total SAT I Score for Applicants Who Graduated

have altered the conditional distributions of GPA given SAT I scores. In effect, many of the lower tails of these distributions were lopped off, especially those with smaller SAT I scores.

Despite sampling 1,000 cases at random, the data obtained were no longer a random sample from the original population because of the inability to obtain all the information required. As a result, the relationship between SAT I score and freshman GPA was estimated to be substantially weaker than it really was. Even with random sampling, if the data generation process reflects a threshold for y below which or above which (or both) observations are lost, the least squares line for simple regression will be systematically attenuated; it will be too flat.[9]

If data had been unavailable because of missing information on SAT I scores, the problems would have been less troublesome. Suppose that students who scored below 1,000 on the SAT I were not admitted to any 4-year college.

[9]For multiple regression, estimates of the regression coefficients will also be systematically in error. But they may be too steep or too flat. Likewise, the intercept may be too large or too small. The problems that can result are sometimes called "sample selection bias." There are statistical procedures available that, in principle, can correct for such problems (Heckman, 1979). But the required assumptions are often heroic, and, in practice, the "corrections" can actually make things worse.

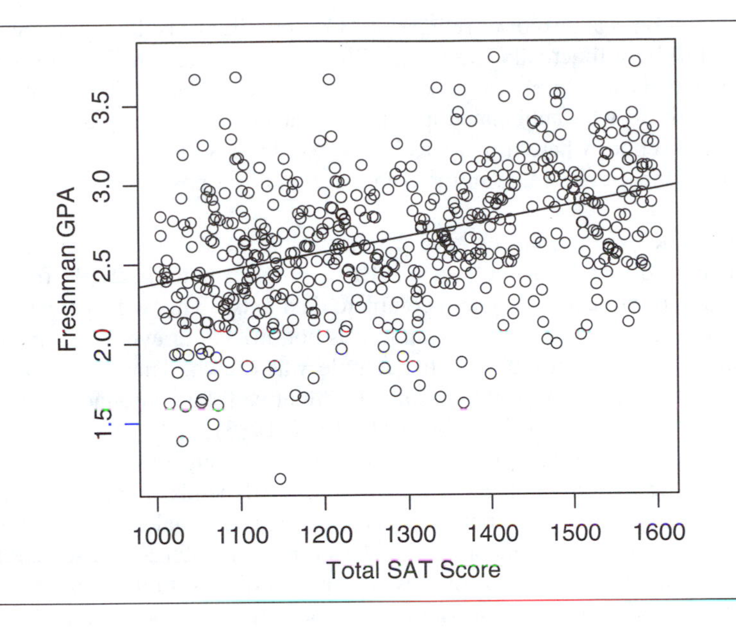

Figure 4.4. Scatter Plot of Freshman GPA and Total SAT I Score for Applicants Who Scored Above 1,000 on the SAT I

For these students, there would be no freshman GPA. Figure 4.4 shows the result.

Although it is a little hard to see, the slope is the same as in Figure 4.2. There is no attenuation. The lack of attenuation follows because we are conditioning on SAT I scores. The observed conditional distributions for GPA are unaffected. We just have fewer of them. However, because we are shrinking the variability of SAT I far more than the variability of GPA, the variance explained by SAT I declines to about 15%. More generally, even with random sampling, if the data generation process reflects a threshold for x below which or above which (or both) observations are lost, the least squares line for simple regression is not, on the average, affected.[10] The variance explained, however, can be dramatically altered.

In practice, the potential distortions in studies of SAT I scores and college performance would be far more difficult to characterize. The likely design would find college administrators collecting GPA information only on students who attended their institutions. This is, in fact, what was done in the University of California study. Then, it would be difficult to determine which parts of

[10]This assume that the relationship estimated between x and y is linear. If the relationship is nonlinear, then losing some of the conditional distributions can lead to biased estimates.

the population scatter plot were missing. One possibility is that the regression line would be artifactually too steep. Students with high SAT I scores who would likely be admitted would likely be admitted elsewhere. And among such students, those who anticipated not thriving at the school in question would enroll in a school where the fit was better. So, high SAT I-low GPA students would be underrepresented in the data set, making a positive regression line steeper.

Under such circumstances, a researcher might be tempted to redefine the population so that the sample in hand is a proper random sample from the population of students for whom complete data exist. This will typically turn out to be a losing strategy. The sample was not, in fact, drawn in this manner; the missing data occurred *after* the sample was drawn. Thus, the processes by which the data were made unavailable might well be confounded with the relationships of interest (Heckman, 1990; Berk, 1983).

Biased regression estimates are not the only risk when convenience samples are treated as random samples. Random sampling depends on independence in the selection process. Without independence, conventional estimation procedures will likely provide incorrect standard errors. Insofar as the selection of one observation increases the chances that another observation will be selected, and insofar as these two observations are more likely to be similar than are independently selected observations, there is more homogeneity in the sample than there should be. Then, the estimated standard errors will likely be too small. This is a very common pattern, and false precision results.[11]

For example, prison inmates who volunteer for particular assignments will often do so with several of their friends. Or they may avoid certain voluntary assignments because members of a rival group are already involved. Likewise, patients who use a particular health maintenance organization (HMO) often enroll their entire families or are assigned to that HMO along with other employees from the same business establishment.

The natural world is no more cooperative. Samples of air pollutants for a particular metropolitan area are often collected by flying a plane over the air space. Oncoming air is directed through filters that extract the compounds of interest. But proximate parcels of air tend to be alike, so that, if the air samples are collected on a continuing basis, the observations are too homogeneous. The same holds for virtually all air quality measures collected by satellites, such as those used to characterize size and composition of aerosols.

Ecological researchers face similar problems. Analyses of biodiversity often begin with counts of the variety of species in a geographical area. Yet these species are not spread randomly over the landscape; indeed, their organization is what ecology is all about. Moreover, their organization will respond to human

---

[11] If the observations tend to be negatively related, then the estimated standard errors will be too large. This seems to be quite unusual, however.

interventions, such as hiking trails, which may provide the most ready access for data collection.

The general point is that the empirical world has structure that typically negates the possibility of random selection unless random sampling is imposed by the researcher. Yet it is common to see statistical inference undertaken from convenience samples as if they were random samples. But because convenience samples are not selected by random procedures, frequentist statistical inference formally does not apply. The probabilities that would be routinely computed have no clear interpretation because there is no clear answer to the question "probability of what?" Moreover, even if such abstractions could be sidestepped, one may obtain very misleading characterizations of the population. Attempts to characterize the uncertainty resulting from sampling can also be thwarted.

4.1.4 Strategy III: Inventing an Imaginary Population

Perhaps the most common response when the data are not generated by random sampling is to proceed as if the data on hand were a random sample from an imaginary population. Such samples are sometimes called "random realizations," and such populations are sometimes called "superpopulation" (because the data can be considered a population). A superpopulation is defined in a somewhat circular way as the population from which the data would have come if the data were a random sample. Imaginary populations do not exist. So, inferences to them do not directly answer any empirical question. However, there may be an important difference between imaginary populations that plausibly *could* exist and those that could not.

The strongest case for inferences to an imaginary population is when there is a population that could actually be produced by some real and well-defined stochastic process.[12] In the natural sciences, many imaginary populations qualify. Examples include where hurricanes make landfall, the Richter Scale values of earthquakes, eddies generated by ocean currents, and particular gene mutations. Thus, it can make scientific sense, for instance, to think about the large set of Pacific storms that could be generated under a particular set of meteorological conditions. And given these conditions and existing understandings of how the conditions lead to storms, it might well be sensible to view a given storm as a random realization (given those same meteorological conditions). Then, several such storms might be considered a random sample from which inferences are made to the population of storms that could be produced under the same conditions.

[12] Of necessity, causal language is used. In the next chapter, inferences about cause and effect will be examined in detail, and key concepts will be clarified. For now, commonsense notions will suffice.

For such accounts to be convincing, however, the conditioning circumstances need to be clearly articulated along with well-accepted accounts of the key chance processes. Often, both will be stated in mathematical terms. The case will be even stronger if it is possible to actually observe a useful approximation of the imaginary population—in this case, a large number of similar Pacific storms. Even though the population may not exist at the moment, a good approximation can be assembled. Finally, with the approximation in hand, there would be empirical evidence on whether a given storm can be usefully treated as a random sample from that population. In short, a relatively small leap of faith is required because, in an important sense, the population could actually exist.[13]

It is difficult to imagine compelling examples for social processes. Yet superpopulation are very commonly assumed, especially for longitudinal processes and especially in economics. Monthly indices for inflation, unemployment, balance of trade, and consumer confidence are treated as random realizations from the populations of such measures that could have occurred.

Consider the month-to-month balance of trade for the year 2000. For the idea of a superpopulation to be more than some slight of hand, one would have to provide a detailed and convincing account of the chance processes by which the monthly balance of trade is produced. In addition, the conditioning factors applicable to the year 2000 would need to be specified. What were the exchange rates between U.S. dollars and the currencies of other countries? What were the interest rates available to businesses and consumers in all of these countries? What were the patterns of tariffs, and what constraints were placed on international trade? Coupled with the stated chance processes, it might then be possible to describe in principle what the population is supposed to be. Yet even this would not really make the case. One would need to find a large set of years sufficiently like the year 2000, assemble a persuasive approximation of the population, and show that the year 2000 is usefully treated as a random sample. Such an enterprise seems quite daunting.

Finally, it is all too common to find studies that simply assert that the data are a random realization from a superpopulation and leave it at that. Saying that something is so does not make it true, and more important, such assertions will usually turn out to be unexamined. It is as if by mouthing the term *superpopulation*, a spell is cast making all statistical inference legitimate.

---

[13]Populations that exist but are not well characterized are not imaginary. For example, there are no doubt a large number of crimes committed in major metropolitan areas over any 12-month period. This could be a population of some interest. Although there is no list of such crimes from which one could take a random sample, the population is nevertheless very real. At the same time, if the population is not well characterized, it would seem a bit silly to try to make a case that the data on hand are a random realization from it (whatever *it* is).

4.1.5 Strategy IV: Model-Based Sampling—Inventing a Friendly Natural Process Responsible for the Data

A final and very popular strategy in the absence of real random sampling is to propose a model by which nature produces the data such that conventional statistical inference plays through. But there is no population, even in principle, and indeed, the entire random sampling framework is abandoned. Inferences are made, not to some well-defined population, but to features of the model claimed to be responsible for producing the data (Thompson, 2002:22-26). Clearly, this is a very different enterprise, but one that is especially popular in what often is taken to be more advanced statistical methods.[14]

The classic approach is to exploit a particular normal distribution that *could exist in theory.* In the univariate case, there is an underlying, real process that, in principle, generates values for some variable, the distribution of which corresponds to a normal distribution. So, no matter what may be going on behind the scenes, it conveniently turns out that about 68% of the values, for instance, would fall between ± 1 standard deviation around the mean. Likewise, about 2.5% would fall beyond 1.96 standard deviations above the mean, and about 2.5% would fall beyond 1.96 standard deviations below the mean. The data on hand are then treated as realizations of this process; "in principle" turns into "in fact."

Thus, for any given data set, those percentages and others should be approximated, and one can proceed in practice just as if the data were a random sample from a normal distribution. Inferences, however, are not made to a real population but to the theoretical distribution responsible for the data. One might use the data, for example, to estimate the mean of the normal distribution from which the data are assumed to be generated.

In regression applications, this account comes in three flavors.

1. Nature adopts a linear model: $y = \eta_0 + \eta_1 x + e$. Each value of x is transformed through multiplication by a constant (i.e., the value of the slope) and addition of another constant (i.e., the intercept). Then, for each value of the transformed x, nature is able to generate a value for the error from a normal distribution, which, when added, yields the value of y. There is no population. Inferences are made back to features of the linear model (e.g., to η_1).[15] Some additional constraints must be placed

[14]Graubard and Korn (2002:73) speak about "superpopulation parameters associated with a stochastic mechanism hypothesized to generate the observations in the population rather than finite-population parameters." Superpopulation inference and model-based inferences would seem to be combined. However, they are using the term "superpopulation" in a different manner than in the previous section and are actually consistent with a model-based approach discussed now. At least that is one way to read them.

[15]For example, if x is family income and y is high school GPA, data would be used to estimate the value of the regression coefficient by which nature links income to high school grades.

on how nature is supposed to function for estimates from the sample to the model to be made in an acceptable fashion. More will be said about this later.

2. The underlying natural process is able to produce a joint normal distribution for the predictor and the response. Then, the simple linear model automatically applies and statistical inference follows directly. Once again, there is no population. Inferences are made to the conditional distribution of y given x that could be produced, with interest usually focused on the regression intercept and slope determining $\bar{y}|x$.
3. For each value of the predictor, the underlying natural process is able to produce a normal distribution for the response. Because, in simple regression, one conditions on the predictor, this account also works in principle. Inferences are made back to the same sorts of model features of interest for the other two flavors. As will be discussed shortly, however, one has to place some additional constraints on how nature is supposed to function for statistical inference to be well justified.

One might think that these three formulations could be relaxed a bit by dropping the requirement that the data are generated by any particular distribution. Thus, one might allow the values of y given x, for example, to be generated through some unspecified distribution. But that only makes the account of how this all comes about more difficult and can produce near-tautologies. This point will be taken up in a bit more depth shortly.

The key question is why any of these accounts should be true. Perhaps the most popular explanation exploits the central limit theorem. It goes like this.

From the central limit theorem, we know, roughly speaking, that the sum of a sequence of independent random variables tends toward a normal distribution as the number of random variables included in the sum increases (Feller, 1968:244-246).[16] Thus, if some measurement is affected by a large number of small, independent measurement errors, the theoretical distribution of measurements will be approximately normal. It follows that a large number of such measurements actually produced would also be approximately normal. A similar story can be told for any set of observations buffeted by a large number of small, independent perturbations. By these mechanisms, therefore, the errors in a linear model could be normal, the joint distribution of x and y could be normal, and the conditional distribution $y|x$ could be normal.

But in a fundamental sense, this explanation just moves the need for a story one chapter back. Why, for example, does nature happen to generate a large number of perturbations (or measurement errors) that are small and independent of one another? What is the actual mechanism? Among the perturbations affecting students' SAT scores, for instance, might be each student's mood,

[16] Actually, the theorem can be weakened a bit to allow for correlations among some of the random variables, but this is a detail that does not fundamentally alter the arguments to follow.

energy level, and ability to concentrate. Even if the effect of each on an SAT score is small, it would seem hard to make the case that these perturbations are independent.[17] Or consider the number of traffic accidents in a given state per day. Surely the number is affected by traffic density and speed; visibility; precipitation; law enforcement practices; and the location, extent, and nature of highway repair activities. As before, even if these effects are small, they are surely not independent; consider rainy days compared with clear days. Allowing for more than one predictor, which we will do soon, might seem to provide some leverage for such problems. Later, we will examine the degree to which this is true.

An interesting variant on the normal distribution is often employed for environmental data. It is common in environmental research to find pollution measures with unimodal distributions having a long right tail; pollution concentrations are generally low, but there are a few instances when they are very high. It is then assumed that nature generates observed pollution levels, conditional on x, in a manner that leads directly to a log-normal distribution (e.g., Millard and Neerchal, 2001:175-179). Typically, the underlying natural machinery responsible for this convenient result is not described in much detail (e.g., Lindgren et al., 1993; Chilès and Delfiner, 1999:56).

But the story line might read something as follows. Suppose that the small, independent measurement errors combine not by addition but by multiplication. In particular, suppose each error alters the measurement by some proportion (which implies multiplication). A log-normal distribution results (which gets its name from the fact that if the logarithm is taken, the distribution becomes normal).

Hence, if one assumes that a large number of small, independent measurement errors combine multiplicatively, uncertainty because of measurement error can lead to a log-normal distribution for the observed variable. Each observation is produced by nature through this error-multiplication process. A variety of other story lines are possible (e.g., Rice, 1995:173), but they all share the multiplicative theme. And for each, the obvious question is why nature would operate in this fashion.

A number of other conditional distributions and stories can be found in the policy-relevant literature. Studies of recidivism, for instance, have exploited the Poisson distribution, the exponential distribution, the Weibull distribution, and the mixed exponential distribution, as well as the log-normal distribution (Maltz, 1984). The basic game remains, however. There is (a) an assumed real process (usually not specified in any detail) by which the data can be produced, (b) those data in principle then have a particular conditional distribution, (c) the

[17] Allowing for some correlations among the perturbations complicates matters because one must, in effect, require nature to produce correlations in very particular ways. Consequently, a more complex and subtle story needs to be spun.

data on hand are from that conditional distribution such that (d) inferences can be made back to parameters of the conditional distribution responsible.

Perhaps the major benefit of the data-from-nature approach is that claims are now being made more explicitly about how the natural and/or social world is supposed to work. Presumably, such claims can be carefully examined with real data, although this seems to be highly unusual. At most, one finds graphical procedures such as Q-Q plots or goodness-of-fit tests in which the null hypothesis is the assumed distribution. A failure to reject the null hypothesis is taken as evidence that nature has cooperated.

There are at least three technical problems with these strategies. First, they depend on treating a failure to reject the null hypothesis as proof that the null is true. The well-known difficulties associated with "accepting the null" will be addressed shortly. Second, the statistical power of such tests is often very weak. As the recidivism example illustrates, there are often several competing distributions that look very much alike so that it takes a great deal of data to tell them apart. Third, it follows that a more relevant issue is which null hypothesis is most consistent with the data. As a technical matter, this is often a very difficult question to answer.

But a deeper problem is that a number of underlying processes may produce data that look somewhat alike, and studying the data on hand cannot determine which machinery is responsible. For example, the Poisson can generate data that look a lot like the normal when the mean of the Poisson is relatively large (e.g., 10). Yet the distributions can behave quite differently, and the statistical tools one might apply can differ as well (e.g., the likelihood functions are different).

The obvious solution is to study the actual processes that are supposed to generate the data, not just the output of the process. Interestingly, this is almost never done. Exactly what is it about homicides, for instance, that might lead to a Poisson distribution for the number of killings per week? Precisely why should the amount of time it takes to find a job be generated by a Weibull distribution? Why, precisely, should the binary event of dropping out of school or not lead to a binomial distribution?

We will return to such questions later in the context of multiple regression and causal inference. We will also see that by including more predictors and by relying on nature to adopt a linear model, the enterprise rests primarily on how nature manufactures the errors. Whether such accounts are any more credible will be considered then.

4.1.6 A Note on Randomization Inference

Recall that under random assignment, a random sampling framework broadly applies even if the number of subjects assigned exhausts the population. With very little assumed (more on that later), one has a sound justification for statistical inference and a number of relatively straightforward inferential procedures. Building on this foundation, there has existed for some time a set of techniques called "randomization tests" that exploit the same basic logic, but when random assignment has *not* been employed (Freedman and Lane, 1983; Edgington, 1986). There also is no requirement that the predictor be a categorical intervention.

The canonical application for simple linear regression would be to test the null hypothesis of no linear relationship between the predictor and the response. The sampling distribution under the null hypothesis is derived from all possible random assignments of cases to predictor values when the predictor and response are linearly unrelated. Inferences are not made to a real population or to a particular model's parameters. Indeed, generalization is not even on the table. The goal is to estimate the probability that the observed association, or a larger one, could have occurred by random assignment alone, if there is really no linear association between the predictor and the response. In practice, this probability can be computed in several different ways, including "resampling procedures" considered later in this chapter.[18]

Because random assignment has not, in fact, been applied, one has to make the case that natural processes lead to a close approximation of random assignment or that this idealization is a useful benchmark nevertheless (Berk et al., 1995: 428-430). The former is typically difficult to do, whereas the latter changes the ground rules. If imaginary random assignment is supposed to provide a useful conceptual benchmark, the meaning of "useful" needs to be explained. Usefulness cannot just be asserted.

One can occasionally find in advocacy settings instructive discussions of how imaginary random assignment can be useful. For example, in litigation over discrimination, the defendant might claim that an observed association between race and salary is just happenstance. Random assignment is then an idealization of happenstance. But even then, one must argue that the idealization is germane. If, for instance, salary decisions are made sequentially so that one decision affects the next, the usual idealization may not be instructive; salaries are not assigned to people independently. The usefulness of thinking about happenstance as random assignment is then questionable.

Randomization tests will not be considered as another possible strategy used in the absence of real random sampling. Randomization tests have not been widely applied in bivariate regression. One reason is that the conventional randomization tests focus on some measure of association, not the regression

[18]Sometimes, the terms "randomization tests," and "permutation tests" are used interchangeably and sometimes not. Sometimes, there is a requirement that the exact randomization distribution be constructed, and sometimes, an approximation is perfectly acceptable. No effort will be made here to sort out these terms (and others). But it is important to distinguish the underlying thought experiment justifying randomization inference, which applies across the board, from the particular procedures used to construct suitable estimates of the relevant probabilities.

coefficient, and extensions to regression with more than one predictor are at best awkward (Edgington, 1983: Chapter 8). In some recent work, Rosenbaum (2002b) argues that the randomization approaches can and should be applied in multiple regression when there is interest in isolating the role of a single predictor among many. He provides a way of overcoming some of the limitations of earlier procedures. A key benefit is that randomization tests are "model free" in the same way that tests exploiting random assignment are. However, the need remains to seriously justify randomization inference when there is no random assignment. Moreover, although Rosenbaum's randomization tests may be applied to observational studies when one or more interventions are the primary concern, their use in multiple regression more generally would seem to be an unsolved problem. More will be said about these issues in subsequent chapters.

4.1.7 Summing Up

There are two widely used generic accounts of how statistical inference is justified, one in which inferences are made to a population and one in which inferences are made to a model. We shall continue to emphasize for now formulations depending on a population, in part because the resulting expositions are more grounded and in part because finding credible models for model-based sampling can be difficult. But where especially relevant, both approaches will be discussed. And as noted above, when we get to more recent statistical developments that tend to be highly model dependent, model-based sampling will be our primary vehicle for trying to answer the question "probability of what?"

4.2 Simple Linear Regression Under Random Sampling

We need now to revisit simple linear regression assuming random sampling to appreciate more fully how sampling can affect statistical inference. For now, we proceed as if all is well. The data are a random sample from a well-defined population.

4.2.1 Estimating the Population Regression Line

Suppose in the population that $\bar{y}|x = \eta_0 + \eta_1 x$.[19] The path of the means can be accurately represented by a straight line. A random sample is taken from the

[19]It is common to represent statistical features of a population with Greek letters. Thus, $\bar{y}|x$ could have been instead, for example, $\mu_y|x$. Alternative notation based on statistical concepts can also be employed. For example, $\bar{y}|x$ could have been instead $E(y|x)$, where E stands for expected value. But in context, the simpler notation used here should be clear.

population so that x and y are now random variables. The goal is to estimate the parameters of the mean function in the population, $\eta_0 + \eta_1 x$, using a random sample from that population. Hence, interest centers on the *estimated* mean function $\hat{y}|x = \hat{\eta}_0 + \hat{\eta}_1 x$.

Define the estimated fitted values (i.e., the regression line) as

$$\hat{y}_i = (\hat{y}|x = x_i) = \hat{\eta}_0 + \hat{\eta}_1 x_i. \tag{4.1}$$

Next, define the residuals as

$$\hat{e}_i = y_i - \hat{y}_i. \tag{4.2}$$

Consider the relationship between

$$y_i|x = \bar{y}|x + e_i \tag{4.3}$$

and

$$y_i|x = \hat{y}|x + \hat{e}_i. \tag{4.4}$$

Equation 4.3 partitions the conditional distribution of y in the population into two parts: the conditional mean and the error. We saw this expression earlier when we were characterizing the conditional distribution of y in a given data set. Equation 4.4 partitions the observed values of y in the sample into the fitted values and the residuals. The fitted values are constructed from x by using the assumed linear form. Clearly, the linear function is, in an important sense, a stand-in for the conditional means. But where this really matters is in the population.

Recall that, in the population, the mean of the errors around $\bar{y}|x$ equals zero. If the assumed linear function holds in the population, the mean of the errors around the linear function for given values of x is also zero. This is because, in the population, the linear function captures the path of the means exactly, and the line can substitute perfectly for the conditional means. It also follows that, if the assumed linear function does not hold in the population, the errors around each conditional mean, now represented in the population by the specified linear function, will not all have a mean of zero. For some values of x, the errors will tend to be larger than for other values of x.

When describing the path of the means in a particular data set, the only penalty for using a linear function when it is not fully correct is a less accurate rendering of the conditional means. That the conditional errors no longer necessarily average to zero does not really matter. With estimation from a random sample to the population, the stakes are much higher, as we shall soon see, because, in the population, x is now related to the errors.

We again apply the least squares criterion, but now to a random sample. As before,

$$RSS(h_0, h_1) = \sum_{i=1}^{n}(y_i - [h_0 + h_1 x_i])^2, \tag{4.5}$$

where (h_0, h_1) are candidate estimates for $(\hat{\eta}_0, \hat{\eta}_1)$ that minimize the residual sum of squares, *RSS*. Solving this problem leads to the same as the formulas we used earlier for description. But now the task ahead is rather more challenging. We are using the least squares formulas as estimators. Are they any good at that job?

The most common measures of "good" rely on the frequentist thought experiment described earlier. The question then is "How do the least squares estimates of the slope and intercept perform in a limitless number of independent random samples from the given population?" A key factor is the relationship between x and e. We will revisit this issue many times in the pages ahead, but a good first approximation is that, if x and e are (loosely speaking) unrelated, least squares estimates of the regression coefficients will be unbiased. For the special case of random sampling from a population, if the assumed linear form accurately represents the path of the means in the population, the least squares estimates are unbiased.[20] Then, the mean of the sampling distribution of $\hat{\eta}_0$ equals the value of η_0 in the population. Also, the mean of the sampling distribution of $\hat{\eta}_1$ equals the value of η_1 in the population. Thus, on the average (over the limitless independent random samples), the least squares estimates will get the population regression line right.

This entire line of reasoning demonstrably works when there is random sampling in fact. It can work without actual random sampling if a good case can be made for Strategy II or III: that nature generated a random sample from a population or the data are a random realization from a superpopulation. We will see soon that the reasoning is a little different for Strategy IV: model-based sampling.

In the population, if the conditional variance for y is constant, the least squares estimators of η_0 and η_1 by the Gauss-Markov theorem have the minimum variance among the class of linear unbiased estimators.[21] That is, for the class of linear estimators, their sampling distributions will tend to cluster most tightly around the population values. On the average, the least squares estimates will be as close as possible. Again, this all depends on random sampling and that same thought experiment.

Some data analysts find little comfort in such reasoning because it has nothing to say about how the estimates perform in any given sample. All of the desirable properties materialize over the long run and then only in an imaginary world of limitless, independent random samples. Not surprisingly, this also opens

[20] This is proven in almost any regression textbook.

[21] Recall

$$\hat{\eta}_1 = \frac{SXY}{SXX} = r(x, y)\frac{\mathrm{SD}(y)}{\mathrm{SD}(x)} = \sum_{i=1}^{n}\left(\frac{x_i - \bar{x}}{SXX}\right) y_i. \tag{4.6}$$

The values of y are combined in a linear fashion if we treat the x as fixed. This is what is meant by a linear estimator.

the door to critics of frequentist statistical inference (Leamer, 1978; Berk et al., 1995).

4.2.2 Estimating the Standard Errors

The sampling distributions have variances and covariances. For the variance of $\hat{\eta}_1$, we have

$$\text{Var}(\hat{\eta}_1) = \sigma^2 \frac{1}{SXX}, \tag{4.7}$$

where σ^2 is the variance around the regression fit.

One implication is that the estimates of $\hat{\eta}_1$ are more variable if there is more variability around the regression line and there is less variability in x. This is why, for the ozone and temperature study introduced earlier, one might want to select the value of x from the extremes of that distribution. The variance of the predictor is then large.

For the variance of $\hat{\eta}_0$,

$$\text{Var}(\hat{\eta}_0) = \sigma^2 \left(\frac{1}{n} + \frac{\bar{x}^2}{SXX} \right). \tag{4.8}$$

The variance of $\hat{\eta}_0$ is larger when there is more variability around the regression line, when the sample size n is small, when the data are not well centered around x, and when the variability of x is small. This motivates some researchers who have a strong interest in the value of the intercept to center x (i.e., subtract the mean of x from each observation). Centering decreases the variance of $\hat{\eta}_0$.

Estimates of the slope and intercept in repeated random samples are related to one another in the following manner:

$$\text{Cov}(\hat{\eta}_0, \hat{\eta}_1) = -\sigma^2 \frac{\bar{x}}{SXX}. \tag{4.9}$$

The sign will depend on the mean of x. And the covariance will be larger in absolute value when there is more variability around the regression line and when there is not much variability in x.

Finally, we need an estimate of the variance around the regression line. Thus,

$$\hat{\sigma}^2 = \sum_{i=1}^{n} \hat{e}_i^2/(n-2) = RSS/(n-2). \tag{4.10}$$

One degree of freedom is lost for the slope and one degree of freedom is lost for the intercept. After dividing by $(n-2)$, the estimator for $\hat{\sigma}^2$ is unbiased. The value of $\hat{\sigma}^2$ estimates the variance around the regression line, which can provide useful information about how good the fit is. The square root, sometimes called the standard error of estimate, approximates the distance between the fit and a typical observation y_i.

The estimated variance is also needed in practice to make Equations 4.7 through 4.9 operational. In particular, the estimated variance $\hat{\sigma}^2$ is used instead of the unknown variance σ^2 in Equations 4.7 and 4.8 to get the standard errors for $\hat{\eta}_0$ and $\hat{\eta}_1$. These standard errors, the estimated standard deviations of the relevant sampling distributions, play a key role in formal hypothesis tests and confidence intervals.

4.2.3 Estimation Under Model-Based Sampling

When model-based sampling is used, one must alter a bit what it takes for statistical inference to work properly. Because there is no population, one's assumptions shift to the model responsible for the data. We shall consider this in more detail shortly, but broadly stated, one has to assume that nature generates the data so that errors around the regression line are unrelated to x.

Presumably, one would know whether this is true if the means by which nature generated the data were well understood. For example, understandings about how nature works might lead to the conclusion that the conditional distribution of y is normal with a mean that depends linearly on x alone and a variance that does not depend on x at all. When the necessary knowledge is not there, however, a popular strategy is simply to assert that nature produced the data so the deviations around the regression line do not depend on x. Such reasoning is close to circular: For statistical inference to apply, assume that nature produces the data so that it does. We shall see later that such reasoning is effectively untestable. The result is another example of assume-and-proceed statistics.

4.2.4 Some Things That Can Go Wrong

What happens if, under random sampling (or one of its proxies), the assumed linear function does not accurately represent the path of the means in the population? As noted above, it is no longer true that the population errors around each conditional mean (as derived from the regression line) average zero. It follows that the least squares estimates of $\hat{\eta}_0$ and $\hat{\eta}_1$ are biased. On the average, they will systematically overestimate or underestimate η_0 and η_1. The bias in the estimates results from a relationship between x and the errors in the population. The role of x in the construction of the conditional means cannot be isolated. The errors and x are correlated.[22] One has the same problem within model-based sampling if, for any reason, the mean of $e|x$ does not equal zero.

[22]Unbiased estimates of the regression parameters require that the e and x are uncorrelated. Independence between e and x is a much stronger condition, denoting that the "entire" conditional distribution of e is unrelated to x. In addition to the mean of e being unrelated, so is the variance of e and the shape of the distribution of e.

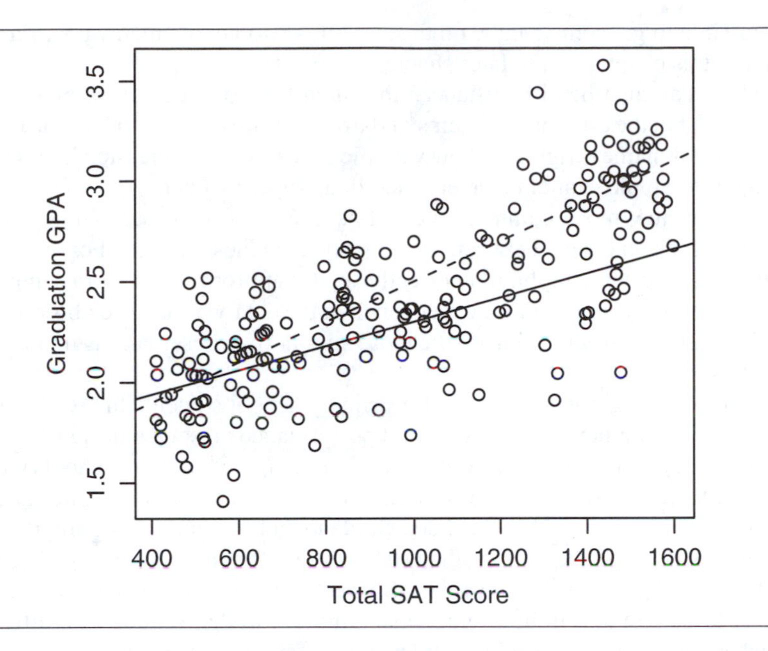

Figure 4.5. Scatter Plot of GPA at Graduation and Total SAT I Score for the Population Showing Biased Estimation

Figure 4.5 provides a visual sense of the confounding and its consequences. Suppose Figure 4.5 is a scatter plot of a population of students with total SAT I score as the predictor and GPA at graduation as the response. The solid line shows the actual population regression line. Alternatively, it is the regression line for the model generating the data. But it is clear that larger positive errors around the line tend also to have larger SAT I values. As a result, the estimated regression line, shown as a dashed line, is rotated counterclockwise. On the average, the regression line estimated from a sample will be too steep.[23]

If the estimates of η_0 and η_1 are biased, the estimates of $\hat{\sigma}^2$ and standard errors will be wrong. If bias matters, and to most data analysts it does, the game of statistical inference is technically over. What may remain is a debate about whether the biases are large enough to matter in practical terms. Sometimes, it

[23]The regression line would be estimated from a random sample but is here overlaid on the population scatter plot where the problem is actually to be found. Also, one might think that one could explore directly in a sample the possible relationship between x and e. As we consider in a later chapter, one can sometimes gain some insight about this using the sample data, but it will always be true for the simple linear model that, by construction, the residuals are uncorrelated with the predictor.

is possible to get some handle on this, and it is a topic to which we will return later in this chapter and in later chapters.

There can also be circumstances in which the estimates of η_0 and η_1 are unbiased, but the estimates of their standard errors are wrong.[24] On the average, the regression line is right, but how variable the estimated regression line is from sample to sample cannot be determined in a proper manner.

One of the most common ways this arises is if a sampling process generates dependence between the observed values of $y|x$. For example, multistage cluster sampling, a perfectly legitimate form of random sampling, almost certainly will produce dependence in the data $y|x$ because observations within a given cluster will likely be more similar than observations in different clusters.[25]

Thus, one might wish to study for primary school students the relationship between the number of days truant and performance on statewide achievement tests. To do so, one might first draw a random sample of primary schools within a state, then a random sample of teachers in each school, and then a random sample of students of those teachers. Students in the same school are likely to be more similar on the average than students in different schools (e.g., because of home backgrounds that are alike). Students with the same teachers are more likely to be similar on the average than students in that school with different teachers (e.g., because teaching styles will differ across teachers).

It follows that a regression analysis using conventional formulas can produce unbiased estimates of the regression line linking truancy to test performance but systematically underestimate the standard errors. In effect, the sampling generates less variability in $y|x$ than one would expect under simple random sampling. Other things equal, the estimate of the residual variance will be, on the average, too small, which in turn will make the estimates of the standard errors too small (see Equations 4.7 through 4.10). Fortunately, there are usually ways to correct these estimates, although a discussion of such procedures is beyond the scope of this book.[26]

Typically far more difficult to handle is dependence that occurs naturally in the data. Consider again the example of ocean water samples to measure the concentration of toxic runoff. There would be dependence in the data if the 7-day interval between samples was not long enough for existing

---

[24] A technical point. When the mean of the conditional errors is zero, and when the variance around the means of y is constant, conventional estimates of the variance of the regression coefficients can be estimated in an unbiased manner. The nonlinear transformation inherent in taking the square root of the variance to get the standard error biases the estimate of the standard error a bit. But in large samples, the bias becomes negligible.

[25] The argument actually has two pieces. First, if one case in a cluster is chosen, the probability that a second case in the cluster is chosen increases, sometimes dramatically. Second, these two cases are more likely to be similar on the variables of interest than two cases from different clusters.

[26] See any good textbook on sampling, such as Steven Thompson's (2002).

pollution levels in the near-shore ocean to be purged by currents and wave action. That is, independence requires that every seventh day begins with a clean slate.

If the researcher knows the sources of the dependence and can capture it through some form of modeling, then it is possible in principle to correct the estimated standard errors. For example, if nature generates the data in a manner that approximates well multistage cluster sampling and if the researcher knows what the clusters are, there is some chance of getting the standard errors close to right. If not, there is not.[27]

Whether the data are derived from random sampling or from nature, another common way in which one may obtain unbiased estimates of $\hat{\eta}_0$ and $\hat{\eta}_1$, and yet have biased estimates of the standard errors, is for the variance around the regression line in the population to not have constant variance. Recall the example in the previous chapter in which money spent on health care was the response and income was the predictor. Higher-income households had greater discretion in how much they spent on medical treatment that was not essential. In the earlier example of ozone concentrations and temperature over the course of a day, there might well be more variability around the regression line on days with strong, gusty winds. In both cases, the use of a single value for σ^2 in the formulas for the relevant standard errors is incorrect.

One can get a feel for the consequences through a very simple illustration. Consider a scatter plot in the population that has more variability around the regression line for very low and very high values of x. There will be more variability in the estimated regression line than can be captured by formulas in which σ^2 is assumed to be unrelated to x. The extra variability happens to fall toward the ends of the regression line where the impact on the fit is greatest (as in a teeter-totter).

If one knows the source of the nonconstant variance and can represent it in the variance function, proper estimates of the regression standard errors can sometimes be obtained. Alternatively, it is sometimes possible to transform the response variable so that the variance of the errors is approximately constant. Log transformations sometimes can be helpful in this regard.

4.2.5 Tests and Confidence Intervals

Assume for now that all is well. Random sampling prevails. Each of the features of the simple linear model holds in the population or in the manner by which nature generates the data. But in order to construct formal significance tests and confidence intervals, one needs to know the distribution of each sample

---

[27] One approach is sometimes called multilevel modeling, which, as a form of regression analysis, will be briefly discussed in a later chapter.

statistic in repeated independent samples. An easy way to solve this problem is to proceed as if

$$y|x \sim \text{NIID}(\eta_0 + \eta_1 x, \sigma^2). \tag{4.11}$$

On top of the assumptions of (a) random sampling, (b) a linear relationship between y and x, and (c) constant variance around the regression line, the conditional distribution of y (or equivalently e) is assumed to be normal. Under random sampling, this is usually an additional assumption. Under model-based sampling, it is commonly built in.

Then, estimates $\hat{\eta}_0$ and $\hat{\eta}_1$ are bivariate normal and

$$(n-2)\frac{\hat{\sigma}^2}{\sigma^2} \sim \chi^2_{n-2}. \tag{4.12}$$

Note that $\hat{\sigma}^2$ is distributed independently of the estimates of the regression coefficients, which simplifies some later calculations.

How sensible is the normality assumption? We addressed this question earlier in the context of possible alternatives to random sampling. But here, the normality assumption for $y|x$ is really just a means to the end of normal sampling distributions for $\hat{\eta}_0$ and $\hat{\eta}_1$. So, one can sidestep the normality assumption and cite the central limit theorem for statistics computed from a sample rather than variables in a population. Roughly speaking, as the sample size increases, the *sampling distribution* of $\hat{\eta}_0$ and $\hat{\eta}_1$ more closely approximates a bivariate normal distribution. Often, that approximation will be quite good even for samples as small as 30.

If the sampling distribution for $\hat{\eta}_0$ and $\hat{\eta}_1$ can be taken as close to normal, one can proceed with confidence intervals and hypothesis tests of various sorts. For simple linear regression, there is little of special importance to say; the game proceeds pretty much as usual. But as a reminder, and to help set the stage for discussion of some other issues, it may be useful to briefly consider what hypothesis tests and confidence intervals formally mean.

For confidence intervals, we begin with some statistic computed from a sample.[28] To keep it all very general, that statistic will be represented by S (e.g., $\hat{\eta}_1$). This statistic is approximately normally distributed with a mean $E(S)$ and a variance $\sigma^2 c$, where c is a known number that can depend on the sample size or on any of the predictors but not on the response (e.g., $1/SXX$). The standard error of S is estimated by $\text{SE}(W) = \hat{\sigma} c^{1/2}$. Now, if the estimate $\hat{\sigma}^2$ has d degrees of freedom and is independent of S, then the $(1-\alpha) \times 100\%$ confidence interval is

$$S - Q(t_d, 1-\alpha/2)\text{SE}(S) \leq E(S) \leq S + Q(t_d, 1-\alpha/2)\text{SE}(S). \tag{4.13}$$

[28]The exposition of confidence intervals and tests to follow draws heavily from Cook and Weisberg (1999).

Recall the meaning of Equation 4.13. Suppose α is .05. Then, in 95% of a limitless number of independent random samples from the same population, intervals constructed in this fashion will contain the population parameter of interest (e.g., η_1). Equation 4.13 does not mean

1. in 95% of a limitless number of independent random samples from the same population, the population parameter of interest will be contained within the interval constructed from the sample on hand; or
2. one is 95% certain that the population parameter of interest is contained within the interval constructed from the sample on hand.

The key error in the first misinterpretation is to forget that, in each independent hypothetical sample, S and $\text{SE}(S)$ will almost certainly differ. And so will the confidence intervals; there is not one confidence interval, but many. The additional error in the second misinterpretation is to use frequentist probabilities to represent a state of mind. How certain or uncertain a data analyst may be is not represented by the probabilities generated in the frequentist thought experiment.

Now recall the canonical test for a regression statistic such as the estimated slope ($\hat{\eta}_1$). Suppose that h_1 is a value for the slope of particular interest in the population. Then

$$\begin{array}{ll} \text{Null hypothesis:} & \eta_1 = h_1, \ \eta_0 \text{ arbitrary} \\ \text{Alternative hypothesis:} & \eta_1 \neq h_1, \ \eta_0 \text{ arbitrary.} \end{array} \tag{4.14}$$

One can then employ the usual Wald test statistic,

$$t = \frac{\text{estimate} - \text{hypothesized value}}{\text{standard error of the estimate}} = \frac{S - h}{\text{SE}(S)}. \tag{4.15}$$

Thus, for example,

$$t = \frac{\hat{\eta}_1 - h_1}{\text{SE}(\hat{\eta}_1)}. \tag{4.16}$$

From the value of t (from the t distribution), one can obtain the conventional p-value. Recall what the p-value represents. If the null hypothesis is true, one would expect to find sample statistics as extreme or more extreme than the sample statistic observed ($100 \times p$-value) percent of the time. For example, if (a) the computed value of $\hat{\eta}_1$ is 2.37, (b) the null hypothesis is that $\eta_1 = 0$, (c) the alternative is that $\eta_1 > 0$, and (d) the p-value is .023, one may conclude that, in a limitless number of independent random samples from the same population, if the value of the slope in the population is 0, one would expect to have an estimated slope of 2.37 or greater about 2.3% of the time. A useful interpretation of the p-value is that it conveys in probabilistic terms the weight of the evidence against the null hypothesis. The p-value is, by definition, not:

1. the probability that the null hypothesis is false or
2. the size of the relationship between x and y.

It is not clear, on close inspection, what the probability that the null hypothesis is false might mean. The null hypothesis is either true or false; there is nothing in between. The size of the relationship between x and y should not be a function of the sample size, but the p-value is.

In practice, of course, it is rare for the p-value to live up to its billing. In particular, researchers often compute a large number of p-values and fiddle with the data in various ways either before p-values are computed or in response to the ones obtained. In certain rarefied situations, p-values can be discounted appropriately, but most of the time, these procedures (e.g., Bonferroni corrections) cannot properly reflect the sequential and dependent relationships between the p-values computed. And in the absence of any correction, the computed p-values are likely to be too small, often very much too small. The weight of the evidence against the null hypothesis looks far stronger than it really is. These problems are hardly special to regression analysis and will not be pursued any further here.

It is common for many data analysts to want to do something more than characterize the weight of the evidence against the null hypothesis. They feel the need to make a decision about whether the null hypothesis should be rejected. A critical value (α) is determined, such as .05, and if the p-value is that small or smaller, the null hypothesis is automatically discarded.

The issues raised by formal tests are also not special to regression analysis, and there are a number of excellent critiques of hypothesis tests in print (Oakes, 1986; Cohen, 1994; Schmidt, 1996).[29] But one issue warrants emphasis because it will figure importantly in later chapters when tests with particular relevance to regression are considered (e.g., "specification tests"). Recall that, as a simple matter of logic, a failure to reject the null hypothesis does not mean that the null hypothesis is true. There will always be a limitless number of other hypotheses, different from the null, that will also not be rejected by the same test. For example, suppose $\hat{\eta}_1 = 3.0$ and the standard error is 2.25. With the usual assumptions, a one-tailed test of the null hypothesis that $\eta_1 = 0$ will yield a p-value of about .20. Given a critical value of .05 level, one would not reject the null hypothesis. However, all of the null hypotheses $-0.69 < \eta_1 < 3.0$ would also not be rejected at the .05 level.

[29] For a thorough and reasonably even-handed airing of these and other related issues, see Barnett (1982).

4.3 Statistical Power

In the context of hypothesis testing, the proper role of statistical power deserves brief mention. Recall that the power of a test is the probability that the null hypothesis will be rejected when it is false. Clearly, one would like that probability to be large.

Yet many studies using regression analysis are criticized for being "underpowered." Even for alternative hypotheses that are of genuine scientific or policy interest, the probability of rejecting a false null hypothesis is small. The culprits can be a small sample size, a lot of variability in y, and/or little variability in x. The usual fix is to collect a sufficiently large sample and/or values of x that are sufficiently heterogeneous so that an acceptable level of power is achieved (e.g., .80). But determing the required sample size or variance of x can be difficult. One must anticipate reasonably well the likely value of the regression intercept and slope, the variance of x (if no special effort is made to collect a heterogeneous set of x values), and the residual variance of y (Kraemer and Thiemann, 1987). Matters are substantially more complicated when there are two or more predictors.

One can sometimes find power analyses applied to data that have already been collected to explain, after the fact, why one or more null hypotheses have not been rejected. Indeed, this is where some "underpowered" criticisms are found. However, post hoc power analyses can be treacherous and even lead to embarrassing paradoxes. For example, the computed p-value and power are hopelessly confounded, so one cannot determine the role of power independently of an offending p-value. Hoenig and Heisey (2001) start with this point, and it goes downhill from there.

A related camp claims that lack of power can be overcome through "meta-analysis" (e.g., Lipsey and Wilson, 2001). The idea is to pool the results of a large number of studies so that, in effect, many small samples become one large sample. Although this has enormous appeal, the gains are usually illusory (Berk and Freedman, 2001). A key problem is that for the statistical inference used in meta-analysis to make any sense, one must treat the set of studies as a random sample from a population of studies. This is dubious on its face. We will return to meta-analysis in a later chapter in part because regression analysis is often employed to examine why the results across some studies differ.

4.4 Stochastic Predictors

To this point in the discussion of statistical inference, x has been treated as fixed. In repeated samples under random sampling or in repeated realizations when the data were generated by nature, x was allowed to vary. But the estimators employed for the simple linear model took x as fixed once it materialized in the data. Once x was known, the relevant mathematical expressions conditioned on x as if it were actually not allowed to vary in repeated samples. The only uncertainty of concern was to be found in the distribution of y given x.

If x is stochastic by design (e.g., simple random sampling of observational units) or is assumed to be generated in a random manner by nature, and if the data analyst wants to treat x as such, one has to proceed a bit differently. There is now random variation in x as well as in y that needs to be taken into account.

Under random sampling, if one is still prepared to assume that, in the population, the mean of the errors conditional on x is zero, estimates of the regression coefficients remain unbiased. Likewise, if nature generates the data such that the mean of the errors conditional on x is zero, estimates of the regression coefficients remain unbiased.[30] But in either case, even if the variance around the conditional means of y is constant, the estimated standard errors will be wrong. The problem is that those standard errors are computed with the sum of squares of x in the denominator. Because x is now a random variable, there is additional uncertainty that is not captured by the fixed x formula. However, if the sample size is not very small (e.g., > 50), the extra uncertainty due to x is rarely of much practical importance. The price for proceeding as usual is not very high.

But when x is taken to be stochastic, some researchers apparently find the assumption that $\bar{e}|x = 0$ too onerous. They favor a slightly weaker pair of assumptions: $\bar{e} = 0$ and $\text{Cov}(x, e) = 0$. In the population or in the process by which nature generates the data, the mean of all the errors is zero and the correlation between the errors and x is zero. The pair of assumptions is weaker because $\bar{e}|x = 0$ implies the other two but not the reverse. Why these weaker assumptions are more palatable for real data sets is at least obscure. It is hard to see how the two assumptions, which are formally less demanding, would be more likely to be true in practice.

Moreover, the least squares estimates of the regression coefficients are now biased. Here, in brief, is the problem.

Consider again the simple regression model but, for ease of exposition, with each variable in units of deviations from its mean,

$$y|x = \eta_1 x + e. \tag{4.17}$$

The least squares estimate of $\hat{\eta}_1$ with mean-deviated variables is

$$\hat{\eta}_1 = \frac{\sum_{i=1}^{n} x_i y_i}{\sum_{i=1}^{n} x_i^2}. \tag{4.18}$$

Substituting Equation 4.17 into Equation 4.18 and simplifying, one gets

$$\hat{\eta}_1 = \eta_1 + \frac{\sum_{i=1}^{n} x_i e_i}{\sum_{i=1}^{n} x_i^2}. \tag{4.19}$$

[30] A very accessible discussion of estimation with stochastic regressors of asymptotic distributions more generally can be found in Johnston's econometrics text (1984: Chapter 7).

In other words, the estimate $\hat{\eta}_1$ is the sum of the "true" slope, η_1, plus the sum of cross products of x and the errors divided by the sum of squares of x. For the $\hat{\eta}_1$ to equal η_1, the sum of cross products would have to always equal zero. That will only be true very occasionally by accident (whether or not x is fixed). For $\hat{\eta}_1$ to be an unbiased estimate of η_1, the far right term would need to have an expected value of zero (taking the expectation of both sides of Equation 4.19). There is no reason to think that such would be the case. Why would the expectation of a sum of the products of two variables necessarily equal zero?[31]

But there is a fallback position. Suppose one multiplies both the top and the bottom of the problematic term by $1/n$. The denominator is then $\sum_{i=1}^{n} x_i^2/n$. Imagine a sequence of samples of increasing size so that n gets increasingly large. Both the sum in the numerator and the sample size in the denominator get large. Under some additional assumptions that are sometimes quite reasonable,[32] it can be shown that, as n increases without limit, $\sum_{i=1}^{n} x_i^2/n$ approaches a nonzero constant related to the variance of x.

Meanwhile, as n increases without limit, $\sum_{i=1}^{n} x_i e_i/n$ approaches zero. That is, the covariance between e and x converges to a value of zero. So, the limiting value is zero, and, in that sense, the problem disappears. The least squares estimator is then said to be "consistent." Consistency serves as the alternative to unbiasedness. In practice, what this means is that, in large samples, the bias in the least squares estimates will be small. There is rarely any formal rule, however, for how large is large. In simple linear regression, practitioners seem to be comfortable with samples of 100 or more.

Some authors, faced with a stochastic x, prefer to assume that x and e are independent. This is the strongest assumption considered here because unbiased estimates of the regression coefficients automatically follow, and the appropriate standard errors can be directly computed. Basically, you get it all. But how plausible is the independence assumption?

There are two stories that can be used to make a consideration of the independence assumption more concrete. First, there is a population consisting of x and e. In this population, both are fixed. But there is balance in the sense that, for every possible value of x, the distribution of e is the same. To take a very simple example, suppose x can take on values of 1, 2, 3, 4, or 5. And suppose e can take on values of -1, 0, and $+1$. There are then 15 possible pairings of x and e, each of which is linked to an observational unit.[33] Random sampling of

[31] The expected value of a variable is essentially the weighted mean over all possible values of that variable. The weights are the probabilities associated with each possible value. Expectations are used here because the mean is not being computed from a data set but from all data sets that could materialize under the frequentist thought experiment.

[32] For example, one cannot allow the values of x to increase without limit as the number of observations increases without limit.

[33] There could be thousands of observational units in the population but still only 15 distinct pairings.

cases from such a population will lead to independence between the (sampled) random variables x and e.

It is hard to think of a real situation in which nature or a researcher would construct such a population. Perhaps in response, the far more popular story abandons a sampling formulation altogether and treats nature as an unpaid but highly skilled collaborator; we are back to model-based sampling. Nature randomly generates the values of x and e so that they are independent. There is no population, only some natural mechanism that produces a very convenient pair of random variables. Nature also goes the next step of linearly combining independent x and e to construct y with the familiar $y = \eta_0 + \eta_1 x + e$. The researcher gets to work with the two random variables x and y. The random variable e is not observable. The goal, as before, is to estimate the values of η_0 and η_1 from the values of x and y. In short, this is the first of the three flavors of models we considered earlier but now with a stochastic x and e generated so as to be independent.

There are certain situations in which at least the first part of the second story for independence maps pretty well to how nature is understood to operate. For example, if e represents random measurement, there will be settings in which it is reasonable to assume that the random errors have a mean of zero and behave as if drawn independently from some distribution and also independently of random x. Thus, x might be the distance from shore of some ocean current thought to be dispersing pollutants. Because ocean currents are turbulent, the distance from shore will be a random variable. That distance may be measured by satellite instruments, which in earlier laboratory experiments may have been shown to measure with a certain amount of noise. One might then be able to argue convincingly that the measurement error is unrelated to the true distance from shore.

But if the truth be told, the differences between the assumptions one can make to obtain acceptable estimates of the slope and intercept when x is stochastic (or when it is not) are, in practical terms, not very important. All are extremely demanding and very hard to justify in practice.

In summary, three definitions of "exogeneity" for a random x have just been considered. They all apply to the population in random sampling or to how nature generates the data in model-based sampling. The strongest form assumes that x and e are independent. The second strongest form assumes that the conditional means of the errors around the regression line are zero. The weakest form assumes that the unconditional mean of the errors is zero and the correlation between x and the errors is zero.[34]

---

[34] When economists worry about exogeneity, it is more likely in the context of regression models for longitudinal data or regression models involving more than one equation in which, for any of several possible reasons, the equations are linked (e.g., the response in one equation is a predictor in another equation). Both of these extensions of conventional regression will be considered briefly in a later chapter.

But it is difficult to construct plausible scenarios for real data in which the case for one of the less demanding forms of exogeneity would be far easier to make than for one of the more demanding forms. So, it is also difficult to see how it would matter in practice. Some may argue that such difficulties stem from limiting the discussion to models with a single predictor. With more predictors, the case for some useful kind of exogeneity would be far easier to make. We will see later that, although in some instances, adding more predictors will make the case for exogeneity more credible, there will often be a high price to pay with respect to other, equally important issues.

Finally, although consistency and other asymptotic properties are comforting to some, the implications for data analysts are less clear. Sample sizes are finite, and for any given sample size, it can be extremely difficult to know how much one can count on theoretical results derived from samples of limitless size.

4.5 Measurement Error

To this point, measurement error has been only briefly mentioned. Measurement error is an important problem but hardly for regression analysis alone. It is also an enormous topic. We shall consider very briefly measurement error as it applies to simple linear regression.

If either x or y is subject to systematic measurement error, the results of a regression analysis, even descriptively in a population, could be very misleading. The response and predictor values used will, on the average, be too high or too low. Then, the fit interpreted could be very different from the true fit.

In practice, data analysts usually assume that any systematic measurement errors are too small to matter. Careful data analysts concerned about measurement error usually try to rely on studies of the measurement process itself, such as engineering and laboratory research on particular instruments. In many policy areas, an alternative to laboratory studies is to collect special data with which one can try to validate the data routinely collected. A controversial recent attempt was to undertake a special and unusually well-conducted sample survey to evaluate the accuracy of statistical adjustments for undercounts in the regular census (Brown et al., 1999).

By random measurement error, one loosely means "noise." Suppose $\tilde{x} = x + \epsilon$ and that $\tilde{y} = y + \nu$. Both ϵ and ν have a mean of zero and behave as if drawn independently, at random, from their own distributions. In a regression analysis, one uses $\tilde{x}$ and $\tilde{y}$ instead of x and y. The impact of the random measurement error in y alone is to leave most of the basic regression results intact. Estimates of $\hat{\eta}_0$ and $\hat{\eta}_1$ retain all of their desirable properties except that the measurement errors are added to the *RSS*; the fit is not as good, and, as a result, the standard errors for $\hat{\eta}_0$ and $\hat{\eta}_1$ are increased.

When x has random measurement error, biased estimates of the regression line follow. In the simple regression case, the slope is attenuated by the following relationship:

$$\tilde{\eta}_1 = \eta_1 \frac{\sigma_x^2}{\sigma_x^2 + \sigma_\epsilon^2}, \tag{4.20}$$

where σ_x^2 and σ_ϵ^2 are the variances of x and the measurement error, respectively. One implication is that if one can obtain an estimate of σ_ϵ^2, one can correct for the attenuation. There will sometimes be such estimates available. Matters become much more complicated when there is more than one predictor, as we will see later. Slopes may be biased upward or downward, the correction of which requires one to build a model of the measurement error process on top of the regression analysis of interest. More will be said on this in a later chapter. Suffice it for now to observe that in order to obtain even reasonably unbiased estimates of the regression line with conventional formulas, there cannot be much systematic measurement error in x or y and not much random measurement error in x as well. The alternative of modeling the measurement error process builds in still more from outside of the data.

4.6 Can Resampling Techniques Help?

Over the past decade, resampling procedures have been developed that can provide information about the sampling distribution of sample statistics using less demanding assumptions about the population from which the data were sampled. The bootstrap is perhaps the most well known of these procedures and can be effectively used to demonstrate some key features of resampling. Other techniques include the jackknife and permutation tests.[35]

Conventionally, what we know about sampling distributions is what can be derived formally. For example, we know for regression analysis that if, in the population, the simple linear model holds, and if the errors are normally distributed, the sampling distributions of the slope and intercept will be normal as well. And we know that, even if they are not normal in small samples, they will be normal in limitless independent samples. But what if:

[35]For the jackknife, each observation is dropped from the data in turn and sample statistics computed. Thus, if there are 200 observations, 200 sample statistics are computed, each based on 199 observations. Variation in the 200 sample statistics provides information about the role of random sampling error.

Permutation tests are the same as randomization tests discussed briefly earlier. In the resampling context, a permutation sampling distribution is either exhaustively constructed, or, more likely, a random sample from the exhaustive permutation distribution is generated (Efron and Tibshirani, 1993, Chapter 15).

1. normality cannot be plausibly assumed;
2. the small sample is too small for the central limit theorem to help much; or
3. in the large sample case, the mathematics are intractable?

Sometimes there are computer-based solutions to such problems. Basically, one simulates what the sampling distribution should look like and uses the simulation results for statistical inference. The trick is that one samples again and again from the single sample on hand (with replacement) as if it were the population. If the sample were generated by sound probability procedures, it is reasonable as an approximation to treat the sample as a stand-in for the population. Sampling over and over from a sample is often called "resampling." The bootstrap is perhaps the most popular instance (Efron and Tibshirani, 1993; Davison and Hinkley, 1997).

One would think that the bootstrap would not be especially relevant to the issues raised in this book. But like any number of procedures, the bootstrap is often oversold. In particular, the bootstrap has been offered by some (Bollen, 1995) as a way to undertake statistical inference for regression models with data that are not random samples. To see why this makes little sense, we will consider the bootstrap in more detail than would otherwise be necessary.

The bootstrap is essentially a simulation of the frequentist thought experiment. To help underscore this, consider the following notation:

- There is a population of N units: $(U_1, U_2, \ldots, U_N)$.
- On each unit, there are measurements $Y_1, Y_2, \ldots, Y_N$, which can be a single measurement per unit or many.
- These measures have a joint probability distribution (in the population) F.
- A random sample of size n (n is usually smaller than N) is taken.
- There are sampled units $(u_1, u_2, \ldots, u_n)$.
- For each, there are measurements $y_1, y_2, \ldots, y_n$, which have a joint empirical distribution function $\hat{F}$.
- The "plug-in" estimate of the population parameter $\theta = t(F)$ is $\hat{\theta} = t(\hat{F})$; one can use the same function for the summary statistic as one would use for the population parameter. To this point, the random sampling process has been characterized through which the data were generated. Now, that process is simulated over and over.
- The B samples drawn from the data set are called bootstrap samples, $\mathbf{y}^{*1}, \mathbf{y}^{*2}, \ldots, \mathbf{y}^{*B}$. In practice, B can be as small as 30 or larger than 1,000, depending on the data and the purpose of the bootstrap.
- The plug-in estimate we compute for each of the B bootstrap samples is $s(\mathbf{y}^{*1}), s(\mathbf{y}^{*2}), \ldots, s(\mathbf{y}^{*B})$.

As the concepts and notation imply, one draws B bootstrap samples from the data. Each sample is of size n. Sampling *with* replacement is employed, using the same basic strategy that was used to generate the data originally. If the data were generated by simple random sampling, random sampling with replacement is used to approximate random sampling without replacement. If the data were generated by stratified sampling, stratified sampling with replacement is used to approximate stratified sampling without replacement. The same sort of logic is applied to cluster sampling.

Thus, one is simulating the frequentist thought experiment but using the data set on hand as if it were the population. This assumes that one knows how the data were generated and that it was some form of random sampling or a naturally produced close approximation.

In practice, the key is being able to find or write from scratch computer code that reproduces the sampling procedures. Most canned software assumes simple random sampling, which is usually well approximated by resampling with replacement. But most large-scale surveys, for example, employ far more complicated sampling approaches. The standard bootstrap software will fail on these applications. Special computer code needs to be written.

For each bootstrap sample $\mathbf{y}^{*b}$, the plug-in estimate $s(\mathbf{y}^{*b})$ of θ is computed. In the univariate case, the plug-in estimate might be the mean or the median. There will be, say, B estimates of the mean. One can use the set of estimates in several different ways. We turn to several popular examples.

4.6.1 Percentile Confidence Intervals

One can construct a histogram of the $s(\mathbf{y}^{*1}), \ldots, s(\mathbf{y}^{*B})$, which provides an empirical estimate of the sampling distribution. The shape of this estimate will, at the very least, provide information about how well the actual sampling distribution corresponds to the normal. However, whether that approximation is good does not really matter if one is going to use the bootstrap results for statistical inference.

A confidence interval can be computed using percentiles. The middle 95% of the estimates, for example, is the 95% confidence interval because it is the range in which the middle 95% of the scores fall. There are a number of variants on this basic theme, some of which can better approximate the true confidence interval in certain situations.

For example, with the studentized bootstrap, the idea is to compute Z scores for the statistic in each bootstrap sample. For each sample, compute

$$Z^{\star}(b) = \frac{\hat{\theta}^{\star}(b) - \hat{\theta}}{\mathrm{SE}^{\star}(b)}, \tag{4.21}$$

where $\hat{\theta}^\star(b) = s(\mathbf{y}^{\star b})$ is the value of $\hat{\theta}$ for the bootstrap sample $\mathbf{y}^{\star b}$ and $\text{SE}^\star(b)$ is the estimated standard error of $\hat{\theta}^\star$ for the bootstrap sample $\mathbf{y}^{\star b}$. Then, the αth percentile of $Z^\star(b)$ is estimated by the value of $\hat{t}^\delta$ such that

$$\#[Z^\star(b) \leq \hat{t}^\delta]/B = \delta, \tag{4.22}$$

where # means to count. For example, if $B = 1{,}000$, the $Z^\star(b)$ for the upper bound of the 95% confidence interval will be the value of $Z^\star(b)$ above which the 25 largest values fall, and the $Z^\star(b)$ for the lower bound is the value of $Z^\star(b)$ beneath which the 25 smallest values fall. Then, the confidence interval is computed pretty much as usual as

$$(\hat{\theta} - \hat{t}^{1-\delta} \cdot \text{SE}, \hat{\theta} - \hat{t}^{\delta} \cdot \text{SE}). \tag{4.23}$$

The studentized bootstrap can work well in a number of conventional applications, and Cook and Weisberg (1999), for instance, use it as the method of choice in their regression package ARC.

4.6.2 Hypothesis Testing

One can use the bootstrap sampling distribution to do hypothesis tests, keeping in mind that the goal is to estimate the sampling distribution of $\hat{\theta}$ *under the null hypothesis*. The bootstrap sampling distribution needs to be shifted so that it is centered on the null hypothesis value. Consider the common case when the null hypothesis is $\theta = 0$. To center the bootstrap sampling distribution around zero, one just subtracts the value of $\hat{\theta}$ computed from the original data set for each of the $s(\mathbf{y}^{*1}), s(\mathbf{y}^{*2}), \ldots, s(\mathbf{y}^{*B})$. Then, one can determine what proportion of the $s(\mathbf{y}^{*1}), s(\mathbf{y}^{*2}), \ldots, s(\mathbf{y}^{*B})$ is as extreme or more extreme than $\hat{\theta}$. That proportion is the p-value. As with confidence intervals, however, there are a number of variations on this theme.

4.6.3 Bootstrapping Regression

The bootstrap can be easily applied to simple linear regression. In the most straightforward case, one samples with replacement as usual but includes values for both x and y; one samples "rows" of the data. Estimates of the slope and intercept (or some other feature of the least squares line) are computed in each bootstrap sample. The result is an estimate of the joint sampling distribution for $\hat{\eta}_0$ and $\hat{\eta}_1$, from which one can easily obtain their marginal sampling distributions. Confidence intervals and tests can then, in principle, be constructed.

Alternatively, one can resample the residuals around the least squares fit for the data on hand. The steps are as follows:

1. Fit a least squares line as usual with the sample data.
2. Take a random sample with replacement of the residuals from this fit, with the sample size the same as the number of observations in the original sample.
3. Add the sampled residuals to the original fitted values to get a "new" set of observations for y.
4. Compute the intercept and slope for this "new" line.
5. Go back to #2 and repeat.

Which method you choose depends in part on how seriously you want to take your model. If the model is suspect, the first method under some circumstances can provide a useful estimate of the standard errors for the biased estimates and even sometimes an estimate of the bias itself (Freedman, 1981). The second method is appropriate if you are willing to bet that your model is sufficiently good for the problem at hand. Another way to think about it is that the first method corresponds to data produced by random sampling from a population and the second method corresponds to data generated by nature using a linear model.

4.6.4 Possible Benefits From Resampling

Despite what some have claimed, the bootstrap occupies a rather small niche in regression analysis. It cannot be used to undertake statistical inference when the data are a convenience sample or a population. If random sampling applies, and if the simple linear model holds in the population, the bootstrap can be a useful tool in small samples when the normality assumption does not hold. It can sometimes be helpful when the model does not hold, but exploiting the bootstrap under these conditions is not a simple or straightforward undertaking.

Alternatively, the bootstrap and resampling more generally can be used as a form of sensitivity analysis, what Gifi (1990: Section 1.5.3) calls "stability under data selection." The empirical distribution of statistics constructed from the many random samples provides a grounded sense of how the results could vary as a function of a particular data generation mechanism.[36] From this, one can gain some qualitative understanding of how sensitive the results are to the particular data on hand. If the conclusions of the research could differ dramatically in random draws of the same size as the original data set, one

[36]If the jackknife is used, then the data are perturbed in a deterministic manner. However, that difference does not materially matter here.

needs to be far more circumspect about any of the findings. The findings are heavily sample dependent.

4.7 Summary and Conclusions

Two chapters back, we started with the data and the conditional distribution of y given x. We then began to impose constraints on the analysis and introduce information from outside the data.

1. We decided to focus primarily on the conditional means because they were likely to be of interest to the data analyst given the empirical questions at hand.
2. In the interest of simplicity, we decided to characterize the path of the means with a straight line.
3. We adopted the least squares criterion because it was simple and convenient. Implicitly, we were imposing symmetry on the errors and placing special weight on the largest departures from the regression line.
4. We considered improving the descriptive analysis with transformations and standardization.
5. With description in hand, we turned to inference from the data to the population. To do that, we assumed the data were produced by random sampling or a natural approximation thereof. Alternatively, we relied on a model of how nature generated the data.
6. When x was treated as fixed, we assumed that the natural world somehow constructed the data in the population so that a straight line passed through each of the conditional means. The result was that the mean of the conditional errors was zero; the mean of the errors did not depend on x. If there was a model by which nature generated the data, we basically relied on the same assumption.
7. For a stochastic x treated as such, alternative assumptions about the relationship between x and e were available, all of which allowed one to disentangle the roles of x and e.
8. We required that the natural world forced all of the conditional variances to be the same.
9. We required no systematic measurement error whatsoever and no random measurement error for x.
10. In some instances, we required that $y|x$ was normally distributed.
11. We imposed the thought experiment of a limitless number of independent samples from the given population.

The first four impositions are essentially judgment calls that do not commit the investigator to any particular worldview. One should certainly scrutinize all judgment calls, and different researchers might make those calls differently, but there always will (and should) be lots of room for discretionary decisions in empirical research.

In contrast, the last seven impositions on the data imply factual statements about the empirical world. If there is a desire to move beyond description of the data on hand, how the data were generated is critical. If random sampling was actually employed, an important empirical matter is resolved. If not, one must make the case that the natural world produced the equivalent of a random sample or constructed the data in a manner that can be accurately represented by a convenient and well-understood model. These are statements about how the natural world works, not just some technical details. And as a statement about how the natural world works, it is subject to all of the conventional rules of scientific evidence. Equally important is the commitment to a world operating at the population level or in nature itself that makes the simple linear model true. Again, this is not a mere technical convenience but a statement about real empirical phenomena. Finally, neither the commitment to a world that produces appropriate samples nor a world that operates by the simple linear model can be directly deduced from the data alone. External information must be brought to bear.

In practice, claims about the natural and social world are always approximations. Then, the question is whether those approximations are good enough. We shall return to this issue near the end of the book. But two observations can be offered now. First, many renderings of the empirical world required for statistical inference are ridiculous on their face. There is no need to argue about how close the approximation is. Second, when it is clear that the quality of the approximation is close enough to consider, the case needs to be explicitly made. One would be hard pressed to find instances in which it really is.

5 Causal Inference for the Simple Linear Model

5.1 Introduction

Causal inference conventionally entails using data and a lot of auxiliary information to learn what might happen if there is an intervention in some social, biological, or physical process. For example, one might want to know what would happen to residential water consumption if the price of water were determined by its marginal cost rather than its average cost. Or, one might want to know what would happen to a wild salmon population if a large number of hatchery salmon were released into the same river system. Or, one might want to know how well first graders would learn to read if class size were reduced a certain amount.

Causal inference is ubiquitous in all manner of policy research and, indeed, is almost second nature. Policymakers are constantly on the lookout for ways to intervene: in national economies, in regional watersheds and airsheds, in local labor markets, in school systems, in agricultural production, in high-crime neighborhoods, in low-income households, in polluted wetlands, and so on. In the language of policy analysis, there is an ongoing search for "policy instruments." In the language of program evaluation, there is an ongoing search for "manipulable variables."

Yet causal inference is at least as controversial as statistical inference, and the payload that needs to be hauled by the simple linear model gets a lot heavier. There was no need whatsoever to consider causal inference when studying $y|x$ by itself, when fitting a descriptive regression line, or when doing statistical inference about that line. Causal inference is something extra that depends fundamentally on information from outside of the data and all of the developments to this point.

There is not space nor is it consistent with the intent of this book to consider long and contentious debates about causality. Judea Pearl (2000) provides an entertaining overview in the epilogue of his recent book, and readers who get hooked will find themselves going back at least 100 years to philosophers David Hume and John Stuart Mill. Here we shall concentrate on relatively recent thinking. In this chapter, the basic concepts and issues are introduced. In later chapters, more focused concerns will be addressed.

We begin with some key definitions to illustrate why causal inference is so difficult and controversial. Readers new to this material may have to work a bit over the next several pages.

5.2 Some Definitions: What's a Causal Effect?

When regression analysis is used to make causal inferences about policy, there is often a model based on econometric traditions. Causal inferences are made from "causal parameters" that are part of that model. Heckman (2000:52-53) provides an excellent explanation of what this means.[1]

> Within the context of a well-specified economic model, the concept of a causal parameter is well defined. For example, in a model of production of output y based on inputs $\mathbf{x}$ that can be independently varied, we write the function $F: R^N \rightarrow R^1$ as
>
> $$y = F(x_1, \ldots, x_N), \tag{5.1}$$
>
> where $\mathbf{x} = (x_1, \ldots, x_N)$ is a vector of inputs defined over the domain $D(\mathbf{x} \in D)$. They play the roles of causes, that is, factors that produce y. These causes are the primitives of the relevant economic theory. Assuming that each input can be freely varied, so there are no functional restrictions connecting the components of $\mathbf{x}$, the change in y produced from the variation in x_j, holding all other inputs constant, is the causal effect of x_j. If F is differentiable in x_j, the marginal causal effect of x_j is
>
> $$\frac{\partial y}{\partial x_j} = F_j(x_1, \ldots, x_j, \ldots, x_N)|\mathbf{x} = \tilde{\mathbf{x}}. \tag{5.2}$$
>
> If F is not differentiable, finite changes replace the derivatives.

Heckman's exposition of causal effects in economics raises a number of issues that will be addressed in this chapter and in several later chapters. Note,

---

[1]Notation has been changed slightly to conform to the conventions in this book, and the equation number is set to fit into the sequence of equation numbers in this chapter.

for example, that Heckman explicitly allows for several "inputs," and we have yet to tackle multiple regression. Still, four points are worth emphasizing now. First, each of the inputs can be manipulated. Manipulation is a key feature of a causal effect. Second, these manipulations can be undertaken one at a time with the other inputs fixed at some particular values. We will be limited to a single input in this chapter, but what it means to "hold constant" when there is more than one predictor will be front-and-center soon. Third, when an input is varied, the output varies in a manner described by a partial derivative (or a numerical approximation). We will see that sometimes this is the same as the slope of the regression fit. Finally, causal effects are defined in the context of a model of how the world is supposed to work. The model should not just be a technical convenience.

Heckman goes on to point out that because the causal effects are really "potential" causal effects, the econometric formulation can be linked to conceptions of causal effects developed by statisticians when the values of x correspond to different "treatments." This is far more than semantics. Causal effects characterize what would happen *if* there were a particular "intervention." Statistical accounts build on this premise.

It is probably fair to say that statistical thinkers focus primarily on "causal effects," perhaps because causal effects lead directly to features of the data that one can examine. Statisticians are interested in characterizing what would happen as a result of some intervention. There has been far less consideration about what an intervention really is, which will get us into some ambiguities later.

Consider a single observational unit: a person, a classroom, a stand of trees, a reach of a stream, and so on. Imagine that there is an intervention: an inoculation, a reduction in class size, a logging road, or a concrete culvert, respectively. The goal is to consider how the single unit would be different (if it is) if an "input" is altered. That is, one wants to know the state of the unit in question with and without the intervention. Intuitive reasoning of this sort led Neyman in 1923 (Neyman, 1990) and later Holland (1986) and Rubin (1986) to propose that a causal effect is understood as some characterization of the two different outcomes, one with the intervention and one without the intervention.[2] It is important to stress that we are *defining* causal effects. These are the phenomena in which we are ultimately interested. How one *estimates* them from data is another matter, to which we shall turn later.[3] For example, a causal effect of

---

[2]See Rubin (1990) for his views on the relationship between Neyman's early work and his own.

[3]There are some terminological problems here. Are causal effects "described," "computed," "inferred," or "estimated" from data? It turns out that one's choice of language can have important implications. We shall favor the term "estimated" because data, along with other information, are used to provide a reasonable guess about what would happen if the intervention were introduced. But "estimation" in this context is different from using information from a sample to infer something about a population.

interest might be the difference in the number of wild salmon returning to spawn if there were a release of a large number of hatchery salmon compared with the number returning were there no release whatsoever. This is the information we want to obtain.

Causal effects are always comparative. There must always be an answer to the question "compared to what?" At the very least, the answer will make explicit what the basis of comparison really is. For example, if the intervention is an arrest in response to domestic violence, a comparison with "business as usual" would need to be clearly described. It might be that the police do nothing more than restore order and leave. But that might or might not include referrals to social service agencies or threats to the perpetrator about what might happen if they should be called back to the same address.

Sometimes, the search for a proper basis of comparison will correct naive assumptions. For example, if the intervention is a logging road in a particular forest, the comparison cannot be to that forest in a pristine state. No such thing exists, and it is not even clear what "pristine" could mean in this context. Evidence of human activity can be found all over the planet.

It also follows that causal effects are defined in a "what if" manner and, as such, are hypothetical. "What ifs" cannot be directly observed. Either the logging road is built or it is not. Yet it is causal effects that we want to estimate; they are the motivation for causal inference. The "what if" logic, formalized as the "Neyman-Rubin Model," is pervasive in statistical discussions of cause and effect.[4]

5.2.1 The Neyman-Rubin Model

The Neyman-Rubin framework can be most easily explicated with a binary intervention. Consider a *single* individual and a job training program. Let y be the response, the number of weeks after completing the program until a job is found. The observed intervention t equals 1 if that person participates in job training and 0 if not. Finally, and a source of potential confusion, let t^* equal 1 if the *hypothetical* intervention is job training and 0 if not. When one asks what *would* happen as a result of job training (compared with the lack thereof), one is asking about the hypothetical intervention that has not actually been introduced. It is the causal effects of this hypothetical intervention that we wish to estimate. We are seeking an answer to a "what if" question.[5]

---

[4]But there are dissenters. See, for example, Dawid's (2000) discussion of causal effects and the following commentary. Dawid (2000:448) describes his position as an "outlier," and there is little doubt that his assessment is correct.

[5]In the actual data analysis, one would have to take into account the real possibility that some of the individuals would not find a job during the course of the study. The response variable would then be "right censored." Although censoring would affect how the statistical analysis was done, censoring does not materially affect the logic of the Neyman-Rubin model.

There are four possible pairings between the intervention that was received and the hypothetical intervention. The outcome, conditional on these four pairs, can be represented as follows:

1. $y|(t^* = 1, t = 1)$: the outcome if, hypothetically, job training were received and it actually was received.
2. $y|(t^* = 1, t = 0)$: the outcome if, hypothetically, job training were received but it was actually not received.
3. $y|(t^* = 0, t = 1)$: the outcome if, hypothetically, job training were not received but it actually was received.
4. $y|(t^* = 0, t = 0)$: the outcome if, hypothetically, job training were not received and it actually was not received.

Only the first and fourth conditional relationships are observable in principle. The second and third reflect "counterfactuals." One cannot observe the outcome for an individual after job training, for instance, if that individual did not receive it. And in practice, moreover, one will only be able to observe any given individual for either the first or last conditional relationship. One of those then becomes counterfactual in a different sense. In any case, these four configurations set the stage for what follows.

Within the Neyman-Rubin model, a causal effect can be defined as the difference between the outcomes under the treatment and control conditions.[6] In this illustration, it is the difference in y had a given subject participated in job training compared with not participating: $(y|t^* = 1) - (y|t^* = 0)$.[7] Hypothetically, y might equal 4 weeks of job search following job training and 12 weeks of job search with no job training at all. This definition is behind much of the work on causality in statistics.

We now have a *definition* of a causal effect that, despite some formal notation, corresponds well to common sense. It represents what we want to know. Unfortunately, this definition cannot be implemented because the individual is either exposed to the treatment or not. Either job training was received or it was not received.

But suppose we shift to groups rather than a single individual. And suppose we reformulate causal effects in distributional terms.

At the *group* level, a causal effect might be defined as a comparison between one or more features of $(y|t^* = 1)$ and those same features of $(y|t^* = 0)$, where y is now a distribution of outcomes for a single group. Thus, one might ask, for a set of 32 potential job trainees, what would happen to them if they had received job training compared with what would happen to them if they did not.

---

[6] One could talk about two different interventions as well.

[7] One might also define a causal effect as the ratio of the two terms.

Although any feature (or features) of the two distributions might be of interest, it is common to focus on the mean. The mean is easy to work with and, under certain assumptions we mention shortly, leads to a definition for the aggregate that is consistent with the definition of a causal effect at the level of the individual unit. Thus, we concentrate on the special case of $(\bar{y}|t^* = 1) - (\bar{y}|t^* = 0)$. This is nothing more than the mean number of weeks until a job is found under the treatment condition minus the mean number of weeks until a job is found under the control condition. Note that this is still a hypothetical comparison of all subjects under the experimental condition to all subjects under the control condition.

Consider again the four possible pairings of the hypothetical intervention and the actual intervention. For the "what if" case when the job training program is received by all, the conditional distribution of y can be unpacked as follows:

$$(\bar{y}|t^* = 1) = (\bar{y}|t^* = 1, t = 1) \times p(t = 1) + (\bar{y}|t^* = 1, t = 0) \times p(t = 0). \tag{5.3}$$

In Equation 5.3, the average time to find a job if job training is received by all depends on what would happen to those who did actually receive job training and what would happen to those who did not, both weighted by particular proportions. For those who received job training, the proportion getting the treatment is used, and for those who did not receive job training, the proportion not getting the treatment is used. Note that the second part of the right-hand side is unobservable and, as such, is counterfactual. There is no way to observe what would happen under the job training intervention for those who did not get it.

For the "what if" case when the job training is not received by all, the same kind of unpacking can be undertaken:

$$(\bar{y}|t^* = 0) = (\bar{y}|t^* = 0, t = 1) \times p(t = 1) + (\bar{y}|t^* = 0, t = 0) \times p(t = 0). \tag{5.4}$$

In Equation 5.4, the average time to find a job if job training is not received by all depends on what would happen to those who actually received job training and on what would happen to those who did not, both weighted, once again, by appropriate proportions. Now the first piece of the right-hand side is counterfactual: There is no way to observe what would happen with the no-job-training intervention for those who received it.

Even though we can now explicitly show the components of an average causal effect at the group level, we are still some distance from being able to do anything useful with data. The counterfactual components remain. In practice, however, there are a number of ways in which the counterfactual problem can be addressed.

The most straightforward way is to assign subjects randomly to treatments. If job training were assigned at random to a subset of potential trainees, for example, the pool of individuals getting job training would, on the average, have the same characteristics as the remaining pool of individuals who did not. Then, in Equation 5.3, the mean number of weeks until a job is found if job training were received is, on the average, the same for those who actually receive job training and those who do not. Similarly, in Equation 5.4, the mean number of weeks until a job is found if job training were not received is, on the average, the same for those who did not receive job training and those who did. The language here gets clumsy, but the point is that there is now a useful way to handle the "what if" for the counterfactual cases.

It follows that a reasonable estimate of the average treatment effect is

$$(\bar{y}|t^* = 1, t = 1) - (\bar{y}|t^* = 0, t = 0). \tag{5.5}$$

One simply compares the experience of the treated group with that of the untreated group. The difference between the two means will be an unbiased estimate of the average treatment effect over individuals if the outcome for any one individual is unrelated to the treatment any other individual receives (Rosenbaum, 2002a:41-42). In some circles, this is called the "stable unit treatment value assumption" (SUTVA), which can often be under the control of the researcher. For example, members of the experimental and control groups can, in many settings, have no contact with one another. Thus, control subjects may have no information about what the treated subjects experienced (and vice versa).[8]

The emphasis of this book is not on randomized experiments or how they can be analyzed. However, it is clear that randomized experiments can, in principle, solve the counterfactual problem. In the absence of random assignment, efforts to make the pools of subjects across interventions comparable on the average boil down to trying to make them conditionally comparable. That is, one uses as conditioning variables features of the subjects that, once "held constant," make the groups the same on the average. We shall return to this issue in depth when multiple regression is discussed.

The "what if" approach to causal effects can be easily generalized to comparisons between several interventions, including a "control" condition, and to interventions that are not categorical (Berk, 1988:159). For example, there might be three kinds of logging roads: a dirt road, a gravel road, and a paved road. Then, there would be three interventions. Or, interest might center on proximity of the road to different ecosystems in the forest (e.g., a meadow or

[8]See Freedman et al. (1998:510-513 and especially footnote 12) for a very accessible discussion of the estimation of average treatment effects in randomized experiments. For a detailed discussion of different treatment effect models that may be applied to randomized experiments, see Rosenbaum (2002a:Section 2.5 and Chapter 5).

a stream), in which case the intervention would be represented by meaningful numerical values. As such, we are back to Heckman's econometric formulation.

However, we need a way to think in still more detail about causal effects and especially how these may be linked to regression analysis. For this, we turn to Freedman's work on response schedules.

5.2.2 Thinking About Causal Effects as Response Schedules

The definition of a causal effect can be embedded in a larger context about how the data that one may observe are generated. Causal effects involve not just the relationships between Heckman's inputs and the output, not just the relationships between observable and unobservable outcomes, but a number of additional features of how nature is supposed to operate. Freedman (2001) makes this explicit in his formulation of response schedules. They represent the full story of what causal effects require within econometric/statistical traditions and help the researcher to formulate causal questions that can make sense. There is no point in trying to estimate causal effects if those causal effects have not been defined in a coherent manner. Estimates of causal effects that have not been properly defined cannot be interpreted in causal terms. One is left with a descriptive regression coefficient indicating solely how the mean of the response differs conditional on particular values of predictors.

Consider again a world in which nature constructs a population or generates the data directly using a linear model. So far, such models have been solely descriptions of how x and y are related. The mean of y is nothing more or less than a transformation of x. As such, the models are silent on what would happen to the mean of y if x were manipulated.

Imagine now a "response schedule" of the following form:

$$y_{i,x} = a + bx + \delta_i, \tag{5.6}$$

where i refers to the observational units of interest, $y_{i,x}$ is the response, x is the "value" or "level" of some intervention, and δ_i is a perturbation, commonly considered to be a random variable with an expected value of zero.[9] Thus, the expected value of $y_{i,x}$ is $a + bx$. In this sense, the response schedule is linear in x, and, because the parameters are not subscripted, the same linear relationship applies to each observational unit. That is, there is some set of observational units that have the exact same response schedule and do not interact. What happens to one unit has no implications whatsoever for what happens to another unit.

A critical point is that the "disturbance" or "error," δ_i, does not vary with x. By some chance process that depends on context, a value of δ_i is chosen and

[9]We are now talking about random variables, which are theoretical entities with probability distributions. Hence, we work with expectations rather than means.

affixed permanently to observational unit i. Then, as different values of x are introduced, systematic variation in the value of $y_{i,x}$ follows.

To help fix these ideas, imagine that one is interested in how the number of homicides in a police precinct is affected by the number of police officers on foot patrol. Local police departments have the option of instituting foot patrol and the number of patrol officers assigned to it. Consider any given police precinct i. The natural processes that determine the number of homicides select at random some value for δ_i. Then, one can determine the number of homicides by adding to δ_i the value $a + bx$, where x is, say, 10 officers, or 15, or 30, or whatever. The value of δ_i is the same no matter which value for x is selected. Thus, a large number of homicide rates could in principle be generated depending solely on the value of x (once δ_i is picked). The response schedule also requires that the values for a and b are the same no matter what the value of δ_i. Finally, the response schedule requires that a and b are the same no matter what value of x or δ_i applies to other relevant precincts. For this application, at least, the response schedule is very demanding of the observable world.

Freedman provides a second kind of response schedule that does not require that errors δ_i be invariant over interventions for a given observational unit. Let

$$y_{i,x} = a + bx + \delta_{i,x}, \tag{5.7}$$

where the $\delta_{i,x}$, with an expected value of zero, is drawn independently and at random from some invariant distribution, given a value for x. This has much the same look and feel as the simple linear model. With x set to some value, the errors in principle generate a distribution for the values of $y_{i,x}$. Thus, we have a response schedule in which, once the value of x is determined, the particular value $y_{i,x}$ is, in effect, sampled at random. Consider again the foot patrol example. The number of officers on foot patrol is determined, which generates $a + bx$. The additional random perturbation $\delta_{i,x}$ implies that the response will vary around $a + bx$ solely as a function of that perturbation. One value, $y_{i,x}$, is then realized at random. But the linear form and a and b are still unaffected by x, the random perturbation, and by whatever may be going on in other relevant precincts. Hence, although the second response schedule is a bit less strict, it is a very long way from permissive.

The main difference between the two models is that in the first, once a random error is attached to a case, it does not change. No matter what the value of x, the error for observational unit i is invariant. In the second model, the errors are not fixed, although the distribution from which they are randomly drawn is. This difference has important implications as one considers how data might be generated. With invariant errors, the intervention is selected independently of δ_i, and one gets to see (X_i, Y_i), where $Y_{i,x} = a + bX_i + \delta_i$. These are the data with which one gets to work. With random errors, X_i is determined, and then, conditional on that value, Y_i is chosen at random from a fixed distribution with a mean of $a + bX_i$.

The first model leads naturally to a causal interpretation for the role of x. Once δ_i is fixed, variation in the response results only from variation in x. In the second model, because both x and δ_i can vary, both are potential culprits, and isolating the role of x is more difficult. For the first model, a causal interpretation requires that x is selected independently of the single error attached to observational unit i. For the second model, a causal interpretation requires that the error is selected independently of x.

Freedman explores how the two kinds of response schedules might fare in a real research setting. He concludes that the first model is less realistic and therefore less useful. It is hard to imagine a world in which a random perturbation, once sampled, does not ever change. Thus, the number of homicides in a police precinct will certainly vary, whether they are observed by day, by week, or by month, regardless of the number of foot-patrol officers. The second model is likely to be a bit more realistic precisely because the perturbations are free to vary. The second model also comports well with a regression formulation and is the conception we shall use. Then, our causal inferences are to the conditional distribution of the response: *What would the conditional distribution of the response be if the value of the predictor were set to x?*

To summarize, response schedules determine if sensible causal questions can be asked, and as such, they precede the data analysis. Although response schedules address issues that by and large are considered in serious discussions of both the econometric formulation and the Neyman-Rubin model, they provide a single framework in which these issues may be examined systematically. In particular, by making the errors a central feature of the causal account, Freedman's response schedule approach requires that the errors be treated as more than a nuisance to be dispatched by a few convenient assumptions. Causal stories must include a plausible explanation of how the natural world generates the errors. Response schedules also can provide a clear link to simple linear regression.[10]

It is important not to forget that all response schedules are hypothetical. They characterize what would happen *if* an intervention were set at some value. Thus, it is like a pudding recipe. If you do thus and so, you get this and that. But as we shall see shortly, the proof of this pudding is not so easily consumed.

5.2.3 What's an Intervention?

Still relatively unaddressed is the nature of an intervention. In Equations 5.6 and 5.7, the features of x are almost totally unspecified. In a real application, we need more.

[10]It is easy to get back to the Neyman-Rubin consideration of treatments. With two different values of x and the prospect of two systematically different values for $Y_{i,x}$, one can characterize a causal effect by comparing the two responses. What is the impact, for instance, of having 15 officers on foot patrol compared with 5?

Like so many of the causal issues raised in this book, the key is whether there is a response schedule that makes subject matter sense, and the test will be, therefore, context specific. A response schedule that works in one setting may not work in another.

But on the matter of what defines an intervention, it is common to require, in the language of Holland and Rubin, that x is "manipulable." As noted earlier, much of what interests us in policy research is manipulable in the sense that conscious human action can change things. A vaccine for measles can be administered. The content of a mathematics curriculum can be revised. Scrubbers can be put on smoke stacks. Dams can be constructed or torn down. In short, human-induced interventions that could easily be imagined with current technology and within existing political systems fit well within the response schedule framework.

Matters get murky if one allows for interventions that depend on technology and/or political systems that do not exist. For example, until very recently, parents could not know before the birth of their child if the child had Down syndrome. Now prospective parents have the option of knowing and then deciding whether they want to continue the pregnancy. In today's world, it makes sense to treat knowledge about genetic defects as an intervention. But what about 20 years ago?

Once one opens the door to interventions that do not appear to be fully realistic, almost anything would seem to qualify as an intervention. Perhaps most commonly, race and sex are taken to be interventions, sometimes cloaked in "but for" legal language. Thus, "but for" Joe's race, he would have been earning $500 more a month. But what does that really mean? In what sense could Joe's race be different? What would the process be? If it would take a science fiction world to make Joe's race manipulable, it is that world, not the one in which we live, to which causal inferences are being made.

In the case of gender, sex-change operations certainly exist. But they do not alter all that there is to gender, and they alter things that are not usually thought to be gender linked. So, if Jane is believed to be making $500 less a month than she would have made had she been male, the policymaker does not really have the direct option of making Jane male. The only real option is to compensate for the apparent inequality through policy instruments that *are* manipulable. For example, Jane might be given a promotion. A lot more will be said about causal interpretations of nonmanipulable variables later. The point for now is that as a practical matter, there is an important difference between predictors that are manipulable and predictors that are not.

There are also more subtle issues. There are times when x can be manipulated, but it cannot be manipulated without manipulating confounders at the same time. Recall that this violates one of the key attributes of the econometric approach to causal effects: One must be able to manipulate causes one at a time. We shall return to this issue after multiple regression is addressed. For now, a simple example should suffice.

A long-standing issue in law enforcement is how lengthy prison sentences should be. It would be good to manipulate sentence length to see whether, for example, longer sentences have greater deterrent effects. However, it is well known that most criminals "age out" of crime regardless of how the criminal justice system intervenes. And there is no way to manipulate the time an offender serves without also manipulating the age at which he or she is released from prison. The prospects are very dim for a response schedule in which the role of x is isolated.[11]

As Lieberson (1985) emphasizes, sometimes interventions are also not reversible. It makes no sense, for example, to ask for a particular watershed what the impact would be on the habitat for certain species of water fowl if the wetlands were restored to their "natural" state. The fact is, we do not know how to do such restorations successfully. Nor, apparently, does nature; there is no way for this x to be set. Thus, x could be set to "polluted," but it cannot be set to "natural."[12] In short, sometimes hypothetical interventions will make no subject matter sense. Then, the prospects for a credible response schedule fail as well.

However, opening the door to natural phenomena as interventions brings into question the centrality of human action in any definition of a causal effect. Much of the literature on causal effects assumes that manipulation requires human agency. But the real issue is less who or what undertakes the manipulation than whether the value of x reasonably could have been different for the given observational unit at the time and place for which inferences are required.

Any number of illustrations exist in which there are policy concerns but little human control over the phenomena: the effect of immigration on local economies, the impact of the demographic age mix on crime, or the influence of the globalization of business on the wages of factory workers in developed nations. For each, the relevant x could have been different. But although x could have been different, conscious human action would, at best, have marginal control over the value of x. Still, a strong relationship might quite properly indicate where one or more human-induced interventions could be important in the future. And causality is central because there is no point in trying to manipulate a variable that is not causally linked to the outcome of interest.

Unfortunately, constructing credible response schedules for such policy-related phenomena can be especially daunting.[13] Perhaps the key point about

---

[11]Keep in mind that the focus here is on conceptions of causal effects. Of course, one could compare inmates of a given age, some of whom had just finished long sentences and some of whom had just finished short sentences. But this is, at best, a way to estimate the impact of sentence length, holding age constant. It does not speak to the conceptions of causal effects and, therefore, whether the empirical exercise makes sense to begin with.

[12]Again, one could certainly compare watersheds that differed in the amount of pollution, but that does not address the definitional issues.

[13]And it would be no less daunting if there were many predictors, as we will see soon.

human-induced interventions is that they are a conscious effort to alter the status quo. Insofar as they do, it is much easier to construct a plausible response schedule. In the absence of some disruption in business as usual, there is the risk that everything seems linked to everything. Exogeneity then becomes nearly impossible to establish, and without exogeneity, there is no response schedule. This is not to say that a credible response schedule can always be constructed for all human-induced interventions, or that no credible response schedule can be constructed for natural interventions. But for policy-related questions of causality, working with systems perturbed by conscious human action is likely to be easier.

Can "theory" help? Some, but usually not enough. Even within economics, which prides itself on formal theory, views are mixed. The "structural approach"—causal models developed from neoclassical economic theory—has been widely criticized even by card-carrying economists for failing to deliver on its promise.[14] As Heckman (2000:49) notes,

> The empirical track record of the structural approach is, at best, mixed. Economic data, both micro and macro, have not yielded many stable structural parameters. Parameter estimates from the structural research program are widely held to not be credible.

Although weak data and inappropriate econometric procedures are in part responsible, inadequate theory is also a culprit. The econometric approach to causal effects is seen by many economists as imposing arbitrary structure on the data. Even when there seems to be a useful theoretical core, key details are missing. In research on water conservation, for example, microeconomic theory makes clear that, if the price of water is increased, people will use less of it. However, efforts to estimate the price elasticity of water consumption get widely different estimates, and there is even some evidence that the relationship may be highly nonlinear and depend on certain features of the household (e.g., household income). Thus, even for moderate-income households, the water bill is so small a fraction of overall household expenses that price increases of the size that are politically palatable may barely get noticed. Within the range of price increases that are viable, there is really very little theoretical help.

Perhaps the largest gap is that available theory used in economics is mostly silent on how to properly characterize the role of the errors in the regression formulation. Angrist et al. (1996:446) observe that "critical assumptions are cast in terms of disturbances from incompletely specified regression functions . . . , rather than in terms of intrinsically meaningful and potentially observable variables." That is, the properties of the errors necessary to

---

[14] And there have long been plenty of more fundamental critiques of neoclassical economics (e.g., Hollis and Nell, 1975; Blaug, 1980).

obtain appropriate regression estimates are made with little or no theoretical justification and in such a fashion that real data cannot effectively be brought to bear.

Almost as important, there are typically a host of ceteris paribus conditions that, in real life, never exist. Policy research on the family, for instance, is often informed by the "household economics" most explicitly linked to the seminal work of Gary Becker. In that formulation, the game begins with the construction of a household. These are the completed transactions of "marriage markets." If these markets are free, if buyers and sellers have accurate information, if price per se has no psychic rewards, then, in the long run, the sorting of individuals into couples is in some sense optimal. But even if one accepts this ideal rendering, how would one ever know if the stated requirements were even approximately true for a given application?

Within the social sciences more generally, the experience is even worse. There is surprisingly little theory that is demonstrably "true enough," at least for the practical problem at hand.[15] For example, it has been remarkably difficult to confirm empirically that more severe punishment for serious crimes actually serves as a general deterrent. Likewise, there is, at best, scant evidence confirming that smaller classrooms by themselves improve student learning, that a more diverse mix of students at the college level improves the quality of education, that educational vouchers improve test scores, or that driver education reduces traffic fatalities among teenagers. There is only a little more clarity on the impact of population growth on environmental quality, the effect of work incentives on welfare recipients, and the influence of transfer payments on subsequent labor market activity.

Moreover, a great deal of what gets called "theory" is not, or at least it is not of the sort helpful for the construction of response schedules. As Leamer (1978) has observed, even the available theory on economics is too blunt to properly inform causal models. Most of the available theories are little more than wiring diagrams. One learns, perhaps, what is related to what and, sometimes, the signs of the relationships. But there is very little that will help with functional forms, how the errors may or may not be related to the intervention, and a number of other essential features of a response schedule. And path diagrams are not response schedules.

In short, although logically, x does not have to be a human-induced intervention, these are the sorts of interventions that will continue to be emphasized in the pages ahead. Human-induced interventions are often key policy concerns and will prove to be difficult enough to handle.

Consider a more extended example. Amendments in 1990 to the Clean Air Act mandated significant changes in vehicle inspection and maintenance

[15]In contrast, there are hundreds of theories in the natural sciences that are demonstrably true enough.

programs for cities with air quality problems. For light-duty vehicles of a certain age, there was to be scheduled testing of tail pipe and evaporative emissions.[16] The inspections could be provided in a decentralized fashion, with vehicles failing the inspection required to undergo repairs. All of the legislated requirements were well within existing technological and organizational capabilities of large metropolitan areas.

Does the response schedule formulation apply? Suppose x is the number of inspections completed in some period of time, and the response is average pollution content of automobile emission measured by remote sensing. Basically, a beam is passed through the exhaust of vehicles as they are being driven so that the measurements can be obtained from a large number of vehicles at almost any time and any place.

There is no question that x can be manipulated. There is ample historical precedent. With the value of x determined, the measurement technology implies that the random perturbations would primarily represent variation in the mix of cars that happens to be tested; the ages, types, makes, models, and emission-control technologies matter. Such variation is likely to be unrelated to x, at least in the short term. It takes a while for the stock of vehicles to turn over. The response function is also not likely to be related to x or to the experiences in other metropolitan areas. Thus, the correspondence between the hypothetical response schedule and the observable world is arguably pretty good. It appears that x can be manipulated and is likely to be unrelated to the errors. We are perhaps on our way; we are nearly ready to collect data with which to estimate the causal effect of automobile inspections using regression analysis.

Consider instead the possible impact of immigration into the United States on the demand for social services in a given city. The value of x might be the number of legal and illegal immigrants establishing residence in any given year. The response could be the number of emergency room visits, calls to police, or elementary school populations with English as a second language (ESL).

In what sense is the number of legal and illegal immigrants manipulable? There are certainly various policy instruments available in the immigration statutes and regulations, but control over legal immigration is incomplete and control over illegal immigration is very weak. There is really no way for human action to "set" the value of x. Even ignoring that issue, another problem is whether there is sufficient knowledge about the errors. How were they generated and exactly what are their properties?

There is also the matter of whether the number of immigrants in one city is related to the demand for social services in a neighboring city. A lot would have to be known about, for instance, the labor market and how common it is for immigrants to live in one city and work in another (e.g., live in the City of Los Angeles and work in the City of Santa Monica).

[16]The testing might involve measuring emissions under idle and at 2500 RPM engine speed.

In the immigration example, any plausible value for the number of immigrants could well have been different. So it makes sense to ask the question, What would happen if it were? The fact that the value of x is determined by forces beyond direct human agency is logically irrelevant. The fact is, x could have been different, and policy researchers can reasonably ask how that might matter.

However, one risks being in an everything-causes-everything situation. To decide if the number of immigrants is related to the errors associated with the number of ESL students, one would have to know a great deal about factors contributing to the number of ESL students: the local housing market, how the local ESL program is defined and administered, the preferences of immigrant parents for such programs, and others. That, in turn, might require an understanding of how zoning regulations affect the price of land, the role of the teacher's union in programmatic matters, and how the experience of immigration changes the preferences that immigrants have for the education of their children. Only if such interlocking processes were well understood would there be some chance of constructing a credible response schedule.

Finally, we return to "interventions" that are effectively not changeable in the world as we currently understand it or in the context where that change is required. These are values of x that really could not have been different. Many are attributes of people: race, gender, height, and other characteristics. But almost any observation unit may have fixed attributes. For example, given the size of the snow pack each winter in the Sierra Nevada, the amount of fresh water that will later flow into California rivers and streams is essentially determined.[17]

What's a researcher to do if the goal is to learn about the effect of some cause that is basically fixed in the world as we understand it? What if, for example, one really wants an answer to the "but for" question about race or sex? If the existing definitions of a causal effect do not fit, the burden falls to the researcher to propose an alternative definition that does. Suffice it to say that this will not be easy. If it were, that alternative definition would already be in widespread use.

However, there will sometimes be ways to reformulate the intervention so that causal effects make sense. In the case of race, for instance, one can manipulate information about race, if not race itself. Thus, a job application could be doctored to show that the job applicant was white or black. Now one may get some traction on the "but for" question. Note that the observational unit

[17]There are other definitions of causal effects in the statistics literature. "Granger cause" is one example (Granger and Newbold, 1986:220-223). But these definitions actually address rather different issues. Granger cause, for instance, addresses whether, conditional on a given set of variables, an additional variable improves forecasting accuracy. Thus, gender may Granger-cause income in the sense that knowing a person's gender may help predict earnings in the future beyond knowing a person's education, occupation, and age. But this is a very different matter from knowing what would happen to a person's income if a person's gender were different. Granger cause is essentially about the existence of a partial correlation that is not zero.

is no longer a particular person. The observational unit is now a particular job application. A lot more will be said about this later, when response schedules for multiple regression are considered.

To summarize, a necessary prerequisite for estimating a causal effect is to define it. Existing definitions of causal inference in the statistical literature are very demanding. If in a given situation none of these definitions can be applied in a manner that is consistent with how nature is believed to work, empirical estimates of causal effects are likely to be nonsense.

5.3 Studying Cause and Effect With Data

Causal inferences are made from a data set to what would happen if x were set at a particular value. Unfortunately, the response schedule approach (and the very definition of a causal effect) creates some thorny complications for drawing such inferences. The fundamental problem is that causal effects cannot be directly observed. A given observational unit can, at best, be studied under one value of x. Then there is no comparative referent. Broadly speaking, there are, in response, two strategies: nonstatistical and statistical. We now consider each in turn.[18]

5.3.1 Using Nonstatistical Solutions for Making Causal Inferences

Two kinds of generic approaches are common for what are nonstatistical efforts to make causal inferences. One can examine the same observational unit under different interventions or examine different units, each under a separate intervention. For example, one could study the diversity of plant life in a forest before and after logging roads are built. Or one could study the diversity of plant life in one forest without logging roads and another forest with logging roads.

The obvious problem with such comparisons is that, in the first case, the observational units may change over time for reasons having nothing to do with the intervention, and in the second case, the observational units may not be comparable before the intervention is introduced. In both instances, causal effects attributed to the intervention may actually result from other factors. These are just more grounded ways of thinking about the need for the perturbations in the response schedule to be unrelated to x.

When the research can be brought into a laboratory or placed in a setting over which a researcher can exercise great control, comparability over time or space can often be approximately enforced. For example, in a chemistry lab,

[18]The "nonstatistical" strategy is sometimes, in the Neyman-Rubin tradition, called the "scientific" solution to the problem of causal inference.

the speed of a chemical reaction with two different catalysts can be observed in solutions that are sufficiently identical for the purposes at hand. That is, the remaining differences are too small to matter. Or, the heat generated by a laser can be measured by comparing the temperature of a surface before it was targeted by the laser with the temperature after. For all practical purposes, the surface would not have changed in a relevant manner between the time the initial temperature was measured and the time the laser intervention began. For most policy questions, however, these kinds of options are not usually available.

5.3.2 Using Statistical Solutions for Making Causal Inferences

As noted earlier, there are solutions available based on aggregating observational units. Comparability is established between *groups* of observational units. Suppose one were interested in the impact of crisis counseling on domestic violence. One would not, for example, compare two households with a history of domestic violence, with one subject to crisis counseling and one not. Nor would one compare a given household before and after crisis counseling. One would compare two groups of households constituted so that the groups were comparable except for their experiences with crisis counseling. Then, the question is not how a given household would be affected by the counseling, but how a group would be affected on the average. Is there, on the average, less subsequent violence in households where the intervention was crisis counseling compared with households where the intervention was business as usual?

Of course groups are not naturally constructed to be comparable. The "gold standard" for comparability is achieved through random assignment to treatment groups. Random assignment guarantees that, on the average, the treatment groups will be balanced no matter how many confounders there are or what their nature might be. For instance, if 75% of the households in the intervention group have children, approximately 75% of the households in the control group do also. Likewise, if 40% of the households in the intervention group have both adults unemployed, approximately 40% of the households in the comparison group do also.

It is worth reiterating that one of the very desirable features of randomized designs is that there is no need to depend on a full response schedule framework; there need be no complete model for how a single observational unit responds. If the goal is to compare a treatment group with a control group using the difference between their means (or proportions) on some response, random assignment allows one to estimate in an unbiased manner the average causal effect as long as one subject's treatment does not affect another subject's response. Statistical inference naturally follows with no additional assumptions; there is no detailed model for the response. In that sense, the inferences are "model free."[19]

If there is a desire to further model the response as a function of the treatment (e.g., impose an additive regression-like model), a response schedule framework can be applied.[20] One's results are still model dependent, but the randomization will at least ensure that x and the disturbances are unrelated on the average. There are a number of excellent books on experimental design using random assignment (e.g., Box et al., 1978; Wu and Hamada, 2000), and there is no need to consider randomized experiments in greater detail here.

Matching is another method commonly used to achieve comparability. Confounded variables on which the groups might differ are designated. Then, the goal is to balance the groups on those confounders. Traditionally, matching has required a large pool of observational units so that, for instance, for each intervention household with children and unemployed adults, there is at least one nonintervention household with the same characteristics. As the number of matching variables increases, finding matches becomes more difficult. Recent developments in matching (e.g., Rosenbaum, 2002a: Chapter 10) can dramatically reduce such problems, but there is never any guarantee that all of the possible confounded variables have been considered; indeed, it is almost guaranteed that some important confounders have not. Then, the investigator must make the case that the comparability is good enough for the purposes at hand. Usually, this will be difficult to do. A discussion of matching is well beyond the scope of this book, but interested readers will find an excellent introductory treatment in Cochran's fine little text on observational studies (Cochran, 1983) and a state-of-the-art discussion in a lengthy paper by Heckman and his colleagues (1997; 1999).

A third method commonly applied to achieve comparability is through "covariance adjustments" that are built into regression with more than one predictor. We will begin considering such matters in the next chapter.

5.3.3 Using the Simple Linear Model for Making Causal Inferences

Suppose, for the moment, that the response schedule formulation is useful and reasonably plausible. Then, with a single x, one can, in principle, apply the simple linear model to describe causal effects and often, depending on how the data were generated, undertake statistical inference as well. That is, the discussion up to this point carries over. But what if x is categorical: treatment versus control?

---

[19]See Rosenbaum (2002a:27-44) for an excellent discussion of how to think about the analysis of randomized experiments and, as noted earlier, Rosenbaum (2002b) for how in principle to undertake inference based on randomization when there is no random assignment.

[20]One might argue model building has already begun with the premise that the intervention one observational unit receives does not affect the response of any other observational unit.

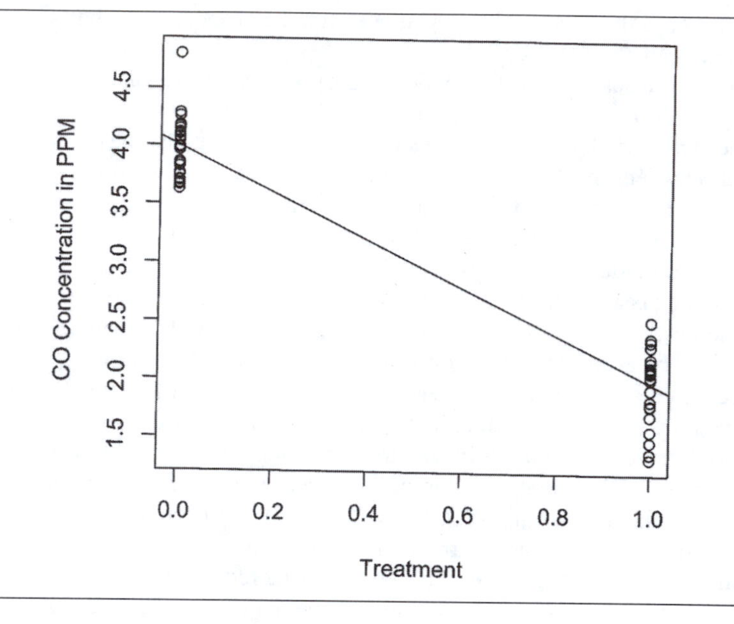

Figure 5.1. Regression of Carbon Dioxide Concentrations on Vehicle Inspection Intervention

For a single binary treatment, the simple linear model can still be applied. Suppose the treatment condition is coded as a "1" and the control coded as a "0." For example, implementing a new mandatory program for inspections of automobile tail pipe emissions might be coded 1 and the situation before the plan might be coded 0.

Consider Figure 5.1, in which, for each of 50 fictitious observations in a given city (some before and some after), the response of average carbon monoxide (CO) concentrations in parts per million (PPM) is plotted against the binary variable for treatment and control conditions. Overlaid is the regression line.

With only two values for the treatment, the regression line goes through both conditional means for CO concentrations. Clearly, average CO concentrations are lower after the inspection intervention. And with the treatment coded as a "dummy variable" (1 or 0), the regression parameters have a neat interpretation. The value of $\hat{\eta}_0$ is the mean of the response before the intervention (4 PPM). The value of $\hat{\eta}_1$ is the difference between the means of the before and after responses (−2 PPM). The sum of $\hat{\eta}_0$ and $\hat{\eta}_1$ is, therefore, the mean of the response after the intervention (2 PPM).

Any other two values could have been used instead of 0 and 1. Then, the fit would have been the same, and it would have been possible to reconstruct the two conditional means. But the 1-0 coding makes the calculations easy. Note, however, that the regression line itself does not really have an interpretation. It makes no sense to consider values of $\hat{y}_i$ for any values of x other than 0 and 1. The regression formulation is just a handy way to compute conditional means for the treatment and control condition and their difference.

If we take the data as a convenience sample or population, statistical tests and confidence intervals do not apply. But had the observations been a simple random sample, or had there been random assignment to treatments, a t-test for the null hypothesis that $\hat{\eta}_1 = 0$ would be the same as a t-test for no difference between the two observed conditional means (i.e., 4 PPM vs. 2 PPM). The test is also identical to an F-test for the null hypothesis that $\hat{\eta}_1 = 0$.[21] Using the simple linear model with a single treatment variable is basically the same as an analysis of variance (ANOVA) with a single factor having two levels. When there are more levels and/or more factors, multiple regression is required, but there is no problem analyzing categorical treatments.

5.4 Summary and Conclusions

Although causal thinking seems to come naturally, causal modeling is difficult to do well. There is nothing in the data by themselves that properly can be used to directly determine if x is a cause of y (or vice versa). There is nothing in simple linear regression that, by itself, will lead to causal inferences. One needs clear definitions of the relevant concepts and then good information about how the data were generated before causal inferences can be drawn. Several lessons follow.

1. The purpose of causal inference is to learn what would happen *if* x were set at a particular value. Causal effects are defined, therefore, in hypothetical terms for different values of x. Causal effects cannot be directly observed. They must be inferred.
2. The intervention and the response need to be thoroughly characterized, ideally within a response schedule framework. Only then is it possible to determine, even in principle, if the desired causal inferences can be appropriately drawn.
3. For these causal inferences to be useful for policy, they must be made to reflect the world as we know it or be well-justified approximations thereof. To be sure, such a world is a moving target. But at any given time, it can be usefully described.
4. A critical element in causal inference is that influences represented by the errors must be unrelated to the values or levels of the intervention. Otherwise, the possible role of the intervention cannot be isolated.

[21] This is only true when the test is for a single predictor.

5. A regression analysis of $y|x$ is absolutely silent on whether any observed patterns are causal. In other words, one cannot use regression analysis to infer cause. We shall see later that the same conclusion holds for multiple regression and regression with more than one equation. Those, too, are just ways to describe conditional distributions.
6. Causal inferences depend on the correspondence between the response schedule conceptualized and how the data were generated. If a case for cause and effect can be made, then regression analysis may be used to estimate it.
7. Conversely, just because a regression analysis can be run does not mean that a cause-and-effect interpretation makes sense.

The last point seems obvious and yet also seems to be routinely ignored. One reason may be that data analysts confuse the estimation of causal effects with the definition of causal effects. For example, suppose in a given occupational category, average salary is computed separately for men and women. Then, the difference between those salaries is given a causal interpretation. What's the problem? Surely one can compare average salaries.[22]

The problem is that the empirical exercise of comparing average salaries is essentially the same activity we undertook in Chapter 2. The means from two conditional distributions are being compared. That alone does not lead to causal inferences. As we will consider in more depth in the final chapter, the comparison may be consistent (or not) with some causal explanation and/or may lead to the formulation and estimation of a legitimate causal model in the future. But no claims can be made that if x is manipulated, the regression equation provides a valid estimate for the outcome. Causal inferences depend fundamentally on information that is not contained in the data. In this chapter, the kinds of information required were specified: (a) a definition of a causal effect, (b) a conceptualization of how the response is generated through an intervention, and (c) a credible case that the conceptualization applies to the situation at hand. Only when these requirements are met are causal inferences appropriate.

In summary, simple linear regression cannot be used to define causal effects. Nor can it be used to infer causal effects. Simple linear regression can sometimes be used to estimate causal effects once a definition and supporting rationale have been provided.

[22]In practice, statistical controls are usually introduced. We will consider the role of covariance adjustments in a later chapter. But it will turn out that whether or not there is an effort to hold confounded variables constant does not affect the argument being made here.

The Formalities of Multiple Regression

6.1 Introduction

Most applications of regression analysis include more than one predictor. In this chapter, we consider multiple regression. In so doing, we need to allow for two complications. There can now be $x_1, x_2, \ldots, x_p$ predictors collected in a $p \times 1$ vector $\mathbf{x}$ and *terms* that can be constructed from one or more predictors. These additions leave the formal theory underlying regression analysis largely unchanged. The vast majority of the material addressed so far carries over nicely. However, some interpretative issues become more complex, and evaluating how well a regression analysis performs is significantly more difficult. We turn now to a quick review of the nuts and bolts of multiple regression.[1]

6.2 Terms and Predictors

As before, our attention is directed to conditional distributions. But now, y depends on $\mathbf{x}$, where the $\mathbf{x}$ is the set of p predictors. Predictors may be the following?

[1]Two notational changes are necessary. First, matrix notation is a major convenience the use of which cannot be postponed any longer. Second, in anticipation of the greater use of model-based sampling in more advanced regression models, the expectation operator will be used to refer to the mean of a population or a feature of the model responsible for the data.

- numerical (i.e., equal interval) even if with a limited range (e.g., only positive);
- categorical (e.g., ethnicity), with binary as a special case; or
- ordinal (e.g., military rank), but this can lead to troubles we will talk about later.

Terms are built from predictors. Thus, one can write

$$E(y|\mathbf{x}) = \eta_0 u_0 + \eta_1 u_1 + \cdots + \eta_{k-1} u_{k-1}. \tag{6.1}$$

There are k regression coefficients (including the intercept) with each of the $k - 1$ terms computed from known values of the p predictors.[2] Even if these functions are nonlinear, the regression equation is linear because the regression coefficients enter the equation in a linear fashion. Each of the $k - 1$ terms is represented by u_j ($j = 1, 2, \ldots, k - 1$). The values for u_0 are an $n \times 1$ vector of 1's, with n equal to the number of observations.

The constraints typically imposed and the information often brought to bear from outside should now be familiar.

1. The concern is with the conditional means of y.
2. The goal is to characterize the path of the means with a hyperplane.
3. The least squares criterion is applied, which imposes symmetry on the errors and places special weight on the largest departures from the regression line.
4. For statistical inference, we assume that the data were produced by random sampling, by a natural approximation thereof from a well-defined population, or through a well-understood data generation process accurately characterized by a model.
5. We assume that the natural world constructed the data in the population so that a hyperplane passes through each of the conditional means. Alternatively, the process by which the data were generated produces errors that are uncorrelated with the terms in the model.
6. In either case, the errors are independent of one another.
7. We require that the natural world forces all of the conditional variances $\text{Var}(y|\mathbf{x})$ to be the same.
8. We require no systematic measurement error for any of the variables and no random measurement error for $\mathbf{x}$.
9. In some instances, we require that $y|\mathbf{x}$ be normally distributed.
10. We impose the thought experiment of a limitless number of independent samples from the given population or a limitless number of independent realizations of the data generation process.

---

[2]Because the $k-1$ terms are constructed from the p predictors, the notation $E(y|\mathbf{x})$ is appropriate.

11. For causal inference, we assume that one of the response schedule formulations applies in the sense that the data were generated as if the world actually operated as the response schedule requires.

As before, the first three requirements are basically judgment calls that affect description of $y|\mathbf{x}$. Statistical inference depends on requirements 4 through 10. Causal inference depends on requirement 11. Requirements 4 through 11 are statements about nature that can be more or less accurate and can sometimes be examined with data. They are not mere technicalities.

6.3 Some Notation for Multiple Regression

At this point, we need to provide the matrix notation as follows:

$$\mathbf{x} = \begin{pmatrix} x_1 \\ x_2 \\ \vdots \\ x_p \end{pmatrix}$$

$$\mathbf{u} = \begin{pmatrix} u_0 = 1 \\ u_1 \\ \vdots \\ u_{k-1} \end{pmatrix}$$

$$\boldsymbol{\eta} = \begin{pmatrix} \eta_0 \\ \eta_1 \\ \vdots \\ \eta_{k-1} \end{pmatrix}.$$

The linear model with more than a single predictor can now be written as

$$E(y|\mathbf{x}) = \boldsymbol{\eta}^{\mathrm{T}}\mathbf{u}. \tag{6.2}$$

6.4 Estimation

Again, we use least squares and minimize

$$RSS(\mathbf{h}) = \Sigma_{i=1}^{n}(y_i - \mathbf{h}^{\mathrm{T}}\mathbf{u}_i)^2, \tag{6.3}$$

where $\mathbf{h}$ is a set of $k - 1$ "trial" coefficients. This leads to

$$\hat{\eta} = (\mathbf{U}^{\mathrm{T}}\mathbf{U})^{-1}\mathbf{U}^{\mathrm{T}}\mathbf{y}, \tag{6.4}$$

where $\mathbf{U}$ is an $n \times k$ matrix of terms (including u_0). The estimates of the regression coefficients $\hat{\eta}$ are unique, given the data. However, no variables can be an exact linear combination of any other variables. Note that one has to invert the cross-product matrix of the terms. If that cross-product matrix is singular because of linear dependence, conventional inversion cannot be done. One way that investigators sometimes in practice create the linear dependence is by including l binary variables for a categorical variable with l categories.[3] A more practical set of concerns surfaces when there is near-dependence, or what is usually called "multicollinearity." We will consider the difficulties that can follow with high multicollinearity in a later chapter.

The residual variance is estimated by

$$\hat{\sigma}^2 = \frac{RSS}{n - k}. \tag{6.5}$$

The estimate of the variance-covariance matrix of the regression coefficients (including the intercept) is

$$\widehat{\mathrm{Var}}(\hat{\eta}) = \hat{\sigma}^2\mathbf{M}, \tag{6.6}$$

where $\mathbf{M}$ is a $k \times k$ matrix through which σ^2 is transformed in the variance-covariance matrix of the regression coefficients (including the intercept). Formally, $\mathbf{M} = (\mathbf{U}^{\mathrm{T}}\mathbf{U})^{-1}$. The diagonal elements in $\hat{\sigma}^2\mathbf{M}$ are the estimated squared standard errors, and the off-diagonal elements are the estimated covariances.

Statistical inference for multiple regression does not create any important new problems. One still requires random sampling or a close natural approximation of it, or data generated by nature through a particular model. However, multiple regression opens the door to a very large number of possible null hypotheses.

For example, there can now be a large number of different nested models to compare. Thus, to test the null hypothesis that all of the regression coefficients are zero save the intercept, one compares the unrestricted model to the model with only the intercept. The restricted model yields a residual sum of squares equal to the sum of squares of y. The unrestricted model produces the usual residual sum of squares. An analysis of variance table and the F-test follow as before. A more detailed discussion of model selection will be undertaken in a subsequent chapter.

Now define the "hat matrix" as follows:

$$\mathbf{H} = \mathbf{U}(\mathbf{U}^{\mathrm{T}}\mathbf{U})^{-1}\mathbf{U}^{\mathrm{T}}. \tag{6.7}$$

[3] In the simplest case, if the variable is male/female and one knows that the observation is not that male, the observation must be female (and vice versa). One of the two possible binary variables is redundant.

For each observation, there is a value h_i that is a function solely of the "input" matrix **U**. The h_i is the ii (diagonal) element of **H** (which is n by n) and is called the leverage of observation i. It indicates the potential "pull" from regression terms an observation has on the regression fit.

The value of h_i is always between zero and one. If there are $k - 1$ terms in the regression equation, the leverages sum to $k - 1$. Thus, the mean leverage is $(k-1)/n$. If n is large relative to $k-1$, individual leverages are unlikely to stand out (and matter). But as h_i approaches one, the regression fit will approach y_i and so y_i pulls hard on the fit. It will generally be true that leverages are greater the farther the observation is from the means of its constituent variables. The hat matrix will figure in some computations ahead and in later discussions of some regression diagnostics.

Finally, we again consider a measure of goodness of fit:

$$R^2 = \frac{SYY - RSS}{SYY}. \tag{6.8}$$

The coefficient of determination, which denotes that percentage of the variance of y "explained" by the set of terms, indicates how closely the observations cluster around the fitted values. Although, on intuitive grounds, a "good fit" certainly seems desirable, on closer consideration, it is often unclear why a good fit is so good.

For example, a well-executed randomized experiment will provide an unbiased and easily interpreted measure of an average causal effect. Statistical inference follows naturally and easily. But a regression model applied to the data may not fit well at all, in part because causes of the outcome not manipulated as part of the experiment are not included; they are simply not of interest. In contrast, a large regression model fit to observational data may fit well but produce statistical and causal inferences that are nonsense. The common reliance in regression analysis on variance explained and other measures of fit is too often a substitute for hard thinking about how useful a model really is.

6.5 How Multiple Regression "Holds Constant"

The regression coefficients estimated by multiple regression are "partial" regression coefficients. Each conveys the change in the expected value of y for a unit change in the values of u_j with the other terms "held constant." What does this mean?

Earlier, we addressed the need to make comparisons between comparable groups, defined by being balanced on the average. Random assignment, properly implemented, was a sure way to achieve balance on the average. Matching was one alternative that could work assuming, among other things, that the necessary matching variables were on hand. Covariance adjustments provided by multiple regression were a third alternative.

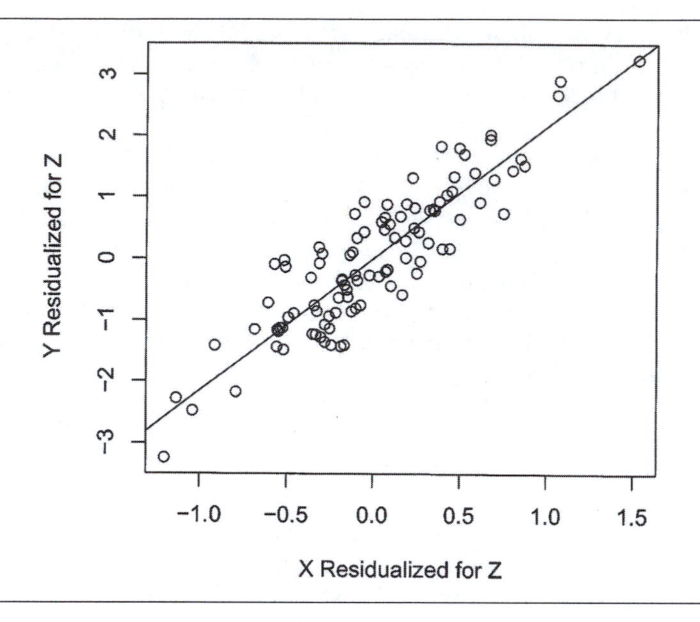

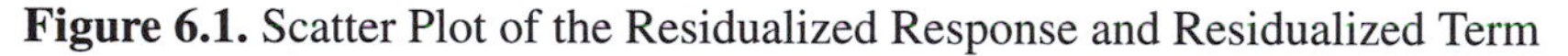

Figure 6.1. Scatter Plot of the Residualized Response and Residualized Term

Consider for now the case of two terms (x, z):

$$E(y|x, z) = \eta_0 + \eta_1 x + \eta_2 z. \tag{6.9}$$

We will focus for now on the regression coefficient for x (η_1). We estimate the parameters of the following two equations:

$$E(y|z) = \alpha_0 + \alpha_1 z, \tag{6.10}$$

$$E(x|z) = \beta_0 + \beta_1 z. \tag{6.11}$$

For each, we compute the residuals, $e_{y|z}$ and $e_{x|z}$. Now consider

$$E(e_{y|z}|e_{x|z}) = \gamma_0 + \gamma_1 e_{x|z}. \tag{6.12}$$

Figure 6.1 is a scatter plot of two sets of such residuals. Overlaid is a least squares line based on Equation 6.12. The estimate of γ_1 will be the same as the estimate of η_1 coming out of the usual least squares formula applied to Equation 6.9. Both estimate the slope as 2.148. In other words, we "residualize" y and x by subtracting out the estimates of their conditional means (which depend on z). Then, the residuals of y are regressed on the residuals of x. Although these are not literally the steps undertaken in least squares estimation

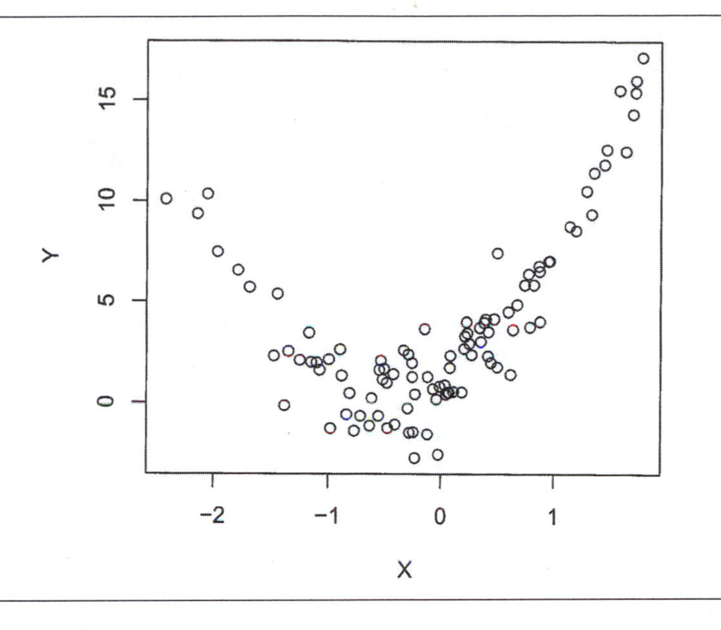

Figure 6.2. Scatter Plot of y on x With x a Nonlinear Function of z

of the regression parameters, this is what happens in effect. A parallel logic applies to what η_2 means. Note that there is nothing in the residualizing process that directly speaks to what holding one or more variables constant might mean in the real world. It is a content-free statistical adjustment. Making the link to how nature is supposed to operate is not in the data nor in the implicit auxiliary regressions. We shall consider this issue in depth in the next chapter.

Likewise, the "partialing" algebra applies if multiple regression is used solely for description of a given data set. There is nothing about the matrix manipulations that depends on random sampling from a well-defined population, or a convenient natural process generating a random sample or random realization.

To help underscore the impact the holding constant operation can have, consider the following example with x and z as predictors. Although y is a linear function of x and z, the relationship between x and z is nonlinear. Figure 6.2 shows a scatter plot of the relationship between y and x ignoring z. The "marginal response plot" that follows ("marginal" because only the two variables x and y are involved) indicates a strong nonlinear relationship. In contrast, the same plot, Figure 6.3, with y and x residualized for z, shows a linear relationship. What is held constant can really matter.[4]

[4]This point can be made just as accurately, but not as dramatically, if x and z are linearly related.

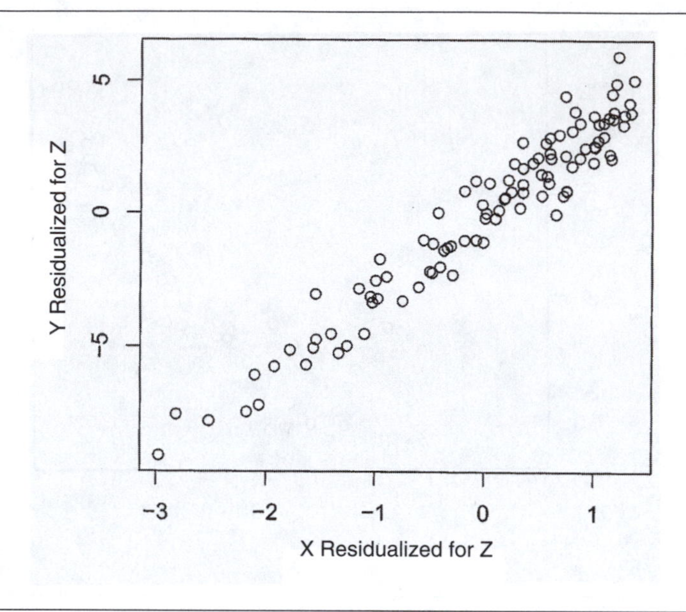

Figure 6.3. Residualized Scatter Plot of y on x With x a Nonlinear Function of z

6.6 Summary and Conclusions

The primary purpose of this chapter is to get on the table the essential formal properties of multiple regression. All of the material discussed before this chapter carries over. The essential new point is what it means to hold things constant. Our job now is to consider how multiple regression can be used in practice.

7 Using and Interpreting Multiple Regression

7.1 Introduction

Multiple regression opens the door to a wide variety of interesting applications. But with the promise comes ample opportunity for serious missteps. There are also some important problems for which there are rarely any definitive solutions. A good place to begin a discussion of using multiple regression is to revisit what the partial regression coefficients convey.

7.2 Another Formal Perspective on Holding Constant

Considered in the previous chapter was the residualization process by which partial regression coefficients are constructed. Equation 7.1 addresses the same issues from a different vantage point. Again, there are only two terms, and we assume that, in the population, the usual regression model holds or that the model used corresponds to the way nature generated the data. In the population, the regression hyperplane goes through the conditional means of y. Stated to allow for data generated by nature, the errors are uncorrelated with the two terms x and z.

The regression coefficient for variable x is

$$\eta_x = \frac{r_{yx} - r_{xz}r_{yz}}{(1 - r_{xz}^2)} \times \frac{\mathrm{SD}(y)}{\mathrm{SD}(x)}, \tag{7.1}$$

where $r_{(.)}$ is the Pearson correlation coefficient and SD(.) refers to the standard deviation. From Equation 7.1, we learn several important things about the partial regression coefficient for x.

- If all of the correlations are nonzero, the marginal response will almost certainly differ from the conditional response. So, omitted variables can be a very serious problem.
- If the terms x and z are uncorrelated, conditioning does not change things; hence, the virtue of randomized experiments. In principle, one gets the same estimate of the regression coefficient even if one leaves out terms related to y. (But including them can improve the fit and reduce the standard errors—see below.)
- If x and z have a correlation of 1.0, the regression coefficient for x holding z constant is undefined. That is an example of linear dependence between terms.
- If x and y are uncorrelated, the regression coefficient for x may still be nonzero, depending on the correlation between x and z and the correlation between y and z. When the bivariate regression coefficient is zero and the partial regression coefficients are not zero, the term "suppressor effect" is sometimes applied.
- If a constant is added to any of the variables, nothing in Equation 7.1 changes. The correlations are all unit free, and the standard deviations are unaffected when a constant is added.
- If any of the variables are multiplied by a constant, the changes in the partial regression coefficient that occur stem from changes in the standard deviations. When y is multiplied by c, the standard deviation for y is multiplied by c, and so the regression coefficient is multiplied by c. When x is multiplied by c, the standard deviation for x is multiplied by c, and so the regression coefficient is divided by c. Because the correlations are all unit free, and because the standard deviation of z is nowhere to be found, multiplying z by c changes nothing. Linear transformations also have no effect on the fit or the standard errors because everything just scales up or down.
- Nonlinear transformations, in contrast, can change everything.
- Each of the above conclusions essentially generalize, if z is a set of terms rather than a single term.

In short, the regression coefficient for the marginal relationship between y and x will typically be different from the conditional relationship between y and

x. Linear transformations do not change anything fundamental, although the metric of the regression coefficients will change. But nonlinear transformations can make an enormous difference. This will have real bite when we consider nonlinear transformations of the data in a later chapter.

7.3 When Does Holding Constant Make Sense?

If the purpose of an analysis is to examine how the conditional mean of the response varies as x_j varies with all other terms fixed, one can proceed with multiple regression without much worry about what sense it makes to think of the other terms as fixed. For example, one could usefully ask, as did the UCLA Gender Equity Study described earlier, what the difference is in average income between men and women, holding academic rank constant. In matching language, one can find those faculty members who have the same rank and see what the salary differences are for men and women. If the regression line for salary as a function of rank for men is parallel to the comparable regression line for women, matching and regression adjustments will, in principle, produce the same estimates of gender differences in salary.[1]

As a descriptive exercise, all is well. One can compare the average salary of men and women, holding constant potential confounders. The result is a summary of how salaries differ on the average by gender, conditional on the values of one or more covariates. *Why* the salaries may on the average differ is not represented explicitly in the regression model, and there is nothing in the summary statistics that directly addresses cause and effect.

Moving to causal inference is an enormous step that needs to be thoroughly considered. To begin, one must ponder, as we did in Chapter 5, whether the causal variable of interest can be usefully conceptualized as an intervention within a response schedule framework. Once again, consider gender. Imagine a particular faculty member. Now, imagine intervening so that the faculty member's gender could be set to "male." One would do this while altering nothing else about this person. Then, repeat the same thought experiment with gender set to "female." Again, only gender changes.

Clearly, the fit between the requisite response schedule and the academic world in which salaries are determined fails for at least two reasons: The idea of setting gender to male or female is an enormous stretch and even, if gender could be manipulated, it is hard to accept that only gender would be changed. In short, the causal story is in deep trouble even before the matter of holding constant surfaces.

---

[1]Because there is a formula at UCLA linking rank to salary, rank can be transformed into a numerical variable.

Recall what the econometric formulation of causal effects requires. It must be possible to manipulate each "input" *independently.* In Equation 7.1, for instance, x can be manipulated while z is unchanged, and z can be manipulated with x unchanged.

Suppose, at a given university, the goal was to increase the success rate at which junior faculty are promoted to tenure. The university administration might decide to provide two kinds of help to all untenured faculty. Each would be offered one sabbatical quarter every other year and $2,000 of research seed money. Both interventions represent manipulation that could be implemented independently of one another, and what it means to "hold constant" is clear: One could offer only the one-quarter sabbatical every other year or only the $2,000 of seed money. The value of the intervention not introduced could remain fixed (e.g., at no sabbatical or no money). There would still be the matter of the errors to be spelled out, but for any *given* untenured faculty member, both "inputs" could be manipulated independently.

In contrast, consider the young sociologist a year or two after appointment. The department chair is concerned about the sociologist's teaching performance in introductory sociology classes and is considering an intervention of smaller class sizes. The response is students' ratings of the professor and the class. But there are a lot of factors besides the intimacy of the setting that could affect the ratings, and many of these would be related to class size. For example, course content is likely to affect student ratings and is also likely to be associated with class size. One can do things in small classes that cannot be done in large classes, so class size might affect course content, and course content might affect class size.

At a glance, the solution is simple; fix course content and vary class size. But how would the department chair manage to do this? The precise meaning of "course content" would need to be articulated and measured. But even if that were accomplished, how would course content be held constant? In effect, one would need to script the assistant professor, all of the questions raised by students, and the professor's answers to those questions. Surely this is not realistic. And if it is not realistic, what sense does it make to think about a response schedule in which course content is held constant? Only if the lectures were taped and no interaction were allowed between the teacher and the students could course content be held constant. But "remote learning" is very different from conventional teaching. A very different response schedule is implied.[2]

[2]One could perhaps circumvent this problem with a convenient definition of course content. For example, course content could be defined solely by the textbook used, and in many institutions, that could be determined by the department chair. But few academics would be comfortable with the idea that the textbook assigned in a course captures most of what there is to class content. Even in a very large lecture setting where there may be very little interaction between students and the teacher, what in the textbook is transmitted to students, how that content is conveyed, and what other materials are introduced can vary widely in a manner that is virtually impossible to control.

In short, even though one could apply regression-based manipulations that adjust for course content being constant, actually holding that content constant would be problematic in an academic department. It makes no sense, therefore, to partial for course content because there is no corresponding operation in reality. And that is the key point: *Covariance adjustments are only arithmetic manipulations of the data. If one decides to interpret those manipulations as if some confounder were actually being fixed, a very cooperative empirical world is required.*

Now consider the kind of canonical causal analysis that undergirds a great deal of policy work: a regression of income on factors thought to affect income, including education, age, occupation, gender, race, and so on. The problems with gender and race have already been addressed. Let's focus on occupation and education. Suppose the goal is to analyze what would happen to income if education were set to particular values, holding occupation constant. Age, race, and gender can be ignored for now and do not, in any case, figure in the point to be made.

There is a set of people for whom the response schedule may be appropriate. Consider one of those people. The first job is to alter education. How would that be done? Public education is free, and with normal progress, a student advances one grade at a time. So, an intervention might be to try to prevent a student from dropping out before graduating from high school. Or, if the interest is in college, one might be able to admit a student regardless of high school performance and offer a scholarship. Of course, there is no guarantee that the student would complete college. In short, altering education is not an easy task, and it is not at all clear what it means then to hold occupation constant, in part because occupation will often be determined a number of years after schooling has ended. How could education in, say, 1995 be altered holding constant occupation in 2005?[3]

---

[3]The relationship between the predictors education and occupation raises an important issue, central in the analysis of social science data in the 1950s and 1960s but largely ignored today: the roles of "intervening variables" and "antecedent variables" (Rosenberg, 1968:Chapter 3). Because, education "causes" occupation, education is an antecedent variable for occupation. Because occupation, in turn, "causes" income, occupation is an intervening variable between education and income. Assuming, for simplicity, that these are the only three variables that matter, conditioning on education will formally leave the relationship between occupation and income unchanged (assuming there is variation in occupation after conditioning on education). Conditioning on occupation will eliminate the relationship between education and income. It will usually not make sense to control for predictors that are antecedent to other predictors. Controlling for an intervening variable is only likely to make sense if its role as an intervening variable is stated explicitly and the consequences of holding it constant are interpreted in that light. For example, if, after controlling for an occupation, education is unrelated to income, it does not mean that education is not a "cause" of income. It means that the effect of education is through occupation. Introducing control variables into a multiple regression equation, just because they are thought to be correlated with other variables of interest and the response variable, risks seriously confusing matters. Here, we are making the additional point that the concepts of "cause" and "holding constant" in this instance are themselves problematic.

Alternatively, one can forego human agency and let nature manipulate education at the same time holding occupation constant. Some interaction between the person, the person's family, peers, and teachers, coupled with a host of other factors, would determine the educational level achieved. Even assuming one could articulate well what this response function would look like, nature now has the problem of altering education at the same time holding constant an occupation that will be determined years later. Again, it is very difficult to think of a response schedule formulation that makes sense.

Might one solve the problem by thinking retrospectively? There is a person with a particular occupation. Nature now manipulates that person's education holding occupation constant. Clearly, this fails because occupation is determined in part by that person's earlier education. How can education for that person be altered assuming no impact on later occupation?

This is not to imply that it never makes sense to apply regression-based adjustments in causal modeling. The critical issue is that the real world must cooperate by providing interventions that could be delivered separately. Thus, in prison settings, it is possible to place an inmate in vocational training and/or provide a substantial amount of gate money. The two interventions are not fundamentally linked. It may then make sense to use regression-based adjustments to consider the causal effect of each of these interventions separately on success in the job market after release.

Likewise, consider efforts to conserve water. For any given household, one can raise the per-unit price of water and/or attach a punitive charge for excessive use. These are separable interventions. Hence, one could, in principle, use regression-based adjustments to estimate the causal effect of each on residential water consumption.

Or, consider prenatal care. One could provide free medical examinations and/or free nutritional supplements. For improving air quality in a city, one could ban diesel engines and/or the use of petroleum-based paints. For moving welfare recipients off of the welfare rolls, one could increase existing forgiveness provisions for earnings and/or shorten the period of time during which welfare payments may be received. Clearly, there is no shortage of examples in which regression-based adjustments can make subject matter sense. But for each application, the case needs to be made.

Finally, we revisit the role of fixed attributes, such as gender and race. Although these are not manipulable and, hence, are not included within the definition of an intervention, one could still imagine that the response schedule for determining income, for instance, could differ depending on race and/or gender.

Recall Equation 5.7,

$$Y_{i,x} = a + bx + \delta_{i,x}, \tag{7.2}$$

where the $\delta_{i,x}$, with an expected value of zero, is drawn independently and at random from some invariant distribution, given a value for x. The coefficients a and b could differ depending on whether the subject is male or female.

For example, the response schedule for males may typically generate higher average income values than the response schedule for females; a is larger for males. Or interventions such as job training (x) may have greater returns for males than for females; b is larger for males. Within this conception, gender for a single person is not subject to change; gender could not have been different. As a result, there is no policy lever to pull with respect to gender; it cannot be changed. Still, one *could* alter manipulable variables whose effects differ for men and women so that the disparities found are ameliorated. For instance, businesses might provide on-site child care so that single parents (usually women) do not have to arrive at work late or leave work early in response to the hours of off-site child-care facilities.

In practice, one could apply simple linear regression separately to a sample of males and a sample of females to estimate the different values of a and b. Alternatively, the different response schedules for men and women could be formulated within a single multiple regression equation. How one would do so will be discussed in the next chapter.

To summarize, there are a number of statistical tools that address the need to hold confounded variables constant. Our interest here has centered on regression-based adjustments. These are, in principle, tools to assist in causal inference. As a technical move, it is easy to apply regression-based adjustments to confounders. Whether it is sensible to do so is an entirely different matter.

7.4 Standardized Regression Coefficients: Once More With Feeling

One of the policy questions that social scientists like to ask is which terms are "most important" or "more important." For example, is social class or IQ more important in determining success in school? Or, what is more important for the wages of factory workers in the United States, the NAFTA accords or minimum-wage legislation? The problem is that, because predictors typically come in different units (e.g., score on the SATs vs. high school grade point average), the metric or "raw" regression coefficients cannot be directly compared to make a judgment about relative importance.

In response, some applied researchers transform each regression term into z scores (subtract the mean, divide by the standard deviation) before applying regression. The result is a "standardized" regression coefficient defined as

$$\hat{\eta}_j^* = \text{SD}(u_j)\hat{\eta}_j. \tag{7.3}$$

Now one can speak about the change in the mean of y for a 1-SD change in u_j, other terms held constant. The new units for all of the terms are standard deviation units. Comparability seems to have been achieved.

There are several difficulties with this kind of standardization. To begin, the process can be very close to tautological. The concept of "important" or the concept of "more important" typically goes undefined. As a result, when asked what is meant by "more important," the common response is that the variable with the larger standardized partial regression coefficient is more important. Why a larger standardized regression coefficient implies greater importance is obscure.

Consider a concrete illustration. Suppose grade point average in college is regressed on grade point average in high school and SAT score. Suppose the metric regression coefficient for high school GPA is .5, and the metric regression coefficient for SAT score is .00075. So the conditional mean of college GPA increases half a GPA point for a 1-point increase in high school GPA. And the conditional mean of college GPA increases three quarters of a GPA point for a 1,000-point increase in SAT score. Those are the facts in this data set.

The standardized regression coefficients might be 1.0 for high school GPA and .25 for the SAT score. Now a 1-SD increase in high school GPA is associated with a 1-point average increase in college GPA, although a 1-SD increase in SAT score is associated with an average increase of 0.25 in college GPA. In what sense is GPA score more important?

Translated back into the original units, an increase of 2 points in high school GPA is associated with a 1-point average increase in college GPA. An increase of 333 SAT points is associated with a quarter of a point increase in average college GPA. Where is the comparability? Implicitly, the standardized coefficients alter the terms by noncomparable amounts in the process of trying to manufacture comparability (here, 2 GPA points vs. 333 SAT points).

The lesson is that "importance" must be defined outside of the data and in such a way that the standardized coefficients are responsive. When such an effort is made, importance is often defined as "variance explained." So, let's examine that.

In the social sciences, it is common to find the standardized regression coefficient, or "beta," defined as follows:

$$\hat{\beta}_j = \frac{\text{SD}(u_j)}{\text{SD}(y)} \hat{\eta}_j. \tag{7.4}$$

In effect, y and each of the terms have been transformed into z scores. Thus, for a 1-SD change in u_j, there is an average change of $\hat{\beta}_j$ SD units in y. In some sense, the relationships are even more standardized.

If one squares $\hat{\beta}_j$, the result is one definition of the variances "uniquely explained" by u_j. So, if $\hat{\beta}_j$ is larger than $\hat{\beta}_k$, it means that u_j by itself accounts for more variance in y than u_k. In that sense, the former is more important than the latter. However, there are other, equally defensible definitions of "unique" variance explained. For example, one can define such an entity for u_j as the amount that the R^2 declines if u_j is removed from the regression equation. This will generally not be the same as $\hat{\beta}_j^2$.

Beta coefficients, whether squared or not, are very popular in many settings. For example, in the study mentioned earlier conducted by the University of California on the relationship between SAT scores and performance in college, the "beta coefficient" is taken to be a measure of "predictive validity." Thus, variables with larger beta coefficients are taken to be more powerful predictors. By this criterion, SAT II scores and grade point averages have better predictive validity than SAT I scores.[4]

Note also that, with standardization via Equations 7.3 or 7.4, the results depend on the relevant standard deviations. As discussed in Section 3.5, two studies could have the exact same values for $\hat{\eta}_j$ and very different values for the standardized coefficients. Thus, the importance of variables is linked not just to how much, on the average, y changes for a unit change in u_j but to the variability of u_j and sometimes y as well. Two very different features of the multivariate scatter plot are confounded. Moreover, the variability of u_j is sometimes consciously manipulated for statistical reasons unrelated to effect size (e.g., to obtain smaller standard errors).

Yet another form of standardization is the elasticity, usually approximated by working with logs of all of the variables. Elasticities were considered earlier. Recall that they translate metric coefficients into units of percentage change and have the clear advantage of being useful theoretical concepts in economics. But when they are used solely for purposes of manufacturing comparability, they too raise the question of what the gains really are.

Finally, what is an applied researcher to do if the relative importance of predictors (or terms) really needs to be assessed? The answer is that importance is probably best defined in subject matter or policy terms. For example, the relative importance of interventions is routinely provided in cost-effectiveness analyses (Levin and McEwan, 2001). The common metric is not standard deviations, but dollars. Thus, every \$100 spent on a particular job training intervention may yield half the impact on the future earnings of welfare recipients as every \$100 spent on providing quality day care for the children of welfare recipients. Day care is two times more cost-effective in its impact on future earnings and might then be declared to be twice as important.

7.5 Variances of the Coefficient Estimates

When there is more than one term in the regression model, the degree of linear dependence among the terms affects the estimated standard errors. Even though

---

[4]No real forecasting is undertaken, however. That would require building a model on one data set and then trying to forecast the response in a new data set; predictive validity actually has nothing to do with forecasting college performance.

this may seem to be only a technical issue, there are important implications for interpretation.

The standard errors for the regression coefficients in multiple regression are affected by the full set of terms, just as the coefficients themselves are. Thus,

$$\mathrm{SE}(\hat{\eta}_j) = \frac{\hat{\sigma}}{\mathrm{SD}(u_j)\sqrt{n-1}}\sqrt{\frac{1}{1-R_j^2}}, \tag{7.5}$$

where R_j^2 is the R^2 for the linear regression of the jth term u_j on all of the other terms in the mean function.

A brief examination of Equation 7.5 will indicate the following:

1. As in the simple regression case, the standard error is larger if the estimate of the residual variance (or standard deviation) is larger.
2. As in the simple regression case, the standard error is smaller if the term in question has more variance.
3. As in the simple regression case, the standard error is smaller if the sample size is larger.
4. This is new: The larger the value of R_j^2, the larger the standard error.

The new insight is that, when terms are added to the mean function, the regression standard errors can be pulled in two directions. The residual standard deviation is often reduced, which reduces the estimated standard errors. At the same time, the degree of linear dependence among the terms can be increased, which increases the estimated standard errors. Ideally, the added terms should be relatively uncorrelated with each other (and to the existing terms in the equation) and highly correlated with the response variable. If statistical inference is employed, small standard errors are desirable; the precision of the estimates will be higher.

It is sometimes not appreciated, however, that Equation 7.5 also has important implications when statistical inference is not undertaken. A large standard error implies that small changes in the values of u_j lead to large changes in $\hat{\eta}_j$. For example, if the observational units included were changed a bit, or if, because of measurement error, the values analyzed were a bit different, $\hat{\eta}_j$ could be substantially different. Moreover, minor changes in which terms are included or in how those terms are defined also can lead to large changes in the estimated value of $\hat{\eta}_j$. In other words, the estimates are very fragile. Variations in the data or the model that should not make a material difference actually do.[5]

In practice, therefore, it is useful to consider the degree to which there is linear dependence among the terms included in the regression model and what

[5]If the large standard errors are being driven primarily by a subset of the R_j^2s, then only those $\hat{\eta}_j$s are at risk.

the implications may be for the stability of the regression estimates (even if the estimates are to be used solely for description). One popular index is the variance inflation factor (VIF), which is essentially the far right term in Equation 7.5:

$$\text{VIF}_j = \frac{1}{1 - R_j^2}. \tag{7.6}$$

The variance inflation factor is a positive number that multiplies the standard error. The greater the linear dependence between terms, the larger the multiplier. However, there is no clear threshold above which one should begin to worry because one's concerns should be linked to how much instability in $\hat{\eta}_j$ can be tolerated, and that depends on the problem at hand. Nevertheless, one common rule based on practical experience is that, if the VIF exceeds 5.0, one might consider ways to make the estimate of $\hat{\eta}_j$ more stable. The value 5.0 is taken to be a threshold above which it pays to think carefully about the consequences of correlations among the terms included in a regression analysis.

It is also important to keep in mind that such concerns need only be raised for estimated regression coefficients of central importance to the research. It is only the R_j^2s for those terms that matter. So, one can include a large number of terms to reduce confounding, even if they are highly correlated among themselves, as long as the R_j^2s for the key terms are not too large.[6]

The various strategies one may employ are discussed in any number of books on regression analysis, and they are not an important concern here. Suffice it to say that among the options are (a) dropping from the model some of the highly correlated terms (because as an empirical matter, they are very similar anyway), (b) imposing constraints on the regression coefficients to allow for more stable estimation, (c) applying nonlinear transformations to the offending terms to reduce the problematic correlations, and (d) employing ridge or Stein estimators (Kennedy, 1998:Chapter 11). The best strategy usually is to collect more and/or better data, but in many situations, that is not possible.

Finally, this discussion of the variances of the estimated regression coefficients implies that doing power analyses for regression to help determine appropriate sample sizes is a daunting exercise. The problem is that one needs to anticipate reasonably well all of the R_j^2s to determine the sample size required for a given level of precision (Cohen, 1988). Such a task can be simplified if there are only a few regression coefficients that will be of interest. Then, only the R_j^2s for those terms need to be specified. In short, although power analyses to determine sample sizes are in principle always a good idea, regression

[6]However, if any $R_j^2 = 1.0$, there is "perfect" linear dependence between u_j and a linear combination of the other terms. Then, the cross-product matrix $(\mathbf{U}^T\mathbf{U})$ is singular. As a result, one cannot obtain unique estimates of the regression coefficients, and the standard errors are undefined. If one wants estimates of the regression coefficients, there is no choice but to try and fix the problem.

applications are one illustration of the difficulties one faces when trying to do power analyses for anything beyond very simple models and tests. In practice, one usually should not take power analyses for complicated models very seriously. They are typically based on too much guesswork.

7.6 Summary and Conclusions

This chapter began with another way to consider what the partial regression coefficients represent. Perhaps the major lesson was that the covariance adjustments built into regression analysis can make an enormous difference in the estimated value of $\hat{\eta}_j$. Regression-based covariance adjustment should not be undertaken casually.

A more subtle point was that one can be misled if terms are included that are not strongly unrelated to the response but are related to the other terms. This was underscored in the discussion of the standard errors for $\hat{\eta}_j$. "Kitchen sink" models are typically not a good solution to model specification even if their complexity per se could be managed.

The most demanding material, however, was the examination of what it means to "hold constant." The technical aspects, discussed in the previous chapter, were not the problem. The problem was the potential incongruence between the mechanics of regression-based adjustments and the natural or social world under study. If the purpose of the study is description, perhaps coupled with statistical inference, the issues raised are beside the point. One can proceed. If potential incongruence is seriously addressed and all is well, causal inference may be justified. But what are the options if, after careful consideration, incongruence remains?

We shall consider such issues in the final chapter. But suffice it to say, one can always stop with description and statistical inference. Both can be extremely useful, and for descriptive work at least, one does not have to import a great deal of external information about how the data were generated. Moreover, all concerns about cause and effect may not have to be abandoned. The descriptive results may provide important insights about what the underlying causal processes could be. In the UCLA gender study, for instance, the descriptive analysis suggested that a key place to look for explanations about average salary differences between men and women was in how rapidly men and women were being promoted. This was a very important lead that refocused the energies of administrators at UCLA. The descriptive studies of climate change described in Chapter 2 also illustrate that good science addressing cause-and-effect relationships can be successfully undertaken without regression-based causal modeling. It is possible to learn some things about cause-and-effect relationships without employing a causal model in which the key causal mechanisms are supposed to be represented.

There also will be times when the causal questions are just too hard. With discretion the better part of valor, it may well make sense to work on other problems. There are lots of very important and very interesting questions that currently are well beyond our grasp. A painful example from my own work is the role of race in death penalty sentences. Descriptions of racial disparities adjusted for important covariates are easily undertaken, even when coupled with statistical inference. Estimating the "but for," however, cannot, in my view, be credibly accomplished (Berk et al., 1993; Weiss et al., 1996).

Some Popular Extensions of Multiple Regression

8.1 Introduction

Multiple regression can be extended in a number of ways. If we are to get on the table multiple regression as it is commonly used, these extensions need to be considered.

This chapter is basically an expansion of material covered earlier: choosing between competing models, working with categorical terms, examining the variance function and its consequences, and using linear regression as a tool for constructing nonparametric smoothers. To these ends, we consider stepwise regression, analysis of variance and covariance, weighted least squares, and a locally weighted regression smoother (lowess). As before, the emphasis will be on interpretation. The statistical theory and details about how to work with the relevant regression models are found in any number of good regression textbooks (e.g., Cook and Weisberg, 1999).

Of necessity, the material will be more demanding without a proportional increase in the number of pages devoted to exposition. Therefore, this chapter and the two to follow are most appropriate for readers who have already had significant exposure to the material discussed. The goals are to provide a brief refresher and then address the kind of interpretative issues emphasized previously.

There will also be an important subtext that will become more salient in the chapters ahead. As complexity is added to the linear regression model, its analytical reach can sometimes be usefully extended. And sometimes, the added complexity can help address some of the problems raised in earlier chapters. But there will be no "magic bullet." It will still be true that all models are wrong—some very wrong. The best one can hope for is that the added complexity will help make some models more useful.

8.2 Model Selection and Stepwise Regression

Much of the formal statistics of regression analysis is phrased in terms of correct models and incorrect models. Good things typically follow from correct models, and bad things typically follow from incorrect models. Yet if one accepts Box's observation that "all models are wrong," the distinction in practice between correct models and incorrect models is not really helpful. Far more relevant is how useful a regression model is. Does a regression analysis legitimately advance the policy or scientific discourse? And with this goal in mind, there are only better models and worse models. Thoughtful researchers will say as much when pressed.

Insofar as one abandons the search for the correct regression model in favor of a search for a useful regression model, the data analysis enterprise is fundamentally changed. The definition of a correct model and the nature of the properties that follow are a matter of formal statistics alone. The policy or scientific application does not matter. Usefulness, in contrast, can only be determined in context and by the users of a regression analysis. Moreover, many of the most visible statistical criteria for model quality no longer formally apply. For example, if all models are wrong, all estimates of regression coefficients are biased. The search for unbiased estimates is a waste of time.

At a gut level, at least, most data analysts recognize that models are more or less useful and not right or wrong. Yet they typically proceed with one foot in each of two camps. They are engaged in what Leamer (1978) calls a "specification search" and, at the same time, still rely at least in part on procedures in which models are either right or wrong. Statisticians have encouraged this tension. They have developed a number of powerful tools to assist in specification searches but often rationalize the techniques with formal derivations in which models are correct or incorrect.

Model selection procedures are a good example. On the one hand, there is lots of talk of models being right or wrong. On the other hand, the goal often is to develop the simplest model that adequately characterizes the data. An "overparameterized" model is to be avoided because it is complicated, fragile, and inelegant, even if that overparameterized model is formally correct.

8.2.1 Model Selection by Removing Terms

In model selection procedures, the theme of correct or incorrect models is typically a starting point. As a formal matter, what are the consequences if a term that belongs in a model is not included? One can get a good sense of how this plays out in an unusually clear exposition by Cook and Weisberg (1999:264-265). What follows is a summary of their discussion.

We will assume that one has data produced by random sampling, or a close approximation to random sampling, or data generated by nature through a particular model. We care, therefore, about statistical inference as well as description. We will need to work with expectations rather than means.

Suppose the correct model is a function of the terms in **U**. Separating **U** into a single term and all of the other terms, the relevant regression model can be written as

$$E(y|\mathbf{U}) = \boldsymbol{\eta}_1^{\mathrm{T}}\mathbf{u}_1 + \eta_2 u_2, \tag{8.1}$$

where $\boldsymbol{\eta}_1^{\mathrm{T}}\mathbf{u}_1$ is a linear combination of all terms save one, and $\eta_2 u_2$ is a product of a single regression coefficient and its term. Assume for now that the usual (constant) variance function holds.

Conditioning on $\mathbf{u}_1$ only, one gets

$$E(y|\mathbf{u}_1) = E[(\boldsymbol{\eta}_1^{\mathrm{T}}\mathbf{u}_1 + \eta_2 u_2)|\mathbf{u}_1]. \tag{8.2}$$

Rearranging a few terms leads to

$$E(y|\mathbf{u}_1) = \boldsymbol{\eta}_1^{\mathrm{T}}\mathbf{u}_1 + \eta_2 E(u_2|\mathbf{u}_1), \tag{8.3}$$

where the last term is the regression of u_2 on $\mathbf{u}_1$. Failing to condition on a term that belongs in the model implies that the linear relationship between the included and excluded terms (i.e., the linear regression of u_2 on $\mathbf{u}_1$) is confounded with the "pure" effect of $\mathbf{u}_1$. This problem was noted earlier.

Consider now some special cases. Suppose that, in the population or in the natural world that generated the data, the expectation of the true regression equation with constant variance for a pair of predictors x and z is

$$E(y|x, z) = 1 + 4x + 5z. \tag{8.4}$$

Now z is dropped, and the result is

$$E(y|x) = 1 + 4x + 5E(z|x). \tag{8.5}$$

The last term is the expectation of z given x multiplied by 5.

1. If the two predictors are independent so that $E(z|x) = E(z)$ (which is a constant), then

$$E(y|x) = (1 + 5E(z)) + 4x. \tag{8.6}$$

There are now two coefficients in the model. The intercept $(1 + 5E(z))$ has been altered, but the regression coefficient is unchanged. This is a restatement of the benefits of randomized experiments; you get the requisite independence between predictors and the correct estimate of the regression coefficient for x.

2. In contrast, if $E(z|x) = \alpha_0 + \alpha_1 x$, then substituting in Equation 8.4 produces

$$E(y|x) = (1 + 5\alpha_0) + (4 + 5\alpha_1)x. \tag{8.7}$$

Note that now, both the intercept and slope have changed. The relationship from x to y via z is now incorporated in the regression coefficient for x. Both the intercept and the regression coefficient for x are wrong. The size of the distortions depends on the values of α_0 and α_1. The larger these are, the larger the distortions.

3. Now suppose that the regression of z on x is a nonlinear function such as $E(z|x) = \alpha_0 + \alpha_1 exp(\alpha_4 x)$. The mean function now becomes

$$E(y|x_1) = (1 + 5\alpha_0) + 4x + 5\alpha_1 exp(\alpha_4 x). \tag{8.8}$$

Clearly, the linear relationship has evaporated, although the truth is still $E(y|x) = 1 + 4x + 5z$. Even the functional form is wrong.

4. There are analogous problems for the variance function when a term is omitted that is related to x and y. The risk is finding a nonconstant variance function even if the variance around the fit is really constant.

A key point of this exercise is to anticipate how important it is within certain model selection perspectives to get the model right. We turn now to formal tests to assist in that enterprise.

8.2.2 Tests to Compare Models

If the data are generated in a fashion that permits statistical inference, there are tests much like ones already described that can help determine which terms should be included in the regression model. The tests allow one to choose between nested models.

If the models are not nested, the tests to be discussed do not apply. More generally, deciding between nonnested models is very difficult, in part because nonnested models can differ from one another in so many ways, each speaking to different features of the data and/or research problem. That is, the first problem is developing a rationale for such comparisons. In practice, this means specifying which difference between two competing models is important. For example, one might be interested in comparing two nonnested models of the same general phenomenon but one with a nonlinear functional form and one with a linear functional form not nested within it. Even if a clear rationale for comparing nonnested models is articulated, however, there are often difficult statistical complications.

It is sometimes possible, for instance, to develop an "encompassing model" that, in effect, broadens the concept of nesting so that formerly nonnested models can be treated as nested. However, the tests that follow rest on very strong assumptions and, even then, can only be justified asymptotically (i.e., in large samples). In any case, tests for nonnested models do not raise any new interpretative problems of the sort addressed here. They just push the interpretative envelope a lot harder. They will not be considered further.[1]

The basic idea behind comparisons of nested models is to capitalize on the following F-test:

$$F = \frac{RSS_{NH} - RSS_{AH}/(df_{NH} - df_{AH})}{\hat{\sigma}^2}, \tag{8.9}$$

where, as before, NH refers to the null hypothesis model, AH refers to the alternative hypothesis model, and $\hat{\sigma}^2$ is from the fit of the model representing the alternative hypothesis.

The general strategy is to start with the largest model that makes sense and tentatively treat that model as the correct model. By "largest," one generally means the model with the most free parameters to be estimated. Then, restrictions are placed on that model to generate the smaller model. Perhaps most commonly, some of the regression coefficients are set to zero, which means that the corresponding terms can be deleted from the larger model. One is testing the null hypothesis that those regression coefficients are zero, and therefore, the smaller model represents the model for which the null hypothesis is true. The larger model represents the model for which the alternative hypothesis is true.

The residual sum of squares from the two models then forms the basis for the F-test. If the residual sum of squares for the smaller model is substantially greater than the residual sum of squares for the larger model, there is evidence that the fit has been importantly degraded. More formally, if the p-value is sufficiently small, researchers will typically conclude that the null hypothesis is false and that the larger model is required; the larger model is, in fact, the correct model.

The same logic may be applied to any pair of models in which the smaller model is nested within the larger model. Indeed, one can begin with the largest model and systematically test all nested models within it. Usually, however, there will be far too many different nested models, which leads to the application of a sequential strategy. That is, an order is imposed on which models are compared so that one may proceed in a linear fashion from more complex to less, or the reverse. We will consider such procedures shortly.

With the correct model determined, there may nevertheless be a temptation to undertake the t-tests for individual regression coefficients. However, the

---

[1] For an excellent review, see Gourieroux and Monfort (1994).

p-values from those tests are no longer valid because they do not take into account the previous tests applied nor the information in the data exploited to arrive at the model currently in favor. Generally, the p-values will be too small, often much too small. Moreover, because joint tests on several regression coefficients will typically have different power than single tests on a particular regression coefficient, one can sometimes arrive at contradictory results. One may fail to reject the null hypothesis that all of a set of regression coefficients are zero and yet reject the null hypothesis that one particular member of that set is zero.

Model selection can lead to the problem of "overfitting." If a goal of a data analysis is to make inferences from a sample to a population or to the natural processes that generated the data (or to forecast), testing lots of different regression models can lead to a final model that reflects far too many idiosyncrasies in the sample. The data analysis process has been made so flexible that data features produced by chance alone strongly influence the results; when a large number of models are tested, one has effectively allowed for a very large number of possible parameters and parameter values. The final fit is then an overfit. Consequently, the inferences drawn can be very misleading. As the saying goes, "If you torture the data set long enough, it will confess." But there is no guarantee that it will tell you the truth.

Overfitting from model selection is a widely understood problem that in practice is too often ignored. One important strategy to combat overfitting is to divide the data into two random samples and use one sample to build a regression model, fishing around in the data as one wills, and to use the other sample solely to determine the amount of overfitting that results. Cross-validation and several related procedures build on this theme (Efron and Tibshirani, 1993:Chapter 17). Cross-validation will be briefly discussed in a later chapter.

8.2.3 Selecting Terms Without Testing

Another strategy to help protect against overfitting is to properly take into account the number of free parameters included in any given model. Larger models may fit better simply because, with many free parameters, the model is more flexible and can better conform to any idiosyncrasies in the data.

Following Cook and Weisberg (1999:272-275), assume that a correct model for the mean function is $E(y|\mathbf{x}) = \boldsymbol{\eta}^{\mathrm{T}}\mathbf{u}$.

Now, re-express the model in the form

$$E(y|\mathbf{x}) = \boldsymbol{\eta}_{\mathcal{I}}^{\mathrm{T}}\mathbf{u}_{\mathcal{I}} + \boldsymbol{\eta}_{\mathcal{D}}^{\mathrm{T}}\mathbf{u}_{\mathcal{D}}, \tag{8.10}$$

where $\mathcal{I}$ and $\mathcal{D}$ refer to the terms to be included and the terms to be dropped, respectively. Now the parameters are estimated for the full model and also for the model with the $\mathcal{D}$ terms deleted. For both, the fitted values can be constructed as $\hat{y}_i$ for the full model and $\hat{y}_{i,\mathcal{I}}$ for the restricted model. It makes sense that, if the smaller model is a good one, the two sets of predicted values will be much the same.

Because we are assuming that the full model is correct, $E(\hat{y}_i) = E(y_i|\mathbf{x}_i)$ and the regression coefficients can be estimated in an unbiased manner. Then, the mean squared error (*MSE*) is defined as

$$MSE(\hat{y}_{i,\mathcal{I}}) = E[(\hat{y}_{i,\mathcal{I}} - E(y_i|\mathbf{x}_i))^2]. \tag{8.11}$$

This mean squared error for $\hat{y}_{i,\mathcal{I}}$ indicates how close the ith fitted value from the submodel is to the corresponding point for the true mean function on the average. Ideally, this value should be small, implying that the larger and smaller model fit the data about equally well.[2]

Equation 8.11 can be re-expressed as

$$MSE(\hat{y}_{i,\mathcal{I}}) = \text{Var}(\hat{y}_{i,\mathcal{I}}) + [E(\hat{y}_{i,\mathcal{I}}) - E(y|\mathbf{x}_i)]^2, \tag{8.12}$$

or as the variance plus the square of the bias. The variance refers to the variability of the fitted values from the submodel for case i over hypothetical random samples or realizations. The bias is the difference over hypothetical random samples or realizations between the conditional mean estimated from the submodel and the true mean represented by the full model. The variance and bias squared combine to generate average disparities between fitted values for case i from the submodel and the true value for case i in the population (or in nature's data-generating mechanism).

This is one important instance of the well-known variance-bias tradeoff. Generally, deleting terms decreases the variance of the fitted values because the fit is smoother. At the same time, deleting terms increases the bias because the fit will usually degrade. The fitted values will, on the average, be farther away from the true values.

But this is all theory. What is to be done in practice? One cannot compute the *MSE* for a given case from a single sample.

One can apply the *MSE* concept by working over all cases in the data and computing a "total mean squared error" defined as follows:

$$\mathcal{J}_{\mathcal{I}} = \sum_{i=1}^{n} MSE(\hat{y}_{i,\mathcal{I}}). \tag{8.13}$$

Total mean square error can be estimated by

$$\text{Mallows } C_{\mathcal{I}} = \frac{RSS_{\mathcal{I}}}{\hat{\sigma}^2} + 2k_{\mathcal{I}} - n = (k - k_{\mathcal{I}})(F_{\mathcal{D}} - 1) + k_{\mathcal{I}}, \tag{8.14}$$

[2]Note that, because $MSE(\hat{y}_{i,\mathcal{I}})$ is for case i, the averages being taken are over a limitless number of independent random samples or random realizations.

where $RSS_{\mathcal{I}}$ is the residual sum of squares for the submodel, $\hat{\sigma}^2$ is the estimated residual variance for the full model (initially assumed to be correct), k is the number of terms in that model, $k_{\mathcal{I}}$ is the number of terms in the submodel, and $F_{\mathcal{D}}$ is the F-statistic for the test to choose between the two. The values of k and $k_{\mathcal{I}}$ help to adjust for overfitting. Mallows $\mathcal{C}_{\mathcal{I}}$ (generally known as Mallows $\mathcal{C}_{\mathcal{P}}$; Mallows, 1973) is driven in part by the $RSS_{\mathcal{I}}$ for the submodel; worse fit, larger value. But the number of regression parameters in the submodel matters too; more parameters, larger value. There will typically be a tradeoff between the *RSS* and $k_{\mathcal{I}}$.

Because an F-statistic around 1.0 indicates that the fit is about as good in the submodel as the full model, promising candidate models will have a Mallows $\mathcal{C}_{\mathcal{I}}$ equal to or less than $k_{\mathcal{I}}$. Note that, if no terms are dropped, the value of Mallows $\mathcal{C}_{\mathcal{I}}$ equals the number of terms in the full model. Thus, the full model is always a candidate.

Note also that $\mathcal{C}_{\mathcal{I}} \leq k_{\mathcal{I}}$ only if $F_{\mathcal{D}} \leq 1$. So it can be useful to delete terms if the relevant F-statistic is less than 1.0. But in short, good submodels will have small values for $\mathcal{J}_{\mathcal{I}}$. And one now has a way to sort through nested models without relying on p-values that are often highly suspect. But the formal justifications still depend on the idea of a single correct model.[3]

8.2.4 Stepwise Selection Methods

Rather than trying all possible nested regression specifications and somehow picking the "best" one, stepwise regression methods consider a sequence of nested model specifications from simple to complex (forward selection) or complex to simple (backward elimination) and pick the "best." Mallows $\mathcal{C}_{\mathcal{P}}$ can be useful in this effort.

Under forward selection, one term at a time is added to the "base model," depending on which mean function has the smallest $C_{\mathcal{I}}$. The smaller the value of $C_{\mathcal{I}}$, the better the submodel.

Under backward elimination, the full model is the starting point, and one term at a time is eliminated based on which mean function has the smallest value of $C_{\mathcal{I}}$. The idea is to select the best model at each step and then drop the term that was deleted from that model.

There are other criteria besides $\mathcal{C}_{\mathcal{P}}$ that can be used, and are often used, to select models: changes in R^2, changes in the *RSS*, t-values, F-values, and others. But the selection statistic is, in some sense, just a detail. The key point is that, to a significant degree, the judgment of the data analyst plays almost no role.

---

[3]Closely related to Mallows $\mathcal{C}_{\mathcal{P}}$ are Akaike's (1974) A Information Criterion (AIC) and Schwartz's (1978) Bayesian Information Criterion (BIC). But for our purposes, they raise no new issues and will not be discussed.

Stepwise regression procedures used to select the correct model can be very misleading. First, the criterion used for choosing between models may not be appropriate for the problem at hand. To return to an earlier question, for example, why is a model that fits better automatically a better model? Second, stepwise methods tend to capitalize on chance, although Mallows $\mathcal{C}_\mathcal{P}$ can help adjust for this problem. Third, the "best" model may be substantive nonsense. There is no necessary correspondence between a selection criterion and a scientific criterion. For example, the best model may include variables for which cause and effect make no sense even though the model is supposed to support causal inference. Finally, given all of the fitting, estimation, and statistical inference applied along the way, the p-values associated with the regression coefficients for the model eventually selected are nearly meaningless.

In summary, with all of the concerns earlier about the role of information formally external to the data and about the need to exercise judgment, one should be uneasy doing model building by algorithm. Whenever possible, it is probably preferable to construct a set of nested models using subject matter knowledge and the data from a "training sample." Then, the final model should be evaluated in a "validation sample." Formal cross-validation procedures can be helpful in the second step (see Efron and Tibshirani, 1993: Chapter 17).

8.2.5 Some Implications

The common tools used for model selection in regression analysis formally depend on one of the tested models being the correct model. This is unlikely, and in any case, there is no way to know if it is true. Therefore, the model selection procedures that follow cannot be taken at face value. However, if one abandons the search for the correct model and instead searches for one or more useful models, some model selection tools can be helpful. In particular, Mallows $\mathcal{C}_\mathcal{P}$ can be used to describe the fit of the model in a fashion that takes account of the number of parameters.[4]

Experience suggests that researchers might usefully consider the subset of nested models in which Mallows $\mathcal{C}_\mathcal{P}$ is smaller than or approximately equal to the number of regression parameters. For these models, one has an operational version of Occam's Razor. Models in which Mallows $\mathcal{C}_\mathcal{P}$ is substantially larger than the number of regression parameters are discarded because the added complexity has little payoff. As a result, some policy implications can also be

[4] As noted earlier, good additional alternatives to Mallows $\mathcal{C}_\mathcal{P}$ are the AIC and BIC. Unfortunately, these three criteria can sometimes lead to somewhat different models because they weight the importance of model complexity a bit differently. If one cannot decide in advance which criterion is most appropriate for the analysis to be undertaken, it often makes sense not to make too much of small differences between the criterion values computed. And ideally, subject matter expertise should play an important role. A model that fits the data a bit worse may be more instructive than a model that fits the data a bit better.

discarded as inconsistent with the regression analysis. Among the remaining models, further winnowing should depend on which models make scientific and policy sense. In the end, one may be left with a single "best" model or, more likely, a few strong contenders. And if the latter, one needs to report that the data cannot effectively distinguish between them; there may be more than one set of policy recommendations consistent with the regression analysis.

It would certainly be helpful if the balance between the fit and the complexity of a regression equation could be more definitively addressed. However, there are both conceptual problems and technical problems (Zellner et al., 2001). For example, Simon (2001) takes a position that one should strive for parsimonious models, not simple models. Parsimony, in turn, represents the difference between the complexity of the phenomenon in question and the complexity of the model. A model is more parsimonious insofar as its complexity is less than the complexity of what it is trying to characterize. Unfortunately, there are lots of ways to define complexity, and in any case, one implication is that model evaluations will be application specific. An instructive attempt to move toward a set of practical tools can be found in Hansen and Yu (2001) and Bryant and Cordero-Braña (2000). A very accessible discussion of earlier model selection criteria—the adjusted R^2, AIC, BIC—can be found in Greene (2000:306).

Despite the absence of definitive guidelines, consider a simple example. Suppose one were interested in a regression analysis of the undergraduate admissions process at a major public university. A key feature of that process is the construction of a score to indicate the "academic potential" of each applicant. Admissions officers review each student's SAT scores, high school grade point average, and measures of the high school's academic quality. From this information, a score between 1 and 10 is generated based on general guidelines and judgment.

In order to learn something about how, on the average, the score is produced, one could regress, for a random sample of the university's applicants, the admissions office's academic potential score on the following:

1. SAT I score (billed as an aptitude test),
2. SAT II score (billed as an achievement test),
3. high school grade point average, and
4. the average score for that high school on a standardized achievement test given to all high school students in the state.

A baseline model including as terms high school grade point average and average score for the high school might have a $\mathcal{C}_{\mathcal{P}}$ of around 8, indicating that the model is not very good. Adding either SAT score produces a $\mathcal{C}_{\mathcal{P}}$ of about 3. Both models are good candidates. Putting in both SAT scores leads to a $\mathcal{C}_{\mathcal{P}}$ of around 6. Overall, a model with grade point average, average high school test score, and *either* SAT I or SAT II is worth further consideration. The model without SAT I or SAT II is probably inadequate, and a model with both SAT scores is unnecessarily complex.

From either of the two acceptable models, one might learn that both a higher grade point average and a higher SAT score are associated with a substantially higher score for academic potential. In addition, coming from a higher ranking high school is associated with a substantially *lower* score for academic potential. One implication may be that, if there are two applicants with the same grade point average and with the same SAT score, the one from the weaker high school may get a higher score for academic potential at this university. Such a finding might indicate that admissions officers are trying to level the playing field or that they believe that grade point averages and SAT scores from students at lower-quality high schools "underpredict" success in college; these students are really stronger applicants than their earlier performance indicates.

8.3 Using Categorical Terms: Analysis of Variance and Analysis of Covariance

We turn now to the use of categorical variables as terms in multiple regression. This will lead to procedures also known as analysis of variance (ANOVA) and analysis of covariance (ANCOVA). Although categorical variables are perhaps most common in data from experiments, categorical variables are routinely found in observational studies as well; the extensions discussed in this section are an essential part of regression analysis. We will also discuss one useful way in which fixed attributes such as gender and race can be used in multiple regression analysis from which causal inferences are to be drawn. However, the fundamental difficulties with statistical inference and causal inference will, by and large, remain.

8.3.1 An Extended Example

For convenience, it is common to code categorical variables so that each category has its own binary variable with a "1" to represent the presence of the attribute and a "0" to indicate the absence of the attribute. Such binary variables are often called "indicator" variables, and the full set of indicator variables for each categorical variable is usually called a "factor."

One alternative is "effect coding," which uses three values: -1, 0, and $+1$. Effect coding meshes more naturally with the output from analysis of variance. But the regression fit is the same whether dummy coding or effect coding is employed. Here, we will emphasize the use of binary indicator variables because of the ease of interpretation within regression.

There is no straightforward way to incorporate ordinal predictors. In practice, one has to either "downgrade" them to categorical variables and code them accordingly or "upgrade" them to equal-interval variables and treat the ranks as real integers. Because the intervals between the values of ordinal variables are unknown and unlikely to be equal, a slope constructed from rank data cannot be sensibly interpreted (unless the variable is literally the rank). It is not clear what a unit change in x really is.

Now suppose one wanted to do a study of the impact of land use on the biodiversity of streams in a given watershed. The 100 sites to be studied are selected by random sampling. Biodiversity is measured by a scale of "taxa richness," which is a function of the number of different kinds of taxa found. The predictor is a factor with three values for three different kinds of land use surrounding where the sample was taken: undeveloped land, farm land, and developed land. In the original data, these might be coded as 1, 2, and 3, respectively. One would not use those values directly in a regression analysis. Rather, one would construct three indicator (dummy) variables as follows:

$$\text{If } x = 1 \text{ then } I_1 = 1; \text{ otherwise} = 0.$$
$$\text{If } x = 2 \text{ then } I_2 = 1; \text{ otherwise} = 0.$$
$$\text{If } x = 3 \text{ then } I_3 = 1; \text{ otherwise} = 0.$$

One can then proceed pretty much as usual. The response can be regressed on the factor, represented by two of the three indicator variables (to avoid linear dependence between the indicator variables). Formally, it does not matter which indicator variable is excluded. But it is often useful to choose the indicator variable that can serve as a common baseline for the other indicator variables.

The intercept represents, as usual, the estimate of the mean of y when all of the xs equal zero. As such, it is the estimated mean of y for the baseline category. Then, each regression coefficient provides an estimate of the difference between the estimated mean of the baseline category and the mean of each category in turn.

In this example, suppose the indicator for undeveloped land is dropped. Then an intercept of 30 is the estimate of the mean number of taxa for sites located within undeveloped land. A regression coefficient of −10 for the urban indicator means that there are 10 fewer taxa on the average in streams within urban sites compared with streams in undeveloped sites. A regression coefficient of −5 for the agricultural site means that there are five fewer taxa on the average in agricultural sites compared with undeveloped sites. Selecting one of the other indicator variables as the baseline would lead to other comparisons in an analogous fashion. But the fit would be the same regardless of which pair of indicators was used.

An F-test for the null hypothesis that all of the regression coefficients are zero (and that, therefore, all of the categories have the same mean for the response variable) with the alternative that at least one of the regression coefficients is not equal to zero is the same as the F-test for a one-way analysis of variance. To test whether a given subset of categories has the same mean, one can just constrain the relevant coefficients and estimate that model. One can then, with the F-statistic, test that model against the full, unconstrained model. If the goal is to test whether a single regression coefficient is equal to zero, the usual t-test will suffice ($t^2 = F$ in this situation).

8.3.1.1 *Two or More Categorical Terms*

The regression model can be generalized to two or more factors. For two factors, one is doing "two-way analysis of variance"; for three factors, one is doing "three-way analysis of variance"; and so on. As long as interest is directed to the differences between estimated means for each of the indicator variables, one can proceed in the same way as above, keeping in mind that the deleted categories within each factor will define the baseline.

For example, suppose we expanded the biodiversity study to include a second factor, season. This might be coded as fall (1), winter (2), spring (3), and summer (4). There would be three new indicator variables, with perhaps summer as the baseline. The intercept now would be an estimate of mean taxa richness measured in the summer for streams within undeveloped land. The regression coefficient for fall is then an estimate of how taxa richness differs in the fall compared with the summer within undeveloped land. The regression coefficient for winter is then an estimate of how taxa richness differs in the winter compared with the summer for streams within undeveloped land. The regression coefficient for spring would do the same but comparing taxa richness in the spring to taxa richness in the summer for undeveloped land. Parallel interpretations now apply for the land-use indicators.

Finally, there is the matter of interaction effects. For ease of exposition, consider a simple two-way analysis of variance in which each factor happens to have only two categories. Thus, we need just a single land-use indicator: undeveloped or not. And we need a single season indicator: summer or not. The regression equation would take the following form:

$$\begin{aligned} E(taxa|\mathbf{x}) &= \eta_0 + \eta_1(undeveloped) \\ &\quad + \eta_2(summer) + \eta_3(undeveloped \times summer). \end{aligned} \tag{8.15}$$

Suppose $\eta_0 = 5$, $\eta_1 = 10$, $\eta_2 = 15$, and $\eta_3 = 5$. So, the average taxa richness when it is not summer and when the land is developed is 5. On the average, taxa richness is increased by 10 if the land surrounding the stream is undeveloped and by 15 during the summer months. Taxa richness is increased by an additional 5 units for samples taken from undeveloped areas during the summer. In other words, the streams in undeveloped areas are especially diverse during the summer. The regression coefficients η_1 and η_2 are sometimes called the "main effects." The regression coefficient η_3 is sometimes called the "interaction effect."

One can also represent these results in a 2×2 table, with taxa values in each cell.

Table 8.1. Main and Interaction Effects for Taxa Richness

	Developed	Not Developed
Not Summer	5	5 + 10 = 15
Summer	5 + 15 = 20	5 + 10 + 15 + 5 = 35

8.3.1.2 *Categorical and Equal-Interval Predictors: Analysis of Covariance*

Consider now a regression model with a categorical and an equal-interval predictor. Regression analyses of this sort are sometimes called analysis of covariance.

Suppose taxa richness is taken to be a function of percentage of land surrounding each stream, say within 200 meters, that is undeveloped. A simple linear regression model follows:

$$E(taxa|\mathbf{x}) = \alpha_0 + \alpha_1 \%\, undeveloped. \tag{8.16}$$

The value α_0 is the average number of taxa when all of the land is developed (i.e., $\%undeveloped = 0$). The value α_1 is how much, on the average, taxa richness changes for a 1% change in the percentage of undeveloped land. The values for the intercept and slope might be 5 and 0.25, respectively.

Now one might ask whether season matters. One kind of answer assumes that there are two parallel regression lines, with different intercepts, as a function of season (i.e., summer and not summer). Thus,

$$E(taxa|\mathbf{x}) = \beta_0 + \beta_1 \%\, undeveloped + \beta_2\; summer. \tag{8.17}$$

The intercept for the fully developed land during nonsummer months is β_0, and the intercept for fully developed land during the summer months is $\beta_0 + \beta_2$. Thus, if β_2 is positive (e.g., 10), the regression line for the summer months is above the parallel regression line for nonsummer months. The slope for both lines is β_1.

Another way to proceed is to examine whether the relationship between development and taxa richness is stronger in the summer. Now, there are two regression lines with the same intercept but with potentially different slopes; that is,

$$E(taxa|\mathbf{x}) = \gamma_0 \;+\; \gamma_1 \%\, undeveloped + \gamma_2(summer \times \%\, undeveloped). \tag{8.18}$$

There are now two slopes. The slope for the nonsummer months is γ_1, and the slope for the summer months is $\gamma_1 + \gamma_2$. If γ_2 is positive (e.g., 0.1), the slope for the summer months is steeper. The intercept for both is γ_0.

Not surprisingly, one can combine the different intercepts and different slopes model as follows:

$$E(taxa|\mathbf{x}) = \delta_0 + \delta_1 \%\, undeveloped$$
$$+ \delta_2 summer + \delta_3 (summer \times \%\, undeveloped). \qquad (8.19)$$

There is now one regression line for summer months and one for nonsummer months. These regression lines have different intercepts and different slopes.

Note that each equation may represent a different theory about how land development might affect biodiversity in different seasons. For example, one theory is that there is more taxa richness across the board in the summer. Another theory is that the role of undeveloped land is more important in the summer than during other times. Because all of the smaller models are nested within the "correct" model (different slopes and intercepts), one can, in principle, determine which theory fits best using nested F-tests. In this case, where the data were generated by random sampling, statistical inference can sometimes be a useful tool.

The same general logic can sometimes be usefully applied when the categorical variable is a fixed attribute such as gender or race and when a causal story is desired. Consider again the example of the score for academic potential constructed by a university admissions office. To keep the exposition simple, high school grade point average (GPA) is the single equal-interval term. The single categorical term is whether an applicant is a member of an "underrepresented" minority.[5]

In principle, grade point average is manipulable in any number of ways. For example, a student can be encouraged to work harder or take easier courses, or a tutor can be hired. There will be some slippage to be sure, but for purposes of discussion, suppose that meaningful variation in a student's high school grade point average could be introduced. Minority status is a fixed attribute of the applicant. Assuming that some form of response schedule applies, an important policy question is whether the response schedule that applies to those underrepresented minorities also applies to others.

Suppose there is a causal effect for grade point average. Different response schedules for underrepresented minorities would mean that the causal effect differs depending on whether a person is a member of an underrepresented minority. One can think of these as "context effects" rather than causal effects. The context changes the way in which the causal effect operates.

With the term *minority* is coded 1 for underrepresented minorities and 0 otherwise, and with *academic score* and *GPA* equal-interval variables, one can represent these ideas with the multiple regression equation

$$E(score|\mathbf{x}) = \eta_0 + \eta_1 GPA + \eta_2 Minority + \eta_3 (GPA \times Minority). \qquad (8.20)$$

---

[5]Because, in many states, Asian Americans are represented in colleges and universities roughly in proportion to their numbers in the general population (or even "overrepresented"), they are often not considered to be an "underrepresented minority."

For one possible set of scenarios, assume that η_0 and η_1 are positive. Then, as before, there are four special cases.

Case I: $\eta_2 = \eta_3 = 0$. There is a single response schedule for underrepresented minorities and all others. The intercept of the single response schedule is η_0 and a slope is η_1. The academic score increases with high school grade point average.

Case II: $\eta_3 = 0$. There are two response schedules. If underrepresented minority status is coded 1 (and 0 otherwise), the response schedule for underrepresented minorities has an intercept of $\eta_0 + \eta_2$ and a slope of η_1. The response schedule for other applicants has an intercept of η_0 and a slope of η_1. If η_2 is positive, the response schedule for underrepresented minorities is parallel to but higher than the response schedule for others. Underrepresented minorities get an across-the-board bump in their academic score.

Case III: $\eta_2 = 0$. Again, there are two response schedules. The response schedule for underrepresented minorities has an intercept of η_0 and a slope of $\eta_1 + \eta_3$. The response schedule for other applicants has an intercept of η_0 and a slope of η_1. If η_3 is positive, the response schedule for underrepresented minorities is steeper than the response schedule for the others, but there is no across-the-board bump for under represented minorities. Underrepresented minorities are better able to translate their high school grade point averages into higher academic scores.

Case IV: η_1 through $\eta_3 \neq 0$. Once again, there are two different response schedules. For underrepresented minorities, the intercept is $\eta_0 + \eta_2$, and the slope is $\eta_1 + \eta_3$. The response schedule for other applicants has an intercept of η_0 and a slope of η_1. With η_2 and η_3 positive, the response schedule for underrepresented minorities lies above and is steeper than the response schedule for others. Underrepresented minorities get an across-the-board bump and are better able to translate their high school grade point average into higher academic scores.

Insofar as Cases II, III, or IV are true, the university admissions office has two or more different response schedules, one for underrepresented minorities and others for the rest. *The way in which high school grade point average affects the academic admissions score is being manipulated.* The university admissions office is not manipulating grade point average, although grade point average, in principle, could be manipulated. The university admissions office cannot manipulate minority status because it is a fixed attribute of all applicants. Rather, the ways in which high school grade point average translates into the admissions academic score is being manipulated. And this is something over which an admissions office can have very direct control. Thus, the ethnic background of applicants has no causal effect. But the decisions by the admissions office about how the background information is used do, in principle, have a causal effect.[6]

To summarize, the use of categorical predictors substantially increases the range of applications for which multiple regression is appropriate. Analysis of variance and analysis of covariance get folded in. Although all of the examples given include no more than two categorical variables, many more can be used if necessary. The primary cost is that interpretations become more complicated. The use of categorical predictors also provides a way to think about response schedules when fixed attributes are involved. One can allow for different response schedules that depend on a context determined by the fixed attribute. Insofar as how those contexts work is manipulable, causal inferences may be justified.

8.4 Back to the Variance Function: Weighted Least Squares

To this point, almost all of our attention has been directed to the mean function. We have assumed, by and large, that the variance function is constant and essentially of little interest. We now turn to regression analyses in which the variance function can be more complicated and an important concern. For example, in a regression analysis of income determination, if there is more variation in the errors for female employees than for male employees, it may imply that income determination for women is less structured.

The nature of the variance function in the population or in the natural process by which the data were generated is basically an assumed feature of the regression model. But once an analysis of data begins, empirical information can be brought to bear. One can examine variation around the regression fit. But note that it is variation *around the fit,* which implies that the variation depends on the fit. This will have some very important consequences.

8.4.1 Visualizing Lack of Fit

In practice, a good place to start thinking empirically about the variance function is with a plot of the regression residuals against the fitted values. Even though the residuals sum to zero (because they are assumed to be deviations from means) and are necessarily uncorrelated with the terms (because any linear dependence has been removed), there may still be important information in them. Generally, there will be three kinds of information of interest:

[6]"In principle," because the job of constructing a plausible response schedule really remains to be done.

1. a pattern in the residuals suggesting that the linear functional form is incorrect,
2. evidence of nonconstant variance around the regression line,
3. outliers and potentially influential observations.

Although these might seem to be three unrelated problems, they are actually closely linked. The residuals being plotted depend on the fitted values, which, in turn, can depend on influential observations. And with a different fit, there will be different residuals. It always makes sense, nevertheless, to examine a residual plot in order to get some overall sense of the relationship between the fit and the data.

There is also a deeper issue implied: Because the mean function and the variance function are necessarily related, it is very difficult to treat both of them as problematic at once. One of them must be taken as correct to consider possible errors in the other. This will complicate the discussion to which we now turn. It is also the beginning of an important lesson. With so much brought to the data from outside, a disappointing model could result from any number of problems. Yet the tools available have to assume some of the problems away to consider the rest. Indeed, it is common to assume that all is well, with the single exception of the particular problem being tackled. How effective such procedures really are will be addressed as we proceed.

8.4.2 Weighted Least Squares as a Possible Fix

If the variance function is not constant, there may be one of two problems or both. First, the mean function may be misspecified, such as when a linear mean function is assumed for a curvilinear scatter plot, or when separate clumps of data suggest that more than one hyperplane is required. Second, the mean function may be correct but the residuals do not have constant variance around the fit. For now, we will concentrate on the second problem and assume that the mean function is correct.

Weighted least squares is an extension of the regression model that allows each observation to be given a different weight in the calculations. To this point, all observations have been given an equal weight. Although differential weighting can serve several purposes, it is a tool that sometimes can be used to address nonconstant variance around the regression fit.

There are two related ways to motivate weighted least squares: (a) developing a variance function that better describes the variance around the fit, and (b) capitalizing on otherwise neglected information in the data about the variance function. We will start with the first motivation, which leads eventually to the second.

Weights can be used in the variance function to address the nonconstant variance. These weights must be known a priori and are fixed, not random, variables. If the weights are a function of random variables, what follows needs to be further expanded into a more general framework. For example, if *estimates* of the different (nonconstant) variances are required, weighted least squares is inappropriate. But the alternative procedures (Greene, 2000: Chapter 12) are, for us, a technical detail.

The variance function can be generalized as follows. Let

$$y_i|\mathbf{x}_i = \boldsymbol{\eta}^{\mathrm{T}}\mathbf{u}_i + e_i/\sqrt{w_i}, \tag{8.21}$$

where $w_i > 0$ and is known. Then, it follows that

$$E(y_i|\mathbf{x}_i) = \boldsymbol{\eta}^{\mathrm{T}}\mathbf{u}_i; \quad \mathrm{Var}(y_i|\mathbf{x}_i) = \sigma^2/w_i. \tag{8.22}$$

The interpretation of the weights depends on how they are defined. Usually, the subpopulation with $w_i = 1$ serves as the reference so that, for example, the cases with $w_i = 2$ have half the variance. Weights are always proportional to the reciprocals of the variances. The larger the weights, the smaller the variance and vice versa.

8.4.2.1 *From Where Do the Weights Come?*

How does one obtain known weights? The most convincing scenario comes from data in which the y_i are summary measures constructed from different samples of known (and varying) sizes. For example, the response might be average longevity in different extended families. Because families differ in size, the means are based on different sample sizes, which in turn affect the variances of the y_i. Likewise, the response might be the mean salary in each of a set of firms or the number of homicides in each of a set of cities.

If for each observational unit, the response is a mean, the $\mathrm{Var}(y_i|\mathbf{x}_i) = \sigma^2/m_i$, where m_i is the number of observations from which the mean is constructed and $w_i = m_i$. This assumes, however, that the observations that go into the mean are independent. In many applications, this will not be true. For example, salaries in a firm are all subject to some budget constraint, at least as a first approximation, and if the salaries are public information, what one employee receives may affect what another employee will bargain for.

If y_i is a sum of m_i independent observations, then $\mathrm{Var}(y_i|\mathbf{x}_i) = m_i\sigma^2$. It follows that $w_i = 1/m_i$. But independence is still an issue, and whether, for instance, homicides within a city are independent is certainly arguable.

In some cases, researchers will assume that $\mathrm{Var}(y_i|x_i) = x_i^2\sigma^2$ (or some other function of a particular predictor), so the variance is a known function of x_i and now $w_i = 1/x_i^2$. How one would know this without looking at the data (which is cheating) is unclear.[7]

---

[7]If the data are consulted first, the weights based on that peek are no longer fixed. Then, as noted above, weighted least squares is inappropriate. Note also that here, $\mathbf{x}_i$ is assumed to be fixed.

Once the weights are obtained and justified, the computations are very straightforward. The new *RSS* objective function is

$$RSS(\mathbf{h}) = \sum_{i=1}^{n} w_i(y_i - \mathbf{h}^{\mathrm{T}}\mathbf{u}_i)^2. \tag{8.23}$$

The fit pays more attention to residuals with larger weights, which makes sense because larger weights imply smaller variances. As the weights increase, the conditional variance $\mathrm{Var}(y_i|\mathbf{x}_i) = \sigma^2/w_i$ will approach zero, and the fit will go right through y_i. This makes sense because the weights are downplaying the role of cases with greater amounts of "noise."[8]

The weighted least squares solution implies one can alternatively transform all of the variables (including the column of 1's for the intercept) multiplying by $\sqrt{w_i}$ and then apply the usual formulas to the transformed data. Then,

$$\hat{y}_i = \hat{\boldsymbol{\eta}}^{\mathrm{T}}\mathbf{u}_i, \tag{8.24}$$

$$\hat{e}_i = \sqrt{w_i}(y_i - \hat{y}_i), \tag{8.25}$$

$$RSS = \sum_{i=1}^{n} \hat{e}_i^2, \tag{8.26}$$

$$\hat{\sigma}^2 = \frac{RSS}{n-k}. \tag{8.27}$$

The only change from the earlier expressions is that the residuals are multiplied by the square root of the weight, which implies that all quantities that depend on the residuals are now also weighted.

8.4.2.2 *So What?*

What are the consequences if one proceeds with the constant variance assumption when it is wrong (i.e., weights are implicitly equal to one)? The problems will be matters of degree, but in some cases, they are serious enough to make a practical difference.

- Although the estimates of the regression coefficients remain unbiased, they are no longer minimum variance linear estimates. On the average, they will be farther away from their population values than would otherwise be the case.
- The estimates of the standard errors will be biased. The bias can be positive or negative. So, all statistical inference is suspect.

---

[8] Only the relative sizes of the weights matter; multiplying the weights by any positive constant gives the same estimates of the regression coefficients.

- The data analysis may overlook part of the subject matter story by assuming constant variance when that is not true. For example, on questions of social inequality, the variance around the fit for subsets of the data can be a very important part of the story. There may be more heterogeneity in income, for instance, for women than for men. Although the first two difficulties only affect statistical inference, this difficulty affects description as well.

Yet hands-on experience with the problems that nonconstant variance can cause suggests that the ordinary least squares results and the weighted least squares results usually will not differ dramatically. Put another way, nonconstant variance is often the least of one's problems. It can make sense, therefore, to try tackling those other problems first.

8.4.3 Evaluating the Mean Function

Now, let's return to mean function and how to consider whether the linear assumption is in error. How we do this is one part of the general strategy of model checking. Model checking is an essential feature of regression analysis and will be an ongoing theme in the rest of the book.

8.4.3.1 *Exploiting Smoothers*

A very useful and simple way to proceed is to fit a smoother to the data and compare that with the linear fit. Disparities between the two often suggest where the linear fit is faulty. In practice, this is easy to do when there is a single predictor. When there are many predictors, special methods have to be employed. One simple and yet very useful approach is to plot the residuals against the fitted values and overlay a smoother. If the smoother is other than straight and flat, there is a pattern in the residuals suggesting that the mean function is inadequate. We will consider fancier methods in later chapters.

8.4.3.2 *Formal Tests*

There are also formal goodness-of-fit tests. Very much like the nested model selection tests considered earlier, the goal is to compare the *RSS* of the model of interest to the *RSS* of a "baseline" model. If the *RSS* of the model of interest is substantially larger than the *RSS* of the baseline model, the model of interest becomes suspect. But everything depends on a critical assumption: *The variance function must be right.* The *RSS* must be allowed to vary as a function of the fit alone.

So, what can be used as the "baseline" model?

- On rare occasions, the residual variance for the correct model may be known. From that, one can easily get the *RSS* for the right model.
- Also on rare occasions, there may be information from other research on what the residual variance is for the correct model. Once again, one can then compute the *RSS* directly.
- There may be replicate observations, that is, two or more values of y from different cases for every value of x. This is common when there is a single predictor. With many predictors, the data may be too sparse to provide any traction. Consider this simple example. The predictors are age and education. The response is income. One would need two or more people and their income values for all possible combinations of age and income. If there are, say, 30 different ages and 10 different educational levels, you'd have 300 combinations, which means you would need a large sample. Imagine if there were five predictors.

  Assuming that there are replicate observations, one computes the conditional means of y, computes the *RSS* around each conditional mean, and combines these to get a total *RSS*. More formally,

$$\hat{\sigma}^{2*} = \frac{\sum_{i=1}^{g} w_i (m_i - 1)\text{SD}_i^2}{\sum_{i=1}^{g} (m_i - 1)} = \frac{SS^*}{df^*}, \tag{8.28}$$

  where there are n observations overall, g subpopulations ($i = 1, 2, \ldots, g$), and m_i observations ($j = 1, 2, \ldots, m_i$) in each group. In effect, the deviations around each local mean are squared and summed to get SS* and df* $= n - g$. One can accomplish pretty much the same thing by estimating the parameters of a regression equation coding each configuration in $\mathbf{x}$ as a dummy variable and proceeding as if $\mathbf{x}$ is categorical. The usual estimate of the residual variance will provide the needed baseline. But sparse data remain a potential problem.

In summary, there is nothing in the procedures just described guaranteed to reveal when the mean function is wrong. Indeed, each approach is limited by one or more untested assumptions and/or by impractical data requirements. And even if one becomes convinced that the mean function is incorrect, there is typically very little in the diagnostic procedures by themselves that indicates how to fix it. This lesson generalizes. An important implication is that one try to use regression analysis in a manner that is less dependent on getting the model exactly right (or even nearly right). A major attitude adjustment is needed. A lot more will be said about this in the final chapter.

8.5 Locally Weighted Regression Smoother

Sometimes, regression analysis can be used as an intermediate step to some other statistical procedure. Lowess is a good example because it not only uses weighted regression as an intermediate step but is itself a smoother that is often used in regression analysis (Cleveland, 1979).

Lowess stands for "locally weighted linear regression smoother." Consider the one-predictor case and an outline of the computational steps.

1. Choose the smoothing parameter f, with a proportion between zero and one.
2. Choose a point x_l and from that, the $(f \times n)$ nearest points on x.
3. For these "nearest neighbor" points, compute a weighted regression line for y on x. The weights are a function of the distance from x_l, with closer values given more weight. The precise weighting function can vary, but one common weighting function decreases linearly with absolute distance from x_l.
4. Construct the fitted value $\hat{y}_l$ for that single x_l as the smoothed value of y.
5. Repeat this for many values of x and connect these $\hat{y}_l$ points with a line.

A major asset of lowess and any number of other smoothers is that no functional form is being assumed. The path of the means determines the fit, with only smoothness or roughness under the data analyst's control.

However, there is a price. The lowess smoother and most other smoothers are rarely used with more than one predictor, and with more than two, they are typically impractical. Because no functional form is assumed, lowess is data hungry, and most data sets quickly become too sparse.

Because no functional form is assumed, there are no parameters to interpret. There are no slope parameters, for example, to indicate the average change in the response for a unit change in a predictor. The overlay of the smoother on the scatter plot is how the story is told.[9]

To illustrate, Figure 8.1 shows a scatter plot with a simple regression line and lowess smooth superimposed. One can see that the lowess fit is responding to local patterns in the data. The linear regression fit assumes a constant slope. The lowess smooth looks to be considerably more steep for $x < -1$ and even for $x < 0$. For $x > 0$, the lowess smooth looks less steep than the linear fit. The dip at $x \cong 0.5$ may be of interest or just the result of sampling error. In any case, a data analyst might well consider a quadratic function for $E(y|x)$

[9] Still, there are fitted values and residuals that can be exploited.

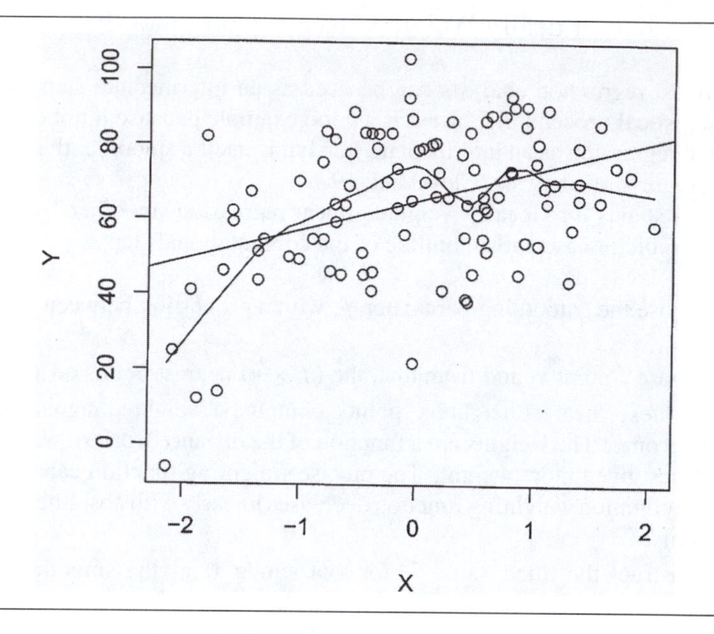

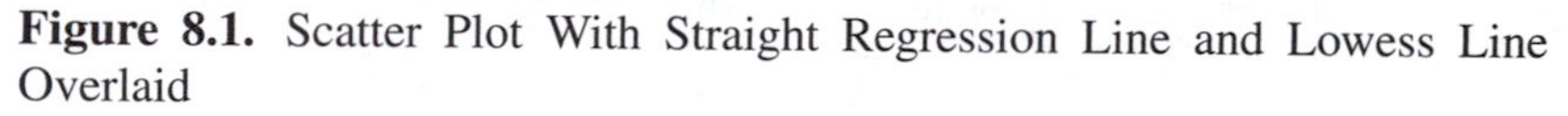

Figure 8.1. Scatter Plot With Straight Regression Line and Lowess Line Overlaid

rather than a linear one. Alternatively, the analyst might decide to characterize the data from the lowess fit directly in much the same terms just employed.

In short, for regression analyses with more than a single term, lowess is used primarily as a diagnostic tool. But it can be used descriptively as well. Examples of both applications will be presented in later chapters.

8.6 Summary and Conclusions

Chapter 8 is a mixed bag of regression extensions and diagnostic tools. Yet there are four broad themes running through the material. First, it is sometimes possible to expand the range of applications to which regression analysis may be applied with very little additional overhead. Regression with categorical terms is an excellent example. Unfortunately, such examples are relatively rare.

Second, there are regression enhancements that appear to be useful until their practical limitations become apparent. Weighted least squares is illustrative. Recall that the weights have to be known, fixed quantities. There are certainly examples of successful weighted least squares applications, but they represent a tiny fraction of the research in which regression analysis is employed.

Third, there is a host of statistical tools developed to address one or more of the assumptions commonly built into a regression analysis. Although some of these tools can be useful, they too often depend on isolating one problem while assuming away all others. Goodness-of-fit tests for the mean function are an example. The data analyst may be forced once again to construct a curious account of the empirical world so that a particular procedure can be applied. The irony is that the whole point of the diagnostic tools is to address dubious assumptions to begin with.

Finally, another problem is that, even when a diagnostic tool can be used sensibly, there will often be very little in the results indicating what can be done to fix the problems found. The lowess smoother is an excellent illustration in part because it conveys more information than most. It will often be apparent where in a scatter plot the mean function fails. But there is no necessary link to why the failure has occurred or how best to fix it. In short, a search for technological cures for the more serious ills of regression analysis will often be frustrated. We shall see in the final chapter that a more hopeful strategy may be to reconsider what can be expected from a regression analysis; aspirations may need to be substantially reduced.

9 Some Regression Diagnostics

9.1 Introduction

The previous chapter raised very directly the role of regression diagnostics. It has long been recognized that there can be a lot of slippage between the model assumed and the "right" model. In response, important research has been undertaken in statistics and econometrics on diagnostic tools that, in principle, can spot problems and, in some cases, suggest remedies. The intent of such efforts is admirable, and the range of tools provided is now vast.

In this chapter, a selection of regression diagnostics will be the major focus. Each is a "case study" of a well-respected or widely used diagnostic tool, although the same issues would arise with any representative cross-section of regression diagnostics. Two broad points will be made. First, there are indeed a number of useful procedures that are relatively easy to apply. Commonly, there is also software readily available. Second, however, the effectiveness of regression diagnostics has been too often oversold. They typically assume that the model is almost right; there is a single problem or a very small number of problems that need to be addressed. In effect, external information is again brought to bear, the credibility of which is too often unconsidered. Equally important, regression diagnostics leave largely untouched concerns about statistical inference and causal inference that also depend on information brought to the analysis from outside.

9.2 Transformations of the Response Variable

To this point, there has been no serious consideration of whether the response variable should be transformed in a nonlinear fashion. By and large, we have used the response variable as it was provided in the data. But that can lead to problems. For example, should one work with income or the log of income? If the log of income is the appropriate form and some other form is used instead, the regression results could be seriously in error.

When the question of how y might be transformed is formalized in a particular manner, there are some potentially useful procedures to provide an answer. We will proceed in some detail to help make some larger points.

9.2.1 Box-Cox Procedures

Suppose the correct regression model in the population is

$$y^{(\lambda)}|\mathbf{x} = \boldsymbol{\eta}^{\mathrm{T}}\mathbf{u} + e \tag{9.1}$$

and, by the scaled power relationship,

$$y^{(\lambda)} = \begin{cases} (y^{\lambda} - 1)/\lambda & \text{if } \lambda \neq 0 \\ \ln(y) & \text{if } \lambda = 0. \end{cases} \tag{9.2}$$

For the transformed value of y, the usual multiple regression model fully applies. Also assume that, in the population, variation around the conditional means is distributed normally.

The value of λ is unknown. If one proceeds as if $\lambda = 1$, a linear function would be applied when a nonlinear function might be required. The results could be very misleading.

Note that the *only* problematic feature of the model is that λ is unknown, and an assumed value of λ may be incorrect. Within a random sample framework, for instance, if the value of λ were known, the regression hyperplane in the population would exactly "go through" each of the conditional means, the conditional variance would be constant, and the conditional distribution of y around the fitted values would be normal. There are no omitted variables, the functional forms for the terms are correct, and there is no measurement error in any of the predictors (and at most only random measurement errors in y). In short, the model is already very nearly right. And if that is really so, there is a widely used procedure developed by Box and Cox (1964) to fix the remaining flaw.

Given the regression model, λ is the single free parameter that needs to be estimated. For technical reasons that need not trouble us here, we actually use a modified power transformation $z(\lambda)$,

$$z(\lambda) = y^{\lambda} gm(y)^{1-\lambda}, \tag{9.3}$$

not Equation 9.2, where $gm(y)$ is the geometric mean of y. Then the profile likelihood function maximized is

$$L(\lambda) = -\frac{n}{2}log[RSS_z(\lambda)]. \tag{9.4}$$

Finding the value of λ that maximizes the $L(z)$ also minimizes $RSS_z(\lambda)$. In effect, the value of λ is found by conditional least squares. That value then makes the scaled power transformation operational; y is transformed to normality, which implies the proper model is being employed (i.e., Equation 9.1).

There are two obvious problems with this approach. First, it is highly unlikely that the model will be correct except for the value of λ. As a formal matter, therefore, $\hat{\lambda}$ will be biased (even in large samples). As a practical matter, then, the issue is how large the bias is. That will generally be very difficult to know.

Second, there is no room for subject matter expertise anywhere in the procedure. The value for $\hat{\lambda}$ produced is supposed to be the "best" estimate. However, the estimated value may be subject matter nonsense. For example, $\hat{\lambda}$ may be -0.13 or 0.46 or 2.15. Such values will probably not make much scientific sense. If it were possible for the data analyst to directly intervene, the more appropriate and scientifically informative values might be 0 (i.e., the log), 0.5, and 2.0. Partly in response to such concerns, newer methods relying on graphical procedures have been developed.

9.2.2 Inverse Fitted Value Response Plots

For purposes of exposition, consider first a single predictor. In regression analysis, we focus on $y|x$. Thus, $E(y)$ is taken to be a function of x. Suppose we reverse roles; we proceed with $x|y$. Now $E(x)$ is a function of y.[1]

Consider the following simple numerical illustration. Assume, for example, that $y = 1, 4, 9, 16$ and $x = 1, 2, 3, 4$. The usual marginal response plot would show y increasing at an increasing rate. The inverse marginal response plot (x on the vertical axis and y on the horizontal axis) would show x increasing at a decreasing rate.

With x on the vertical axis and y on the horizontal axis, an *inverse* regression function is fit to the data. This is done by considering various transformations of y. In this case, it is apparent that the proper fit is to raise y to the $1/2$ power. The fit is nonlinear, but the fitted values go right through the means of x.

Using our previous notation, let $\hat{\lambda} = 0.5$. Returning to the marginal response plot and transforming y with $\hat{\lambda} = 0.5$, the fitted values of $y|x$ form

[1]The use of expected values implies that we have a random sample from a population or that we will be making inferences back to a model responsible for generating the data. But the same issues arise in descriptive analyses of a data set for which one might use the mean rather than the expected value.

a straight line. That is, the best (nonlinear) fit of the inverse marginal response plot produces in the estimated value of λ, the transformation needed to make the usual marginal response plot linear. Of course, with a single term, one would probably have arrived at the same result without the inverse response plot.

In practice, one can entertain the set of scaled power transformations and allow for more than one term. Plotting y against more than two terms is not feasible, but generalizing from the inverse response plot, one can make use of an inverse fitted value plot. The basic idea, thanks to Cook and Weisberg (1994), is to

1. fit the usual linear regression using the untransformed y,
2. plot the fitted values on the vertical axis and the untransformed response variable on the horizontal axis,
3. find the value of λ for y that produces the best fit, and
4. use that value of lambda in the scaled power transformation of y for $y^{(\lambda)}|\mathbf{x} = \boldsymbol{\eta}^{\mathrm{T}}\mathbf{u} + e$.

However, for these steps to work, a key assumption must be made: All of the terms linked to the response must be linearly related. For any given term u_j, we require that for $(j = 1, \ldots, p)$

$$E(u_j|\,\boldsymbol{\eta}^{\mathrm{T}}\mathbf{u}) = a_j + b_j\,\boldsymbol{\eta}^{\mathrm{T}}\mathbf{u} \text{ for } j = 1, \ldots, p. \tag{9.5}$$

In other words, the conditional mean of any term is a linear function of $\boldsymbol{\eta}^{\mathrm{T}}\mathbf{u}$, or, more generally, a regression of any linear combination of terms on another set of those same terms will be linear. A good indication of whether this assumption is correct is if all of the scatter plots between the terms look to be approximately linear. If they are not, some transformations might be considered, or, through a generalization of the Box-Cox procedures described earlier, one can try to transform all of the terms so that they approximate the multivariate normal distribution. Linearity among the terms then follows automatically.

Here's the logic. In order to compute the fitted values with the transformation of y unknown, values for the regression coefficients and intercept need to be known. They are typically not known. But they can be usefully estimated, even if λ is not known, if all of the terms are related as in Equation 9.5. The risk for inverse fitted value plots is that if any of the terms are related to one another in a nonlinear fashion, the nonlinearity will "spill over" into the apparent relationship between the fitted values and the response. The wrong transformation of the response could easily result.

How does one actually estimate the value of λ? Because there are now only two variables to plot, one can proceed as before trying various values of λ to maximize the fit. Some software (e.g., ARC) allows the data analyst to do this interactively. As different values of λ are specified, the relevant inverse bivariate regression is performed and the fitted values are overlaid on the inverse fitted value plot. The best value of λ is determined by a visual judgment about the quality of the fit or some more formal fit measure. One advantage is that if certain values make subject matter sense, the data analyst can experiment with trial values for λ in that neighborhood.

Once the value of λ is determined, y can be transformed accordingly. The transformed y is then regressed on the original terms, in part because we have assumed that the right-hand side of the regression equation is correct as specified.

To help fix these ideas, suppose the correct model is

$$\log(y) = 1 + 1x + 1z + e, \tag{9.6}$$

with x and z linearly related but not especially strongly.

The data analyst does not know that the response is $\log(y)$. The first step would be to check the scatter plot matrix. In this case, the scatter plot would show that x and z are linearly related, but the correlation is not large. If the relationship were highly nonlinear, a transformation to linearity would need to be considered.

The marginal response plots would show that there is a strong nonlinear relationship between the response and both x and z. Figures 9.1 and 9.2 both show the response increasing at an increasing rate.[2]

In part because Figures 9.1 and 9.2 look very similar, perhaps a transformation of the response is needed. So, the second step would be to regress the response (as is) on x and z and then plot the fitted values on the vertical axis and the response on the horizontal axis. The result can be seen in Figure 9.3.

In a third step, various scaled power transformations of the response would be tried until the fit for the regression of the fitted values on the untransformed response was acceptable. In this case, λ would be estimated to be close to 0 (for the log). The R^2 using the log transformation is .98, which declines as values for λ larger or smaller than 0 are inserted in the scaled power transformation.

In a fourth step, the log transformation is applied to the response, which in turn is plotted against the fitted values. Figure 9.4 shows that the transformation inferred from the fit of Figure 9.3 leads to the correct relationship: The log of y is linearly related to the linear combination of x and z.[3]

The final step would consist of regressing the transformed values of y on x and z. One would then recover the parameter values in Equation 9.6.

What would have happened if the terms were related in a nonlinear way? Suppose that the mean function were really linear and that $z = x^2 + v$, where v represents the usual errors. Figure 9.5 shows the inverse fitted value plot. One can see a parabola on its side that derives solely from the nonlinear relationship

---

[2]Because, at this point, the researcher does not know that the response is really $\log(y)$, both graphs use y for the response.

[3]Note that, again, the response variable is on the vertical axis.

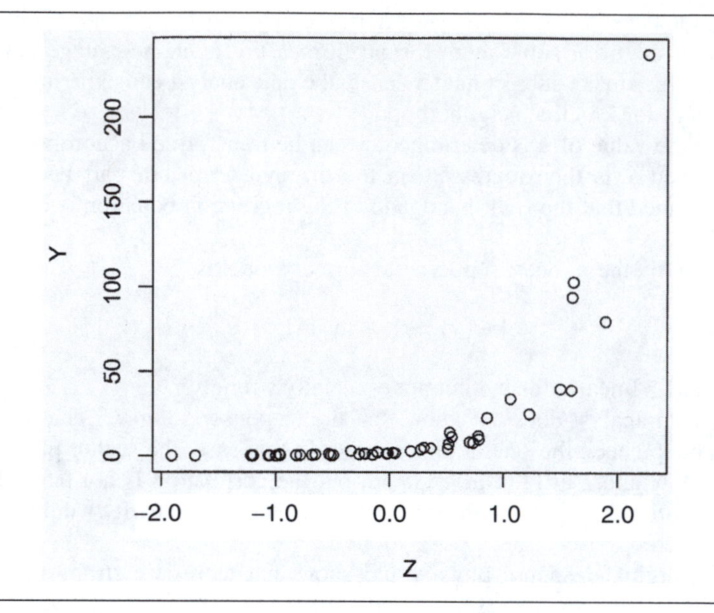

Figure 9.1. Scatter Plot of y Against z

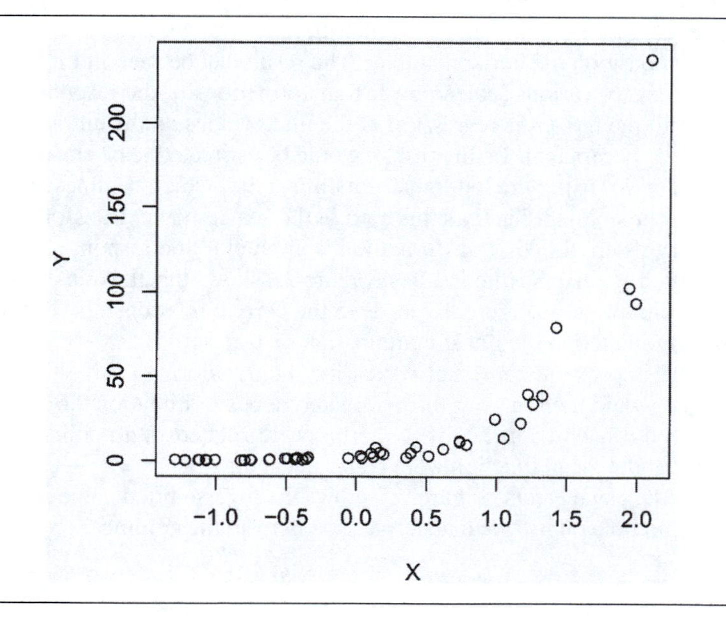

Figure 9.2. Scatter Plot of y Against x

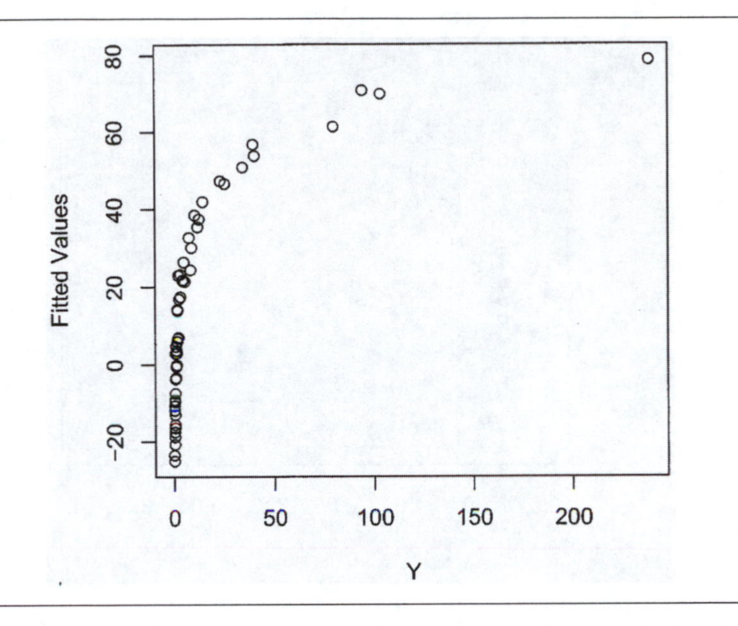

Figure 9.3. Inverse Fitted Value Plot of the Fitted Values Against y

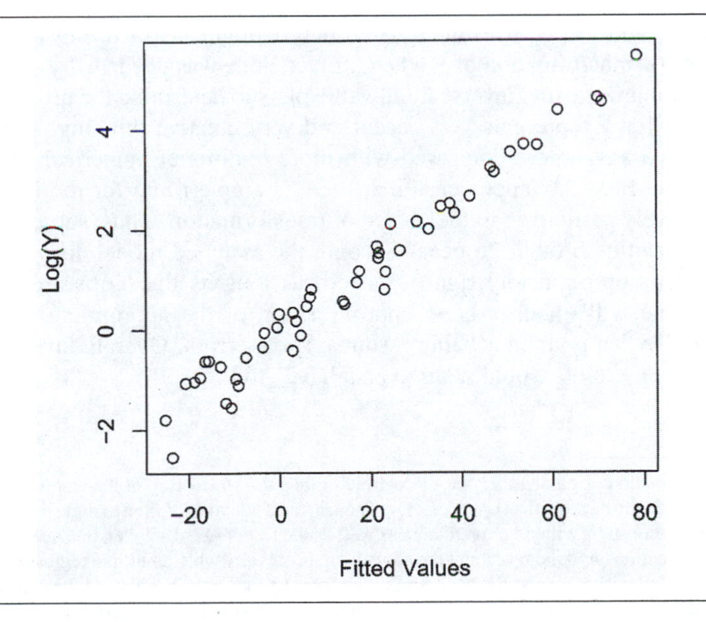

Figure 9.4. Plot of the Transformed y Against the Fitted Values

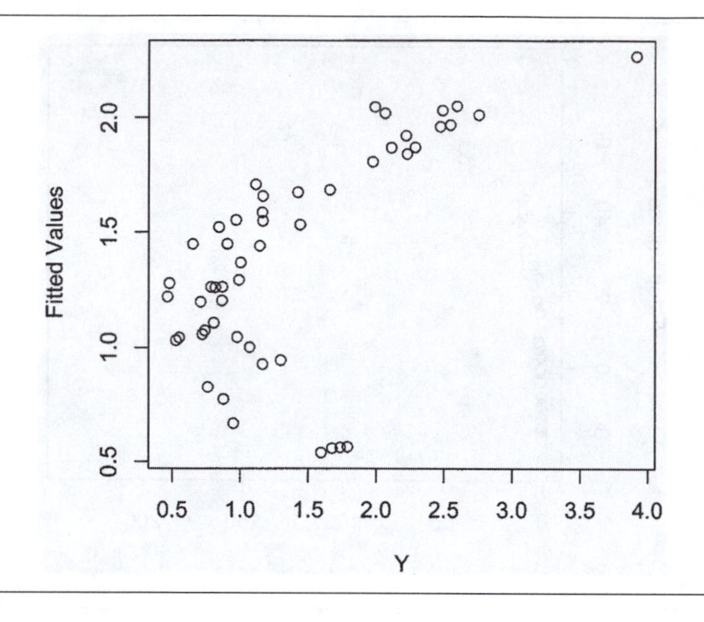

Figure 9.5. The Fitted Values Against Untransformed y With z Omitted

between z and x. As a result, a data analyst might begin trying to find an appropriate transformation of y when, in fact, none was needed.

To summarize, using inverse fitted value plots to determine the proper transformation for y represents very recent and very creative thinking. There are at least two advantages compared with more traditional numerical solutions such as the Box-Cox approach. First, there is ample room for the investigator to actively participate in the choice of transformation. Thus, subject matter expertise can be brought to bear. Second, the assumed model does not have to be even approximately right. Indeed, as long as the terms are linearly related, one will obtain a good approximation of the appropriate value for λ. Note also that nothing is being assumed about errors. Overall, inverse fitted value response plots would seem to be a handy tool.[4]

[4]Transformation of predictors is far more difficult than transformation of the response because there will typically be more than one predictor. Then, a transformation of even a single predictor will affect its relationships with other predictors as well as the response. Moreover, one needs to apply the transformation taking into account the adjustment process by which multiple regression "holds constant." Methods to address the need for predictor transformations are beyond the scope of this book and in any case would not raise any new points going to the interpretative issues. Interested readers will find an excellent discussion of predictor transformations in Cook and Weisberg (1999: Chapter 16).

However, there are also some important limitations. Perhaps the most obvious problem is that there is really no way to know if variables not in the data set, which might otherwise be included in the model, have the requisite linear relationships. Thus, the investigator would need to make the case that the omitted terms meet the necessary linear assumption. This will be very difficult to do. And once again, information external to the data is central. Cook and Weisberg (1999:321) suggest that the procedure is robust to modest violations of linearity. Although this may provide some real comfort on the average, the implications for a given data set are unclear. Perhaps in the future, more specific guidance will be available.

When there are important omitted variables, one may well obtain misleading results, regardless of whether y needs to be transformed or not. And this leads us right back to where we have been: Even if the correct transformation is found, one still needs to construct and estimate the parameters of the right (or nearly right) model. Inverse fitted value response plots have little to say about this or any of the other fundamental concerns that have been raised.

9.3 Leverage and Influence

Most data analysts appreciate that regression results can be distorted by a few observations that are atypical of the rest of the data. When there is a single term or even two terms, one can often spot possible problem observations in a two-dimensional or three-dimensional scatter plot. For more than two terms, scatter plots that are linked so that selected values in one plot are highlighted in all others can also be helpful. Once candidate points are identified, they can be deleted to determine if they make a difference in the fit.

If the difference in the results is substantial, the first matter to consider is *why* those few observations are so deviant. If this results from an error in the data themselves, the error needs to be corrected or the affected cases need to be dropped. If the values are legitimate, the choices are more ambiguous and usually depend on subject matter expertise. On the one hand, the problematic observations may differ from the rest for uninteresting reasons, and to simplify the conclusions, they can be dropped from the analysis. On the other hand, they may represent new and important information, in which case, it will usually be important to keep them. In other words, what one does with deviant observations is not primarily a statistical matter. External information is critical. The statistical problem is finding these observations in the first place. And in particular, when there are more than two terms, graphical methods often will not suffice. Other approaches are needed.

9.3.1 Influential Cases and Cook's Distance

A good, commonsense place to start is with considering how the fit changes if a single observation is deleted. If the fit does not change much, that observation is not influential. If the fit changes a lot, that observation is influential. This idea can be made more formal and rigorous.

Let $\hat{\eta}_{(i)}$ be the vector of k regression coefficients (including the intercept) for the fit with the ith observation deleted. As usual, let $\hat{\eta}$ be the vector of k regression coefficients (including the intercept) for the full data set. Then, $(\hat{\eta}_i - \eta)$ is a measure of distance in vector form. The sign of the difference is generally of no interest, and it would be useful if there were some way to standardize the distance so that it is unaffected by the units in which the variables are measured. These considerations lead to Cook's Distance, defined as

$$D_i = \frac{(\hat{\eta}_{(i)} - \hat{\eta})^{\mathrm{T}}(\mathbf{U}^{\mathrm{T}}\mathbf{U})(\hat{\eta}_{(i)} - \hat{\eta})}{k\hat{\sigma}^2} = \frac{(\hat{\mathbf{y}}_{(i)} - \hat{\mathbf{y}})^{\mathrm{T}}(\hat{\mathbf{y}}_{(i)} - \hat{\mathbf{y}})}{k\hat{\sigma}^2}. \quad (9.7)$$

$\mathbf{U}$ is the $N \times k$ matrix of terms, including an initial column of 1's for the intercept. Thus, $\mathbf{U}^{\mathrm{T}}\mathbf{U}$ is the cross-product matrix that comes into play for generating predicted values. The denominator standardizes the formula by a scale factor to take account of the variability around the regression fit and the number of coefficients. Thus, Cook's Distance is a standardized average squared disparity between the two sets of coefficients. Alternatively, Cook's Distance can be viewed as the sum of the squared differences between the two sets of fitted values divided by a scale factor so that, in effect, one gets the average (over coefficients) disparity between the two fits in units of the residual variance.

Each value of Cook's Distance can be hard to interpret by itself. There is some lore to suggest that values of D_i in excess of 0.5 may need to be examined, and values of D_i in excess of 1.0 could well be problematic. In addition, it can be instructive to examine the relative size of D_i for each observation i. Observations for which values of D_i stand out may need to be scrutinized.

Observations singled out by Cook's Distance, whatever the screening rule, can be dropped from the analysis to determine if the results change enough to alter any overall conclusions. If they don't, the regression analysis may be considered robust to influential observations in the data set. If they do, one has to make a policy or scientific decision about whether the influential observations should be included. Alternatively, it is often useful to report two sets of results, one with the influential observations included and one with the influential observations excluded. Readers can then make the decision about which analysis should be preferred. They may also decide that there is insufficient information to determine which analysis is preferable.

Now recall that the variance of the residuals is

$$\mathrm{Var}(\hat{e}_i|\mathbf{x}_i) = \sigma^2(1 - h_i), \quad (9.8)$$

where h_i (leverage) is a function of the terms in the equation and represents distance from the means of those terms. A larger value for the leverage h_i sets up the potential for substantial influence on the fit, depending on the value of y_i.

The variances of the residuals over repeated samples depend on the associated leverage. Residuals with less leverage have less variance.[5] Sometimes, the different variances can muddy the waters when residual plots are examined. However, one can correct for the unequal variances as well as the scale of y and arrive at a studentized residual,

$$r_i = \frac{\hat{e}_i}{\hat{\sigma}\sqrt{1 - h_i}}. \tag{9.9}$$

Each studentized residual has a mean of zero and a variance of one, which helps in making comparisons. One also can now see from another perspective what Cook's Distance means. In particular,

$$D_i = \frac{r_i^2}{k} \times \frac{h_i}{1 - h_i}. \tag{9.10}$$

Note that both the residual and the leverage weigh in. Larger studentized residuals lead to a greater Cook's Distance, other things being equal. Larger leverage also leads to a greater Cook's Distance, other things being equal. So, influence is a function of outliers in both the "x direction" and the "y direction." By themselves, neither large leverage nor a large residual imply large influence.

Cook's Distance is a very useful diagnostic tool that can help researchers make decisions about atypical observations affecting the regression fit. However, Cook's Distance is not without its problems. For example, influence is defined one observation at a time. This can mask the impact of several observations that are influential. At a deeper level, implicit in most discussions of Cook's Distance is that any problems that surface reside in the data. The model is correct in the sense we have been using. But because this is never demonstrably true, it will often be unclear whether an influential observation results from data problems or modeling problems. For example, an observation may be influential because of a failure to properly transform the response or because of systematic measurement error in y that happens to be associated with large values of the predictors. Cook's Distance is a good illustration of another diagnostic tool that can spot potential problems but then not provide much guidance about why there are problems to begin with or what to do about them.

[5] Consider the case of a single predictor. If the regression line is rotated slightly around the mean of x, the fit will change most for observations far away from that mean. The fit near the mean will change least. The same basic principle applies to the case with many predictors.

9.4 Cross-Validation

Capitalizing on chance patterns in the data can be a serious problem if the goal is to generalize from a sample to a population. In developing a regression model, data analysts often make a series of decisions forcing the model to conform to the sample as much as possible. Many regression tools encourage such "overfitting": sequential fitting algorithms, Box-Cox transformations, inverse fitted value plots, and others. Then, generalization back to the population is undermined; the fit responds far too much to sampling error and not enough to stable features of the population.

In response, it is often suggested that researchers make a clear distinction between a "training" data set and a "testing" data set. Model building is done on the former, and model assessment is done on the latter. It follows that building and evaluating a model with the same data can be very misleading. The model is likely to look better than it really is.

For example, suppose one were interested in per capita water consumption in a random sample of cities as a function of the price of water and housing density. Price is set by the policies of the local water utility, and household density is determined by zoning regulations. Higher prices should be associated with lower water use, other things being equal. Cities with denser housing should use less water per capita because outdoor water for landscape would be less. But the existing theory and literature are silent on possible interaction effects and potential transformations for the response and the two predictors.

Acting in an exploratory mode, the researcher develops a model. There are estimates of the intercept and two slope coefficients: $\hat{\eta}_0$, $\hat{\eta}_1$, and $\hat{\eta}_2$. Various measures of fit are then computed, such as $\hat{\sigma}^2$. But the researcher has so massaged the data that $\hat{\sigma}^2$ is probably optimistic compared with the true σ^2 in the population or in nature.

Therefore, a second random sample of the same size is taken from the same population. The regression coefficients estimated from the *first* sample ($\hat{\eta}_0$, $\hat{\eta}_1$, and $\hat{\eta}_2$) are applied to the measures of water prices and housing density from the *second* sample to generate fitted values. From these fitted values and the values of the response variable (in the second sample), another estimate $\tilde{\sigma}^2$ can be obtained. Insofar as the two estimates are roughly the same, there is no evidence of overfitting that really matters. If the two estimates substantially differ, there is evidence of overfitting. Measures of fit from the first sample need to be discounted.

Special kinds of scatter plots can also be instructive. For example, suppose that the model developed in the first sample was applied to the second sample, but with new least squares estimates of the regression coefficients computed. From these and the data in the second sample, a new set of residuals could be constructed. A plot of these residuals against the residuals in the second sample, when the regression coefficients from the first sample are used, will often indicate which observations are driving potential overfitting.

It is rare for researchers to have access to a second random sample from the same population. Using a random sample from a different population can be very misleading; if the fit degrades when applied to the second set of data, it will not be clear if overfitting is the problem or if a different model for the second population is required.

In response, some researchers divide a single random sample into a random subset for model building and one or more random subsets for model testing. However, a relatively large initial sample is required. Therefore, there are resampling alternatives based on either the bootstrap or the jackknife (Efron and Tibshirani, 1993: Chapter 17).

In the case of the bootstrap, one begins with the model estimated in the full sample, presumably vulnerable to overfitting. From this is computed the averaged squared deviation between the observed values of the response and the fitted values of the response.[6] This value may be too optimistic. Then, for each of the B bootstrap samples, the values of the regression coefficients are estimated. Each of these, in turn, is applied in the *original* sample to obtain B estimates of the averaged squared deviation between the observed values of the response and the fitted values of the response. The average of these B estimates provides a more valid measure of average fit. Some further steps are required, but they need not trouble us here. (See Efron and Tibshirani, 1993:247-249.)

Cross-validation can be a useful diagnostic tool for overfitting. One must be very clear, however, that cross-validation has no implications one way or another for how "valid" the model is more generally. Indeed, one could easily cross-validate a model that is patently wrong. Moreover, if a model is demonstrably a product of significant overfitting, it is not clear what follows. Which particular features of the model have capitalized excessively on chance are not routinely revealed. The only recommendation may be to get another data set and try again.

9.5 Misspecification Tests

Under the rubric of model misspecification tests are a very large number of "significance tests" addressing various assumptions about the regression model. The basic idea usually is to pose a null hypothesis that a particular feature of the model is "correct" and formally consider whether the null should be rejected for an alternative that implies some flaw in how the model is formulated. Kennedy (1998:78-79) organizes such tests into ten categories, from which we will select "tests for exogeneity" (sometimes called Hausman tests) for illustrative purposes. Such tests address a critical issue in the regression model, namely, the relationship between u_j and e. Recall that a key part of whether a

[6]This is just $\hat{\sigma}^2$ unadjusted for the number of regression coefficients in the model.

model is the right model depends fundamentally on any relationship that may exist between u_j and e.

Consider, for example, the evaluations of the Special Supplemental Nutritional Program for Women, Infants, and Children (WIC). The goal of the program has been to avoid preventable physical and medical conditions by improving the diets of low-income women who are pregnant, breastfeeding, or postpartum. This is to be achieved by providing supplemental foods and nutritional education. Besharov and Germanis (2001) observe in their review of WIC that most of the research attempting to evaluate the efficacy of WIC has been nonexperimental. Women receiving WIC benefits are compared with women not receiving WIC benefits, but in part because program participation is voluntary, it is likely that the experimental and control groups are not comparable in a number of ways. Selection bias can result. And as Besharov and Germanis (2001:36) observe,

> Careful regression analysis often can reduce selection bias, but even in the best of circumstances it cannot do so completely. The results of a regression analysis are, however, of limited credibility when the differences between participants and nonparticipants are large and little data are available about their social, economic and personality characteristics with which to explain differences in outcomes....

Such concerns translate into dependence between the terms in the regression model and the errors. In principle, therefore, tests for exogeneity could be instructive. But in order to examine the relevant properties of exogeneity tests, a brief excursion into instrumental variables is needed.

9.5.1 Instrumental Variables

The exposition can be kept relatively simple if we consider the case of a single predictor. For our purposes, the points to be made will generalize sufficiently well to multiple regression without having to work with matrices.

Recall the earlier discussion of stochastic predictors. Using the same notation, the simple regression model with, for ease of exposition, mean-deviated variables is

$$y|x = \eta_1 x + e. \tag{9.11}$$

The least squares estimate of $\hat{\eta}_1$ is

$$\hat{\eta}_1 = \frac{\sum_{i=1}^{n} x_i y_i}{\sum_{i=1}^{n} x_i^2}. \tag{9.12}$$

Substituting Equation 9.11 into Equation 9.12 and simplifying, the result is

$$\hat{\eta}_1 = \eta_1 + \frac{\sum_{i=1}^{n} x_i e_i}{\sum_{i=1}^{n} x_i^2}. \tag{9.13}$$

If x and e are correlated, the expected value for the far right-hand term will be nonzero, and the numerator will not go to zero as the sample size increases without limit. The least squares estimate will be biased and inconsistent. The correlation could be the result of random measurement error in x, one or more omitted variables correlated with x and y, the incorrect functional form, and a number of other problems.

Suppose one could find a variable z that was correlated with x but not correlated with e. It might then be possible to use z in place of x. Here's how. Replace x with z as follows:

$$\hat{\eta}_1^* = \frac{\sum_{i=1}^n z_i y_i}{\sum_{i=1}^n z_i x_i}. \tag{9.14}$$

Substituting Equation 9.11 into Equation 9.14 and simplifying, we get

$$\hat{\eta}_1^* = \eta_1 + \frac{\sum_{i=1}^n z_i e_i}{\sum_{i=1}^n z_i x_i}. \tag{9.15}$$

But from our previous discussion of estimation with stochastic predictors, if the top and the bottom of the far right-hand term are multiplied by $1/n$ and n grows without limit, that term converges to zero (thanks to the assumption that z and e are uncorrelated). Hence, the instrumental variable estimator $\hat{\eta}_1^*$ is consistent. In other words, if an instrumental variable z can be found, one can obtain consistent estimates of the slope even if x and e are correlated.

How does one find such a variable? In most applications, instruments are found and justified either by subject matter theory or information from how the data were collected. Suppose, for example, one is interested in the amount of money a household spends on goods and services as a function of income. If the variables come from a sample survey, it is reasonable to assume that there will be the least random measurement error in reported income. Hence, a regression of consumption on income will yield biased and inconsistent estimates of $\hat{\eta}_1$.[7]

Greene (2000:379) argues that, if one could ascertain the number of checks written by the head of a household over the period of interest (e.g., by examining the checkbook), that number might serve as an instrument. It would likely be highly correlated with income and uncorrelated with the measurement errors (which are the source of the problem).

A second strategy is to construct instrumental variables from the existing data. For example, one could rank people in the data set on their reported

---

[7]Suppose that $x_i^* = x_i + v_i$, where v_i is measurement error with a mean of zero and constant variance and is drawn at random from some distribution. Instead of regressing y on x, y is regressed on x^*. So, by substitution, the actual regression run is $y_i = \eta_1 x_i^* + (e_i - \eta_1 v_i)$. Note that v_i is now contained both in the regression term x_i^* and the error term $(e_i - \eta_1 v_i)$. As a result, x_i^* is correlated with the errors.

income and use the ranks as an instrument. This assumes, however, that the random measurement error has not altered the ranks.

For both instruments, one assumes that the problem is solely random measurement error in x. If there are also omitted confounders, then the justifications for both instruments are undermined. The general point is that finding and justifying instruments becomes much more difficult if the relationship between x and e could result from more than one problem with the regression model. One has to make the case that the instrument is at least uncorrelated with the errors, and if the potential correlation between x and e could result from any of several problems with the regression model, each of those problems needs to be addressed. A great deal of credible information not contained in the data must be brought to the analysis.

For example, although there may be no correlation between the number of checks written and the random measurement error in reported income (insofar as a respondent's records could be consulted), the number of checks might well be correlated with any number of omitted variables folded into the errors. To make the case that such correlations did not exist would require a very grounded and lengthy discussion. Taxes paid, for instance, would presumably be related to reported income and consumption and would thus be a confounder. Moreover, taxes paid should be related to the number of checks written. Showing that such correlations did not exist would take a lot of credible information.[8]

Consider now the multiple regression case. Suppose there is reason to think that all of the terms are correlated with the errors. Thus, if there are p terms (excluding the intercept), there will need to be p instrumental variables. The multivariate instrumental variable estimator is then

$$\hat{\eta}^* = (\mathbf{Z}^{\mathrm{T}}\mathbf{U})^{-1}\mathbf{Z}^{\mathrm{T}}\mathbf{y}. \tag{9.16}$$

But now, one must make the case that each instrument is uncorrelated with e. This comes up most forcefully in simultaneous equation modeling, which will be addressed briefly in the next chapter. For our purposes, the main point is that the effort to address the correlation between u_j and e requires yet more information brought to the analysis from outside. There is nothing in the data by themselves that can determine whether one has a valid instrumental variable.[9]

---

[8] There is sometimes an embarrassment of riches: more than one instrument for each term correlated with the errors. Then, the problem can become which to choose and/or how to combine them.

[9] One can also employ an instrumental variable estimator for a subset of $\mathbf{U}$, $\mathbf{U}^*$. In any case, the literature on instrumental variables is vast. A useful treatment that is now a bit dated can be found in Bowden and Turkington (1984). An excellent example of recent advances can be seen in the article by Angrist et al. (1996).

9.5.2 Tests for Exogeneity

The basic idea is very simple. Suppose that a single term u_j is thought to be correlated with e, and there is an instrumental variable z_j correlated with u_j but not with e. One could ignore the potential problem with u_j and apply the usual least squares estimator. One could, thanks to z_j, also use an instrumental variable estimator. If u_j is correlated with e, the least squares estimate will be biased and inconsistent. But the instrumental variable estimator, even though biased, will be consistent. So, in large samples, a substantial disparity between the two indicates that, indeed, u_j is correlated with e. The null hypothesis is that u_j is not correlated with e, in which case, both estimators are consistent and in large samples will produce very similar estimates.

This logic can easily be generalized to a subset of terms $\mathbf{U}^*$ thought to be correlated with e. And one might think that a relatively simple test statistic follows. For a variety of technical reasons, however, such is not the case (Greene, 2000:383-385). But there is an alternative and more operational formulation developed by Wu (1973) that is represented by

$$y = \boldsymbol{\eta}^{\mathrm{T}}\mathbf{U} + \boldsymbol{\gamma}^{\mathrm{T}}\widehat{\mathbf{U}}^* + e. \tag{9.17}$$

$\mathbf{U}^*$ is the subset of the terms in $\mathbf{U}$ thought to be correlated with the errors in the original regression model. $\widehat{\mathbf{U}}^*$ are the fitted values from the regression of $\mathbf{U}^*$ on the instrumental variables $\mathbf{Z}$. An F-test, on the set of $\boldsymbol{\gamma}$ coefficients for the null hypothesis that all of those coefficients are zero, is a test of the null hypothesis that the suspect terms in $\mathbf{U}^*$ are uncorrelated with the errors in the original regression model.

All of the issues raised earlier about the use of instrumental variables remain relevant. But there is a new wrinkle that applies not just to tests for exogeneity but any misspecification tests in which the null hypothesis is that all is well: It is not clear what to do if the null hypothesis is not rejected.

To begin, there are the usual problems of power and Type II errors. The researcher may well fail to reject the null when the null should be rejected. More important is the old saw that there are a very large number of other null hypotheses that would also not be rejected. In the case of tests for exogeneity, these alternative null hypotheses would imply that u_j and e are correlated. Thus, when the null is not rejected, one cannot logically conclude that all is well. The real issue is the likely size of the correlation between u_j and e and then how much bias remains in regression estimates obtained.

For example, if, for a single instrument, γ is estimated at, say, 1.5, the researcher may fail to reject the null hypothesis that $\gamma = 0$. But perhaps all of the null hypotheses $-0.5 < \gamma < 3.5$ would also not be rejected. In short, as a logical matter, tests for exogeneity cannot determine if u_j and e are uncorrelated. And as a logical matter, analogous problems are inherent in tests of any null hypothesis that the regression model is correct. Testing one's way to the correct model does not seem to be a useful strategy.

Would exogeneity tests have helped in the evaluation of WIC? If Besharov and Germanis (2001) are correct, the null hypothesis would have been rejected.[10] The claims of Besharov and Germanis would have been strengthened. However, with the null hypothesis rejected, it is unlikely that clear guidance about remedies would follow. Any single predictor or subset of predictors (or even all predictors) could be correlated with the errors and for any of several different reasons. Even less clear would be the meaning of a failure to reject the null hypothesis. A failure to reject the null hypothesis would not necessarily mean that all was well.

The general lesson is that when the null hypothesis is rejected, and if the assumptions of the test are met, useful information may be conveyed. However, it is typically difficult to know how to respond to the bad news, and if the null hypothesis is not rejected, one cannot conclude that the errors and the predictors are necessarily uncorrelated.

9.6 Conclusions

Regression diagnostics of all kinds are widely available in statistics and econometrics. It is hard to quarrel with their motivation. They acknowledge, at least implicitly, that it is hard to construct a satisfactory regression model, let alone the correct one. And they offer tools to address many key vulnerabilities.

At the same time, the usefulness of the existing diagnostic tools can be easily overestimated. To begin, they leave untouched such questions as whether the manner in which the data were generated justifies statistical inference or whether a sensible response schedule has been or can be formulated. Thus, they cannot help with the bedrock issues raised earlier.

The existing diagnostic tools are also rather focused. At their best, they can pinpoint the existence of a particular problem if that is the only potential problem with the model. But even then, there may be little guidance about the cause of the problem or what can be done. And if there are several potential problems, the diagnostics can fail to find real difficulties, or they can find difficulties that are not real.

Because there are often several potential problems with any regression model, the best strategy may be to work sequentially from one's best guess about the most serious problems to those that are perhaps less serious. There is no guarantee that such an approach will work, and a lot will depend, of course, on how the model is to be used. For example, if one aspires only to describe relationships in a population, correlations between the predictors and the errors may not be very important. One implication is that the more demanding the

---

[10]This assumes, of course, that, for any given study, statistical power was sufficient.

uses to which the model will be put, the more weight the regression diagnostics will be asked to carry.

Finally, diagnostics relying on formal tests must be handled with special care. Like all statistical inference, they depend on random sampling, a natural approximation, or on a credible data-from-nature formulation. Then, they provide only a thumbs-up or thumbs-down decision rule, which leaves unaddressed how serious the problem really is. And on top of all of the well-known difficulties with the testing paradigm, a key problem for regression diagnostics is the inherent ambiguity of what it means when the null hypothesis is not rejected.

10 Further Extensions of Regression Analysis

Many would claim that, on a scale of 1 to 10, the technical sophistication of the regression models considered so far would score no higher than a 3. Consequently, it is natural to wonder if higher-tech modeling can be used to circumvent the problems discussed in earlier chapters.

By and large, the answer is no. More sophisticated models are generally developed to address more complicated empirical questions, not to patch up holes in the existing technology. Thus, they tend to pass over the kind of difficulties discussed earlier. The older problems do not disappear. Nor is their impact any less important. We turn now to a brief sample of more complex models to make this point.

10.1 Regression Models for Longitudinal Data

Most of the data considered so far have been "cross-sectional." The observational units are measured at the same moment in time or are treated as such. But what if the data are observed longitudinally, for example, a single cross-sectional unit (e.g., a person, business firm, or country) followed over time?

Moreover, time really matters in the analysis; *when* things happen counts. For example, one might be interested in how the yearly number of homicides has varied with the unemployment rate over the past four decades for the County of Los Angeles. One might treat the number of homicides as the response variable and the unemployment rate as a predictor.

In many important ways, nothing changes formally when time series data are analyzed within a regression framework. Interest still centers on $E(y_t|\mathbf{x}_t)$ and $\text{Var}(y_t|\mathbf{x}_t)$, where all that has changed is the subscript. The data are now indexed in time by $t = 1, 2, \ldots, T$ time periods. Thus, the data are usually organized with rows as points in time and columns as variables.

But longitudinal data can provide some new and interesting analysis possibilities and some special difficulties. One of the enrichments is that it is possible to consider the time "lag" in any associations. For example, one can ask whether unemployment is more strongly related to homicides in the same year or a year or two later. How long does it take for unemployment to translate into crime? Likewise, one can ask how homicide might be related to itself in the future. Although the number of homicides one year might be strongly associated with the number of homicides in the next year, what about that association five years later? This might be relevant for a "contagion" understanding of violence associated with rival gangs.

Another enhancement is that it is sometimes possible to untangle causal direction. There may be, for example, two response schedules, one in which y is the response and x is the intervention, and one in which the roles are reversed. If the analysis is undertaken so that change in x at an earlier time is related to change in y at a later time, one has made a commitment to the response schedule with x as the predictor; y cannot cause x.

But there is also a down side in working with longitudinal data. Perhaps the major problem for regression analysis is that the errors will often not be independent. Errors closer in time to one another will tend to be more alike than errors farther apart. Especially when coupled with using lagged values of the response as a predictor, proper estimation of the key regression parameters becomes more difficult. Consider now the multiple regression framework to see how all this plays out.[1]

10.1.1 Multiple Linear Regression for Time Series Data

If all that one cares about is description of a given longitudinal data set, one can apply multiple regression as usual. But if the data are a random sample from a population or can be treated as such, and if there is interest in statistical inference, it is necessary once again to consider carefully a formal model in the population.

[1] See Hamilton (1994:Chapter 7) for an unusually thorough, formal discussion.

However, time series data are rarely random samples from a real population, and it is typically difficult to make the case that nature produces time series data in a manner consistent with random sampling from a population. For time series data, therefore, the model-based sampling is especially common, and inferences are made to a joint distribution that nature could construct, typically with special interest in regression parameters characterizing the joint distribution. That is, attention is directed toward a model of how nature is supposed to operate.

The standard multiple regression model, whether it resides in the population or represents how nature generates the data, contains $k - 1$ terms (where k is the number of regression coefficients plus the constant) in the usual form,

$$E(y_t|\mathbf{x}_t) = \eta_0 + \eta_1 u_{t,1} + \cdots + \eta_{k-1} u_{t,k-1}. \tag{10.1}$$

To justify the usual least squares estimation, nature must have constructed the population or generated the data so that $E(e_t|\mathbf{x}_t) = 0$, $\text{Var}(e_t|\mathbf{x}_t) = \sigma^2$, and $\text{Cov}(e_t, e_s) = 0$ (where t and s are any two time periods with $t \neq s$). In time series parlance, the errors are "covariance stationary." For any arbitrary point in time, the expected value and variance of e given x is the same. And for any two arbitrary points in time, the errors are uncorrelated.[2]

Implicit, once again, can sometimes be the thought experiment of a limitless number of independent random samples from a fixed population. Thus, there is a limitless number of sampled values for any time point. But because it is often very difficult to square this conception with understandings about how the data were actually generated, researchers commonly use one of the three flavors of model-based sampling. Nature (a) generates a joint distribution of the response and the predictors, (b) generates a conditional distribution of the response given the predictors, or (c) adopts a linear model. The third is perhaps the most popular. Conditional on the predictors (but not the lagged values of the response) and a model, the errors behave as if drawn independently at random from some specified distribution (although allowance will be made for correlated errors shortly). Randomness comes from the errors alone, which nature produces in a very convenient manner.

As stressed earlier, a commitment to any of these thought experiments is a commitment to how nature is supposed to function. Good practice dictates that sound scientific arguments are brought to bear. Too often, however, researchers are silent on such matters.

---

[2]The errors are "weakly stationary" if the means, variances, and covariances of the errors are the same despite arbitrary displacements of time. Strong stationarity means that the joint distribution of the errors is the same despite arbitrary displacements of time.

10.1.1.1 *Lagged Response Variables*

Important complications are added if the model includes one or more lagged values of the response. Suppose the model is now

$$E(y_t|\mathbf{x}_t) = \eta_0 + \eta_1 y_{t-1} + \eta_2 u_{t,1} + \cdots + \eta_k u_{t,k-1}. \tag{10.2}$$

With y_{t-1} on the right-hand side, one must revisit how the errors are related to the predictors. Even if **U** and e are uncorrelated (or independent), least squares estimates will be biased. The problem is that because the errors are carried along in the lagged values of the response variable, those lagged values are associated with earlier values of e. For example, e_t and y_t are related in models like Equation 10.2. At time $t + 1$, y_t is a predictor. So, in that role, y_t is necessarily related to the errors. This formally biases the estimate $\hat{\eta}_1$, and because, by Equation 10.2, y_{t-1} is also related to **U**, the other estimated regression coefficients will be biased as well.

However, if earlier values of y are uncorrelated with later values of e, the least squares estimates are consistent. More formally, consistency follows if nature guarantees that the $E(e) = 0$, the $\text{Cov}(\mathbf{U}_t, e_t) = 0$, the $\text{Cov}(y_{t-1}, e_t) = 0$, and as the number of observations increases without limit, the covariance matrix of the predictors (including y_{t-1}) converges to a symmetric positive definite matrix.[3] Whether all this is plausible needs to be argued on a case-by-case basis. It will often be a hard sell if anyone is paying attention.

If $\text{Cov}(e_t, e_s) \neq 0$, then the least squares estimates are not even consistent. An alternative estimator is required. One option is an instrumental variable estimator discussed in any number of econometrics texts. But with the prospect of correlated errors now raised, it is necessary to consider these correlations more thoroughly.

10.1.1.2 *Correlated Errors*

For the moment, suppose there is no lagged response variable, and that Equation 10.1 is correct but the $\text{Cov}(e_t, e_s) \neq 0$. One of the key assumptions for least squares estimation is violated. With $E(e_t|\mathbf{x})$ still zero, least squares estimates are unbiased.[4] However, the conventional formula for estimating the standard errors is incorrect. The dependence among the errors has been ignored. Another problem is that the failure to exploit the information in the errors leads to inefficient estimates of the regression coefficients; their sampling distributions will in theory be more variable than if that information were properly used.

---

[3]A necessary condition is that $-1 < \eta_1 < 1$. Otherwise, the mean and variance grow without limit. Also, slight variations in the assumptions about the errors also work, but they do not materially change the burden that nature has to carry.

[4]They are also unbiased for any of the usual variants on this theme (e.g., x and e are uncorrelated).

More formally, let

$$\text{Cov}(e_t, e_{t-r}) = \text{Cov}(e_t, e_{t+r}) = \gamma_r, \tag{10.3}$$

where $\sigma^2 = \gamma_0$ and r is the lag. That is, the covariance is symmetric with respect to lag direction.

The relevant correlations are

$$\text{Corr}(e_t, e_{t-r}) = \frac{\text{Cov}(e_t, e_{t-r})}{\sqrt{\text{Var}(e_t)\text{Var}(e_{t-r})}} = \frac{\gamma_r}{\gamma_0} = \rho_r. \tag{10.4}$$

It follows that $\text{Var}(e_t) = \gamma_0 \mathbf{R}$, where $\mathbf{R}$ is the "autocorrelation" matrix such that $\mathbf{R}_{tr} = \gamma_{|t-r|}/\gamma_0$. That is, an autocorrelation is solely a function of the time interval between the two errors for any value of t, and $\mathbf{R}$ is a $T \times T$ matrix filled with autocorrelations. (The autocorrelation at a lag of 0 is 1.0, and these fill the main diagonal.) The usual least squares formulas ignore $\mathbf{R}$ when the regression parameters and their standard errors are estimated.

Estimating the error variance requires $\widehat{\mathbf{R}}$. Because, in a real data set, there is only a single residual in each cell of $\mathbf{R}$, the cell entries cannot be estimated directly cell by cell. One must construct a model of the autocorrelations and estimate that model's parameters. With that done, the autocorrelations follow.

There are two popular approaches, but both require weak stationarity; the means, variances, and covariances of the errors are constant with respect to arbitrary displacements of time. Only the lags matter.

The first formulation is called "autoregressive" (AR) and has the following structure:

$$e_t = \theta_1 e_{t-1} + \theta_2 e_{t-2} + \cdots + \theta_p e_{t-p} + v_t, \tag{10.5}$$

where v_t behaves as if generated independently from some convenient distribution (i.e., "white noise"), often the normal. The second is called "moving average" (MA) and has the following structure:

$$e_t = v_t - \phi_1 v_{t-1} + \phi_2 v_{t-2} + \cdots + \phi_q v_{t-q}. \tag{10.6}$$

In practice, p and/or q are two or less. AR models imply that the regression errors are a function of regression errors at earlier points in time (hence the term "autocorrelated") plus an initial random perturbation. The θs are typically constrained so that with longer lags, the correlation between errors declines gradually.[5] MA models imply that the regression errors are a linear combination of a contemporaneous and earlier random perturbations. The usual constraints on the ϕs imply that the autocorrelation between the errors does not gradually decline with longer lags but drops to zero after a certain lag.

One can, in principle, use the regression residuals to determine which of the two formulations (or a combination of the two) fits the data best. The AR

[5] For example, if the model includes a single θ, the absolute value of that θ is less than one.

and/or MA parameter estimates can then be used to provide the off-diagonal elements in **R**. If the model for the errors is already known, one can estimate the regression parameters and the error parameters at once with maximum likelihood procedures. The estimates then have all of the desirable asymptotic properties, at least in principle. And they can be employed when there is a lagged response variable as well.[6]

10.1.1.3 *Finding "Serial Correlation" in the Residuals*

How one determines whether the errors are autocorrelated to begin with depends in part on the error model postulated. Still, it is often useful to compute a set of autocorrelations at various lags. The number of lags depends on the total number of observations and whether there is reason to suspect autocorrelations at long lags (e.g., "seasonal effects"). Many conventional statistical packages will compute the "autocorrelation function" with a single command.

There are also several possible statistical tests for autocorrelation. The old war horse is the Durbin-Watson statistic, which basically tests the null hypothesis that the autocorrelation at a lag of one is equal to zero. However, the usual Durbin-Watson test is biased in the presence of a lagged endogenous variable. The Q test is a more recent and general test based on the χ^2 distribution. It tests the null hypothesis that all autocorrelations from lag 1 to lag p are equal to zero (where p is determined by the researcher). Finally, if one has a formal model of the errors, it is possible to test the coefficients of that model. For example, one can test the null hypothesis that all of the coefficients in an autoregressive model are zero. Each of these options, and more, are discussed in most intermediate-level econometrics books (e.g., Greene, 2000).

10.1.1.4 *Implications*

To summarize, longitudinal data of the sort just described are fully compatible with regression analysis (and other forms of analysis, too). But the price will often be additional complexity and the need for one or more additional models to shore up the regression model of the mean function. In particular, there will commonly be a need for a somewhat elaborate model of how the errors are produced. Consequently, still more information must be brought to the data from outside, which must be carefully scrutinized. Why would nature, for instance, generate the errors through a moving average model?

---

[6]One might incorrectly think to use $\widehat{\mathbf{R}}$ as the weight matrix in weighted least squares. However, the weighted least squares procedure assumes that the weight matrix is known. In this case, the weight matrix would be estimated from the data. Treating the estimated matrix as known would ignore an important source of uncertainty.

Table 10.1. Five Years of Data on Homicide and Unemployment for Two Cities

Year	City	Homicides	Unemployment (%)
1960	A	450	5.6
1961	A	467	5.7
1962	A	480	5.3
1963	A	446	5.8
1964	A	571	5.2
1960	B	455	5.9
1961	B	461	5.2
1962	B	490	5.0
1963	B	451	5.5
1964	B	579	6.2

But the main point is that the added complexity and technical apparatus do not really address any of the important problems raised earlier. We are not really any better off. Indeed, new issues have arisen.

10.2 Regression Analysis With Multiple Time Series Data

Suppose that one has homicide rates over time for a number of cities. That is, the response is y_{it}, where i refers to cities and t refers to time ($i = 1, 2, \ldots, N$ and $t = 1, 2, \ldots, T$). There are N time series, each of length T. Suppose also that there is a set of predictors $\mathbf{x}_{it}$ as well. Some of these predictors may characterize the cities: the unemployment rate, the consumer price index, the proportion of the city's population under the age of 25, the clearance rate for the local police department, and so on. Some of the predictors may characterize time periods: season of the year, average outside temperature, number of daylight hours, and the like. Such data can go by the name of multiple time series, panel data, or pooled cross-section time series data (Hsiao, 1986).

Table 10.1 shows how such a data file might look for two cities (A and B), five years, and one predictor. The rows are years nested within cities. With two cities and five years, there is a total of $N \times T = 10$ observations. In practice, the data file would likely contain many more observations: more time periods, more cross-sectional units, or both.

One could analyze these data within the linear regression framework we have been using: There would be a single response variable and a single predictor. But there would be nothing in the model explicitly addressing possible differences between cities or between years. More generally, one is assuming as usual that the variability in homicides can be properly captured with the unemployment rate and whatever other subject matter predictors one would include on the right-hand side. In addition, the possibility that the errors may be correlated over time and within each city is unaddressed. To consider such concerns, another set of elaborations is necessary.

10.2.1 Fixed Effects Models

Consider a simple extension of the linear regression model,

$$y_{it}|\mathbf{x}_{it} = \alpha + \beta_i + \gamma_t + \boldsymbol{\eta}^{\mathrm{T}}\mathbf{u}_{it} + e_{it}, \tag{10.7}$$

where (for now) e_{it} meets all of the necessary regression assumptions. Each β_i allows for a different intercept for each cross-sectional unit (here, city), and each γ_t allows for a different intercept for each time period (here, year). In practice, one could include $N - 1$ and $T - 1$ indicator variables for each city and time period. In principle, the regression fit represented by $(\alpha + \boldsymbol{\eta}^{\mathrm{T}}\mathbf{u}_{it})$ is just shifted up or down for each city and time period. Interactions between city and time can be built in, as can interaction between city and/or time and any of the other terms in the model. For example, one can allow for a different relationship between unemployment and homicide in different cities. However, as product variables are added to the regression model, it can rapidly become quite unwieldy and even produce linear dependence among sets of predictors.

Equation 10.7 is called a fixed-time and group-effects model because the indicator dummy variables are treated as fixed. That is, they are the same as any other fixed terms; estimation is undertaken assuming that their values are unchanged over random samples or random realizations. As such, one can proceed with least squares as usual.[7]

10.2.2 Random Effects Models

The main practical problem with fixed effects models is the large number of parameters that may need to be estimated. These can lead to complicated interpretations and high multicollinearity. An alternative that addresses these problems, but adds others, is random effects models.

---

[7]One can simplify the regression model by mean-deviating the data as follows:

$$y^{\star}_{it} = y_{it} - \bar{y}_{i.} - \bar{y}_{.t} + \bar{y}_{..} \tag{10.8}$$

and

$$\mathbf{u}^{\star}_{it} = \mathbf{u}_{it} - \bar{\mathbf{u}}_{i.} - \bar{\mathbf{u}}_{.t} + \bar{\mathbf{u}}_{..}, \tag{10.9}$$

where the three means are for time periods, cases, and total observations, respectively. After running the regression on these "mean-deviated" observations, one can recover the different intercepts, if that is desirable.

For ease of exposition, the indicator variables for time periods are replaced by one or more functions of time included within $\mathbf{x}_{it}$ to control for smooth fixed effects of time (e.g., a linear trend). The new model specification is

$$y_{it}|\mathbf{x}_{it} = \alpha + \beta_i + \eta^{\mathrm{T}}\mathbf{u}_{it} + e_{it}, \qquad (10.10)$$

but the β_i is now random and represents a single random variable that shifts the intercepts for cities and is constant over time.

In addition, nature generates the data so that each of the following is true for all i, t, j:

$$\begin{aligned} E(e_{it}) = E(\beta_i) &= 0 \\ E(e_{it})^2 &= \sigma_e^2 \\ E(\beta_i)^2 &= \sigma_\beta^2 \\ E(e_{it}\beta_j) &= 0 \\ E(e_{it}e_{js}) &= 0 \\ E(\beta_i\beta_j) &= 0. \end{aligned}$$

The β_i is really just a new set of errors with the same basic properties as e_{ij} and uncorrelated with it. The model is sometimes called a "variance components model" because one can treat the sum of β_i and e_{ij} as a new error with two random and uncorrelated components. Conveniently, the number of parameters to be estimated can be dramatically reduced. The $N - 1$ regression coefficients for cities under the fixed effects model have been replaced by σ_β^2 in the random effects model. This is very convenient indeed.

But does it make sense? Here, nature would have to generate homicides something as follows. In a given city, the mean number of homicides each year is $(\alpha + \beta_i + \eta^{\mathrm{T}}\mathbf{u}_{it})$. The values of α and η do not change from year to year and are also the same in the other cities. Thus, the association between unemployment and homicides, for instance, is the same one year to the next. The same goes for other predictors, such as the homicide clearance rate for the police. There is also a random perturbation, β_i, generated once for a given city that is thereafter also constant. Why this particular kind of error is only generated once and not every year would need to be explained. It is very difficult to think of some important feature of cities, related to the number of homicides, that materializes by chance a single time and then does not ever change. And why nature generates the intercept at random but not the regression coefficients would also require considerable discussion.[8]

The realized value for the number of homicides each year is generated by nature with the addition to $(\alpha + \beta_i + \eta^{\mathrm{T}}\mathbf{u}_{it})$ of a random error that is

[8]If the cities were a random sample from a well-defined population, the assumption of random intercepts could be more easily justified. But then why not random regression coefficients as well?

uncorrelated with any of the predictors, with itself from year to year, and with the randomly selected (but then fixed) value of β_i. The variability in these errors is also constant from year to year. Why nature produces such friendly errors would have to be grounded in a credible discussion of exactly how chance factors function in the production of homicides. It is difficult to imagine such a case being made. Why exactly, for instance, is the underlying variability in the errors always the same? Why is the amount of "noise" in the system the same from year to year?

But nature is not finished. The random errors are generated so that they have the same variance and are not correlated across cities. Why the amount of noise in the production of homicides is the same across cities would need to be addressed. Also, there are no chance effects operating at regional or state levels, only at the level of a city. If such effects existed, the errors would be correlated across certain cities. Thus, changes in state penal codes, coordinated law enforcement efforts at the county level, the parole policies of state prisons, drug sweeps aided by federal authorities, and any number of actions by relevant law enforcement agencies across cities are either included in $\mathbf{u}$ or are not important.

When a researcher proceeds with Equation 10.10, a very precise statement is being made about how the natural and social worlds function. Although this is true of any model, the point here is that the statistical convenience of random intercepts necessarily commits the researcher to a theory that can be extremely difficult to justify. There are, of course, a host of variants on random effects models that could allow for more complex processes. But these are no less demanding of nature. For example, one could allow for the errors to be correlated over time within a given city, but then one needs to formulate a model for how nature generates those correlations.

10.2.3 Estimation

There are a large number of estimation procedures. Most produce biased estimates and depend, therefore, on asymptotic properties. But the most popular procedure can be found in all of the major statistical packages.

10.3 Multilevel Models

Multilevel models are a relatively recent development that actually has much in common with earlier regression models for multiple time series data. Not surprisingly, therefore, the proper analysis of multilevel data raises many of the same issues, and the formal tools are closely related. A key similarity is that in both cases, the data are nested. There are a number of excellent textbooks available, including Kreft and de Leeuw (1998) and Bryk and Raudenbush (2002). For our purposes, it is only necessary to work through a simple example.

The school accountability movement depends fundamentally on the use of standardized tests through which students, teachers, and entire schools can be compared. One of the most common uses of multilevel models is to study factors associated with the performance of school children on standardized tests. Because notation gets very heavy very fast, we will consider only two predictors.

Suppose the response variable is performance on a standardized achievement test. The two predictors are the household income of a student and a school's student-teacher ratio. The former reflects the socioeconomic background of the child, and the latter represents the school resources allocated for teaching. The data are a random sample of ten high schools and then all seniors in each high school. Students are nested within schools.

For this example, the students are at the "micro" or "first" level. And for these students, let

$$score_{ij} = \eta_{0j} + \eta_{1j} income_{ij} + e_{ij}, \tag{10.11}$$

where parameters are subscripted as 0 and 1, i refers to the student and j to the school, and e_{ij} is the usual error term. The subscript j attached to the slope and intercept implies that each school has its own equation.

The researcher would like to systematically characterize the similarities and differences in these equations across schools. One strategy would be to employ a fixed effects model, much like the one described earlier, with indicator variables for schools. In principle, one could allow for different intercepts and different slopes. But this may be unsatisfactory for at least three reasons. First, allowance would have to be made for the possibility of different error variances in the different schools. Second, the number of parameters to be estimated could be very large. Third, the role of the student-teacher ratio, which operates at the level of entire schools, has not been considered. In response, one might specify the following relationships (as but one of several possibilities) for the *parameters* in the first-level model. One might write

$$\eta_{0j} = \gamma_{00} + u_{0j} \tag{10.12}$$

and

$$\eta_{1j} = \gamma_{10} + \gamma_{11} ratio_j + u_{1j}, \tag{10.13}$$

where school-level errors u_{0j} and u_{1j} are uncorrelated with each other and the student-level errors e_{ij}.

The intercept is now a random variable with γ_{00} the grand mean across schools and u_{0j} the source of the uncertainty. Note the similarity to the random effects model described above. The slope is now, via school-level regression coefficients γ_{11} and γ_{10}, a linear combination of the student-teacher ratio and another set of random errors u_{1j}. The student-teacher ratio of a school is allowed to affect how each student's background translates into test performance. Much as in the early evaluations of television programs such as *Sesame Street*, perhaps students from more affluent backgrounds are better able to take advantage of available educational resources.

Substituting Equations 10.12 and 10.13 into Equation 10.11,

$$score_{it} = (\gamma_{00} + u_{0j}) + (\gamma_{10} + \gamma_{11}\, ratio_j + u_{1j})\, income_{ij} + e_{ij}, \quad (10.14)$$

which simplifies to

$$\begin{aligned} score_{ij} &= \gamma_{00} + \gamma_{10}\, income_{ij} + \gamma_{11} ratio_j \times income_{ij} \\ &\quad + (income_{ij} \times u_{1j}) + u_{0j} + e_{ij}. \end{aligned} \quad (10.15)$$

Equation 10.15 is a conventional linear regression with a main effect for income and an interaction effect between income and the student-teacher ratio. As such, there is nothing very mysterious. However, the errors no longer have constant variance because of the product of income and the school-level errors associated with the first-level slope parameter. Applying least squares to Equation 10.15 will produce unbiased estimates of the two regression coefficients and intercept but, because of the usual constant variance assumption, will get the estimates of the standard errors wrong. However, there is a wide variety of consistent estimators that do a much better job with the standard errors.

The multilevel framework can be generalized beyond this simple example in a number of ways:

- Using many predictors, but at the risk of very high multicollinearity[9]
- Employing a mix of random and fixed effects for different coefficients
- Using binary response variables (see below)
- Allowing for nonconstant variance and dependence for the first-level errors

More relevant for our purposes is how realistic multilevel models are likely to be in practice. Equation 10.11 is just a simple linear regression but with all of the difficulties already discussed. Here, for example, one would have to consider at some length how nature operates so as to make the first-level errors uncorrelated with income (or, more likely, some set of regression terms), and why the variance of those errors is constant across children who differ in many important ways. And what does it mean to say that the two regression

[9]When multilevel models are constructed, it is common not to do the substitution illustrated in Equation 10.15. It may then not be apparent how many interaction terms are being added to the model and how hard the multicollinearity envelope is being pushed. It is often very useful to do those substitutions and estimate the resulting model with ordinary least squares. (Recall that the estimates of the regression coefficients are, in principle, unbiased.) Then, one has easy access to all of the usual regression diagnostics, including those for multicollinearity. Careful examination of those diagnostics can be very enlightening and rather humbling.

parameters at the first level are random variables generated by Equations 10.12 and 10.13? The random intercept raises the same sets of concerns discussed under the random effects models for multiple time series data. But now nature also determines that student income translates into test performance through a linear function not just of the student-teacher ratio but of another random error operating at the level of schools. Why linear? Why are the errors at the school level unrelated to the student-teacher ratio? And why would nature not allow the two school-level errors (for the student-level intercept and slope) to be related? They both function at the level of the school.

Even very simple multilevel models can require complicated stories of how nature generates the data. The complexity of the necessary accounts is then likely to outstrip any existing understandings about how nature really operates, at least in the social and policy sciences. In such a scientific vacuum, the only possible response to any question about "why" may be "why not?" And in such a setting, almost anything goes.

In short, the lesson is once again that fancier models do not, by and large, fix the kinds of problems discussed in earlier chapters. Or if they do, the usual price is a new set of difficulties.

10.4 The Generalized Linear Model

Linear regression is a special case of a larger set of regression formulations subsumed under the "Generalized Linear Model" (GLM). Logistic regression and Poisson regression are two other special cases. By considering the GLM, even briefly, the reach of regression analysis can be extended substantially.[10]

10.4.1 GLM Structure

As before, we let $\mathbf{u}$ be a $k \times 1$ vector of terms derived from $\mathbf{x}$. In the population, the terms are related to y via a linear combination $\boldsymbol{\eta}^{\mathrm{T}}\mathbf{u}$. Or, nature generates the conditional means of y using this expression.

The mean function is given by $E(y|\mathbf{x}) = M(\boldsymbol{\eta}^{\mathrm{T}}\mathbf{u})$, where M is the "kernel mean function." Likewise, there is a variance function, $\mathrm{Var}(y|\mathbf{x}) = v(\boldsymbol{\eta}^{\mathrm{T}}\mathbf{u})$. Thus, within the GLM scheme, the argument in the mean function figures in the variance function. A particular kind of nonconstant variance around the fitted values can be built in.

There is a "canonical mean function," which serves as the "default" mean function, depending on the nature of the response. For normal errors, the

---

[10]The organization of this exposition draws heavily from the fine exposition by Cook and Weisberg (1999: Chapter 23). The classic reference is McCullagh and Nelder (1989).

default is linear. For binomial errors, the default is logistic; for Poisson errors, the default is exponential ($exp(\eta^{\mathrm{T}}\mathbf{u})$); and for gamma errors, the default is reciprocal ($1/\eta^{\mathrm{T}}\mathbf{u}$). In other words, the canonical mean function is determined by the conditional distribution of the response.

However, none of the added flexibility negates the key assumption that the errors are unrelated to the predictors in any of the several ways considered in earlier chapters. This rules out random measurement error in the predictors and systematic measurement error in the response and the predictors, omitted variables, and incorrect functional forms. One must also still rely on information from outside of the data for proper justification of causal inference and statistical inference. The game has not really changed all that much.

10.4.2 Normal Models

When one can assume that the errors have a normal distribution (or, alternatively stated, that $y|\mathbf{x}$ is normal), the canonical choice for the kernel mean function is linear. This is nothing more than the linear regression model we have been considering all along but with the requirement of normal errors. We have also considered already a wide variety of functions for $M(.)$ based on a transformed response.

10.4.3 Poisson Models

For Poisson regression models, the errors have a Poisson distribution that explicitly depends on $\mathbf{x}$. The conditional mean equals the conditional variance. Poisson regression models are most commonly applied when y is a count and the events in the count are independent.

The canonical kernel mean function is the exponential, $exp(\eta^{\mathrm{T}}\mathbf{u})$. This implies that if the logarithm is taken of both sides, the regression coefficients are multipliers of the count. For example, if a regression coefficient is -0.29, then the exponentiated regression coefficient is about 0.75. For every unit increase in that term, the count is reduced by a multiplicative factor of 0.75.

Examples of potential count response variables include such things as the number of commercial plane crashes per year, the number of wildfires in national forests each year, the number of teenage suicides per week, and the number of sea mammals caught in gill nets per year. But in each case, one would need to make the argument that the underlying events are independent and that the conditional mean and conditional variance are the same.

Often, these two conditions are related because a lack of independence makes it unlikely that the conditional mean will equal the conditional variance. Independence can be especially problematic when the events that go into the counts can interact. For example, if the unit of observation is schools and the response is the number of dropouts per year, one would have to assume that whether or not one child drops out is unrelated to whether another child drops out. Given peer pressure, this is probably a stretch.

10.4.3.1 *What If the Conditional Mean and Variance Are Not Equal?*

Perhaps the common and easily diagnosed problem with Poisson regression is that the conditional mean and variance are not the same. Typically, there is "overdispersion" because of heterogeneity among the observational units that is not accounted for in the model. If the data analyst assumes that the mean function is correct, the extra heterogeneity is not because important predictors have been overlooked or improperly represented in the model. The problem lies elsewhere.

It is common to use λ_i as the conditional mean of the Poisson process generating the data. One can directly address the situation in which the conditional variance exceeds the conditional mean by allowing $\lambda_i|\mathbf{x}_i$ to be a random variable, in much the same spirit as the random effects models examined earlier (McCullagh and Nelder, 1989: Section 6.2.3; Scrucca, 2000).

To help keep the notation straight, let $exp(\boldsymbol{\eta}^{\mathrm{T}}\mathbf{u}_i) = \mu_i$ (not λ_i). Now let μ_i be a parameter in a gamma distribution that generates θ_i which, in turn, determines the particular Poisson distribution from which y_i is realized. Between μ_i and y_i has been inserted a new random variable θ_i. More heterogeneity is being built in.

The gamma distribution from which nature generates the values of θ_i has a second parameter $1/\phi$. It then follows that

$$\mathrm{Var}(y_i) = \mu_i + \mu_i^2\phi = \mu_i(1 + \mu_i\phi), \tag{10.16}$$

where, for $\phi > 0$, there is overdispersion. Should $\phi = 0$, the usual Poisson model holds. In practice, one can use $(1 + \mu_i\hat{\phi})^{-1}$ as a weight in an iterative regression procedure, with the estimate of ϕ obtained from an earlier iteration (Breslow, 1984).

There are several other motivating frameworks that can lead to Equation 10.16. One popular version exploits the negative binomial distribution (Long, 1997:230-238).[11] But for our purposes, the main point is that a researcher who adopts this approach is committing to a very precise theory about how natural and/or social processes generate the data. Why two sequentially produced random variables? Why the gamma distribution determined in part by μ_i?

[11] The negative binomial distribution represents the probability of there being N independent trials to see M successes. N is the random variable, and we condition on M. For example, given the need for five successes, what is the probability of that happening in five trials, six trials, seven trials, and so on?

Table 10.2. Sample 2 × 2 Contingency Table

	Hired = 1	Not = 0
Female = 1	12	6
Male = 0	16	4

10.4.4 Poisson Models for Contingency Tables

Poisson models are very closely related to "log-linear" models used to analyze contingency tables because the raw numbers in each cell of a contingency table are counts. Basically, each *cell* in the table becomes an observation. The response is the count in that cell. The terms are binary variables that indicate which cell in the table is involved. So, all of the issues raised earlier can sometimes apply.

For example, suppose there are two variables: gender and whether or not in a pool of job applicants a person is hired. The data could be organized as in Table 10.2.

In this simple example, the cell counts might be assumed to be the sum of a row "effect" and a column "effect." Then, one would estimate the following Poisson regression: $E(y|\mathbf{x}) = exp(\eta_0 + \eta_1 gender + \eta_2 hired)$. This may or may not fit the data well. If not, one could include an interaction variable that is the product of the two main effects: a 1 for the cells in which both main effect variables are one and a 0 otherwise. Within this formulation, the interaction variable (hired × gender), when added to the equation, will represent any association between the two, holding the marginal distributions of hired and gender constant. In this illustration, the regression coefficient associated with the interaction effect would likely be the key parameter of interest. A negative regression coefficient, which would translate into a fractional multiplier, would mean that female applicants would be less likely to be hired than male applicants. As before, it matters a great deal for statistical inference how the data were generated. However, insofar as the point of the analysis is to estimate an association, not a causal effect, concerns about response schedules and related matters fall away. This is a theme to which we will return in the next chapter.

10.4.5 Binomial Regression

Suppose that y is a binary outcome: arrested or not, school dropout or not, made a profit or did not, at war or at peace, and so on. Then, let y_i be a binomial random variable with θ_i as the probability that $y_i = 1$. But now let θ_i be a function of a linear combination of terms so that one can write

$$\theta(\mathbf{x}_i) = M(\eta^{\mathrm{T}}\mathbf{u}_i). \quad (10.17)$$

What should the kernel mean function M be? One could use any number of different functions as long as they are smooth and bounded at zero and one. Perhaps the most popular is the logistic, written as follows:

$$M(\eta^{\mathrm{T}}\mathbf{u}_i) = \frac{exp(\eta^{\mathrm{T}}\mathbf{u}_i)}{1 + exp(\eta^{\mathrm{T}}\mathbf{u}_i)} = \frac{1}{1 + exp(-\eta^{\mathrm{T}}\mathbf{u}_i)}. \tag{10.18}$$

The logistic is an S-shaped function that is bounded at zero and one. It is symmetric and nearly linear for more than half of its length. Another feature is that, consistent with the discussion so far, the variance is a function of the mean, so no additional parameter is required. The nonconstant variance is addressed directly.

One can also write equivalently the expression for logistic regression as

$$\log_e\left(\frac{p_i}{(1 - p_i)}\right) = \eta^{\mathrm{T}}\mathbf{u}_i. \tag{10.19}$$

The expression to the left of the equal sign is the "logit." In the logit form, one can more easily see the connections to what was covered under the linear regression model, and it is the form with the most straightforward interpretation.

If both sides of Equation 10.19 are exponentiated, the regression coefficients become odds multipliers. A one-unit change in the term u_j multiplies the odds of the outcome by $\exp(\hat{\eta}_j)$, other terms held constant. For example, if the regression coefficient is 0.30, the odds multiplier is 1.35. If the regression coefficient is -0.30, the odds multiplier is 0.74. A regression coefficient of 0.0 leads to an odds multiplier of 1.0.

The parameters for logistic regression are typically estimated via maximum likelihood procedures. Therefore, all of the desirable properties of the estimates are only justified in larger samples. And all of the other concerns raised about linear regression still apply.

10.4.5.1 *Elaborations*

As an alternative to the logistic function, some investigators, especially in economics, prefer the cumulative normal. This leads to a probit form of binomial regression. The fit is much the same except for the extreme tails.

The probit regression coefficients are often reported in standard deviation units and have essentially the same interpretation as they do in linear regression. A common justification is that the "real" response is an equal-interval latent variable. The data contain only an indicator variable for whether the response is or is not above some threshold. For example, if the underlying latent response is frustration, the manifest response may be a violent act when that frustration exceeds some threshold of self-control. Still, the regression coefficients represent the change in the average value of the latent variable in standard deviation units for a one-unit change in the term.[12]

---

[12] See Long (1997:Chapter 3) for an excellent discussion of logit versus probit models.

Overdispersion can be an issue in binomial regression as well as Poisson regression. The problem can occur when there are $m > 1$ independent trials for θ_i; that is, there is more than one realization from the underlying binomial distribution for a given value of θ_i. For example, there may be 31 high school students who use one set of materials to study for the SATs and 43 matched students who use another set of materials. So, there are 31 trials in the first case and 43 trials in the second. Logistic regression assumes that the variance around the fit is $m_i\theta_i(1 - \theta_i)$.

But if, for example, the responses are correlated over the m trials, the data can become "lumpy," and overdispersion can result. For example, each of the elementary schools in a school district may be modeled as having the same probability of receiving money from the state for building improvements. But whether one school in the district receives money may well be related to whether another school does.

The "solution" to such problems is to treat θ_i as a random variable generated by nature from a beta (not gamma) distribution. This leads to a weighting function and an iterative regression estimator (Williams, 1982). Once again, nature must act in a very complicated way that would be almost impossible to evaluate with data. There are also some artificial restrictions on the values key parameters can take.

Finally, there are extensions of binomial regression that are not formally part of the generalized linear model but retain much the same flavor. These include the following (Long, 1997):

- multinomial logistic regression for categorical responses with more than two categories;
- ordinal logistic regression when there is an inherent ordering among the categories; and
- conditional logistic regression, developed in part for case-control studies when there is matching.

The overall point is that binomial regression and its extensions tackle new problems created by categorical response variables. The old problems associated with linear regression remain, and some of the new ones are not necessarily solved. By now, this is the same old story.

10.5 Multiple Equation Models

Multiple equation models contain two or more equations, each with its own response variable. The equations are constructed so that they are statistically related. Three kinds of statistical relationship are popular.

First, the equations may be related through their errors. For example, in very much the same spirit as multilevel models, there may be a regression equation for students in each of ten primary schools. The ten regression equations may have errors that are correlated across schools, perhaps because all are in the same school district and are administered by the same bureaucracy. Chance factors at the level of the school district may tend to affect all of the students in similar ways regardless of their school. No new issues relevant to our concerns are raised by such models.

Second, one or more of the variables in a regression model may be seen as indicators of one or more latent variables that cannot be measured directly. In addition to the usual regression equation, now including symbols for the latent variables, there are other "measurement" equations representing how the indicators are linked to the latent variable. For example, social class can be seen as a latent variable with education, income, and occupation as indicators. In that sense, the latent variable is a "cause" of the realized values of the indicators. Although latent variable models add a number of new concepts and depend on extremely complex views of how nature is assumed to operate, there are no new issues relevant to our concerns here. The differences are differences of degree. Still, if some of the applications discussed earlier seem to stretch credibility, latent variable models will often seem over the top.

Third, the equations may be linked because the response variable in one equation is taken to be a predictor in one or more other equations. In the recursive case, there is a set of cascading relationships. Thus, for example, the conditional mean of y depends on x, and the conditional mean of x depends on z. The response variables y and x may be related to a number of other predictors as well. For the system to be recursive, we require that the errors in the two equations, usually assumed to meet the least squares assumptions, be uncorrelated across equations as well. The key interpretive point is y's dependence on x and x's dependence on z.

To illustrate, the assertiveness of graduate students may be related on the average to the amount of mentoring they receive, and the amount of mentoring may be related on the average to the prestige of their first academic jobs. At the same time, the errors from the mentoring equation are uncorrelated with the errors from the prestige equation. In practice, recursive multiple equation models can have a large number of equations linked in this cascading fashion.

In the nonrecursive case, the conditional mean of y, for example, depends on x and the conditional mean of x depends on y. The conditional mean of either or both y and x may be related to z and a number of other predictors. We will soon see that compared to the errors for recursive models, the errors for nonrecursive models are not nearly so cooperative. But the key interpretative point is the mutual dependence between y and x.

To illustrate, in big city police departments, the average amount of crime may be related to the proportion of crimes that are cleared by arrest, and the average proportion of crimes that are cleared may be related to the amount of crime. The average amount of crime may also be associated with the proportion of the male population under the age of 25 in a city. The clearance rate may be linked to the number of police officers. Just like for recursive models, a large number of equations may be involved.

There are really no new statistical issues of the sort that have been our main concern. Consider, for instance, the risk of "simultaneous equation bias" common in nonrecursive models. The response variables from one equation, when used as predictors in other equations, will be correlated with the errors in those equations. To see why this is true, consider two multiple regression equations, each much like those discussed earlier:

$$y_i = \alpha_0 + \alpha_1 x_i + \alpha_2 z_i + e_i \tag{10.20}$$

and

$$x_i = \beta_0 + \beta_1 y_i + \beta_2 w_i + v_i. \tag{10.21}$$

A least squares estimate of α_1 will require an estimate of the covariance between y_i and x_i. But because x_i in Equation 10.21 is a function of y_i, which in Equation 10.20 is a function of e_i, e_i cannot be pulled out of the estimated covariance. It is confounded with x_i. Consequently, a least squares estimate of α_1 will be biased and inconsistent. The estimate of α_2 will likely be biased and inconsistent as well.

The general lesson is that in nonrecursive models, trying to estimate the regression coefficients with ordinary least squares is problematic because the errors are correlated with predictors. We have seen this particular problem several times now, and one solution, just as before, is to employ an instrumental variable estimator. There are some additional complexities to be sure, but for our discussion, those are details.

More important for our purposes is that it is very difficult to talk about, let alone specify, multiple equation models without slipping into causal language. Should one look at $y|x$, $x|y$, or both? If one or the other, a natural justification may be that x causes y or that y causes x. If both, what does the apparent simultaneity mean?[13]

It is not surprising that multiple equation models have been the key tools for many researchers who study complicated cause-and-effect relationships. When used in this fashion, regression with multiple equations is often called "structural equation modeling" (SEM). The regression equations are explicitly meant to represent the mechanisms by which causes have their effects. That is, they are supposed to reveal what the value of one or more response variables would be if a given predictor is set to a certain value, other predictors held constant. Causal inference is now front and center.

Much of the existing practice is presented in a number of texts (e.g., Duncan, 1975; Bollen, 1989; Greene, 2000; Kaplan, 2000), although the nature of causal

[13] One popular explanation is that, if the process represented could be observed carefully at short enough time intervals, one would see x affecting y one moment and y affecting x the next. The apparent simultaneity is a result of observing the data at too coarse a time interval.

inference is not usually considered in great depth. However, the work of Judea Pearl, now summarized in a widely discussed book (Pearl, 2000), has made causal inference for structural equation models a very visible issue. Loosely stated, the claim is made that one *can* routinely do causal inference with regression analysis of observational data. Given the stance toward causal inference taken up to now in this book, Pearl's claims need to be carefully examined.

10.5.1 Causal Inference Once Again

10.5.1.1 *A Brief Refresher on Response Schedules*

Recall the earlier discussions of response schedules. A response schedule applies to a single observational unit: a person, a household, a city, a stand of trees, a stream, a business firm, and so on. A response schedule provides a formal structure in which to consider what the value of the response y would be if an input x were set to some value. More commonly, the inputs are a vector $\mathbf{x}$.

Thus, response schedules can, in principle, be applied to a wide variety of policy questions. How many handguns, for example, would be turned over if a city's buy-back program offered $20 per weapon? What would be the impact on a stream's sediment loading if a new housing development were not permitted to become closer than 200 yards? What would the unemployment rate for the United States be if the minimum wage were set at $10 an hour? What would be the reading scores of fourth-grade students in a school district if class size were 20 students? What would be the number of cars running the red light at a particular intersection if an automatic camera to record violators were installed? How much water would a particular household use per month if there were fines levied for use 25% greater than that household's average past use? What is the probability that a prison inmate would find a job after release, after having participated in a 20-week job training program in prison? How many salmon would return to spawn in a given watershed if its three dams were removed?

These are questions posed within a particular setting so that, for instance, the number of returning salmon would depend on which watershed was targeted for dam removal and when the demolition might occur. The response schedule is setting specific as well. Thus, there are no salmon (and there never were as best we know) in streams feeding into the Gulf of Mexico. Context really matters and cannot be abstracted away. Indeed, in many applications, it will make good sense to take the different contexts into account with particular context variables. Recall that this was a way in which fixed attributes could be usefully included in response schedules.

The scenarios implied also include an input that could be manipulated in the world as we know it. Gun buy-back programs, for instance, have been tried in a number of jurisdictions. One could easily imagine zoning laws and/or building codes to protect nearby streams. Class size requirements have actually been legislated in California and elsewhere.

More problematic would be four other technical requirements if the role of the causal input is to be isolated:

1. the errors are drawn independently of the x;
2. the response schedule coefficients are not altered by x;
3. the response schedule for any given observational unit is unaffected by the experiences of other observational units; and
4. confounded variables can be held constant.

For each of the questions posed, a case would have to be made that all of these conditions were at least approximately true. Otherwise, the response schedule formulation would not apply. And without such a formulation, the "what-if" questions cannot be answered.

The important point is that a credible response schedule is a necessary condition for causal inference. Moreover, there is rarely much information in the data themselves about making the case one way or another. The key information comes from outside of the data.

10.5.1.2 *Judea Pearl and Fellow Travelers*

Pearl's contribution and others like it (Spirtes et al., 1993; Glymour and Cooper, 1999) provide a formal logic for determining which conditional distributions can be estimated from the data. Sometimes, this is advertised as inferring causal relationships, typically from observational data. In fact, the enterprise *begins* with a set of possible "causal" models taken as given. Causality is not discovered. It is built in.

Pearl's key heuristic device is a directed acyclic graph (DAG), which is essentially a conventional path diagram with a number of formal mathematical properties attached. These properties need not trouble us much here for reasons that will be apparent shortly.

Pearl's (2000:44) opening move is to define a "causal structure" as follows:

> A causal structure of a set of variables V is a directed acyclic graph (DAG) in which each node corresponds to a distinct element of V, and each link represents a direct functional relationship among the corresponding variables.

A functional relationship is, in Pearl's (2000:32) words, "convenient language for specifying how the resulting distribution would change in response to external interventions." This is very similar to the language used by Freedman (2001) initially to characterize response schedules. For Pearl, then, a "causal model" is basically a more detailed causal structure in which the relevant equations and parameters are specified. Yet Pearl's causal model does not include many of the details that Freedman provides for response schedules.

There is no serious discussion about how nature is supposed to behave in order for the response schedule takes the form it does.

With these definitions in hand, one of Pearl's central concerns is "inferred causation" (Pearl, 2000:45-48). Pearl relies on the concept of a latent structure, which is a proposed causal structure for the data on hand. Two latent structures are equivalent if, with a proper choice of parameters and functional forms, they imply the same conditional distributions. Each latent structure in a set of such structures is "minimal" if it can produce the same conditional distributions and only those. A structure is consistent with the data if it reproduces the observed conditional distributions. Ideally, latent structures should be minimal and consistent with the data. Finally, with $\hat{P}$ as the distribution of the data, "inferred causation" is defined as follows:

> Given $\hat{P}$, a variable C has a causal influence on variable E if and only if there exists a directed path from C to E in every minimal latent structure consistent with $\hat{P}$.

Loosely speaking, if every minimal structure consistent with the data requires that the C and E are linked by a directed path, one has inferred a causal relationship. Pearl provides a set of algorithms for determining when this is true.

One is certainly free to define concepts as one chooses, but Pearl's contribution (Section 3.4) is to provide tools for winnowing down a set of proposed causal models and then determining for this subset whether they speak with one voice about a particular causal relationship. This can be useful, but for each of the candidate models, causality is already built in; it is assumed. Cause and effect is *not* being discovered from the data. In fact, data only enter the process after the candidate causal models are specified. And there is not any requirement that the candidate causal models make much sense.

It is this last feature that is perhaps the most troubling. There are precious few real applications in Pearl's definitive book. Most of the examples are cartoons designed to assist in the exposition. But consider the illustration called "Example: Sex Discrimination in College Admissions" (Pearl, 2000:128-130). This is supposed to be a "real" example. The policy concern, despite the title, is the role that gender might play in *graduate* admissions to the University of California's Berkeley campus.[14] The point of the example is to show how DAGs can help formulate direct and indirect causal effects.

Figure 10.1 is a reproduction of Pearl's DAG. One can see that gender is assumed to directly cause an applicant's career objectives, choice of academic department, and admissions outcome. Choice of department is also directly affected by career objectives. And the admissions outcome is also directly

---

[14]This example is described in Freedman et al. (1998:17-20) and is taken from Bickel and O'Connell (1975).

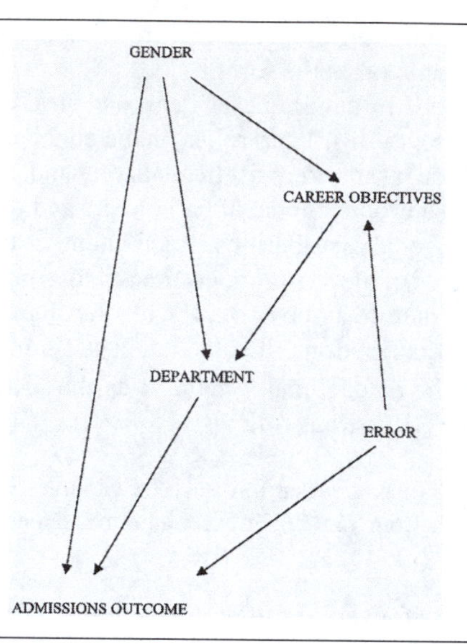

Figure 10.1. Admissions to Berkeley

affected by the choice of department. A key complication is that the unobservable error, which might include such factors as "aptitude," affects both career objectives and the admissions outcome.

Pearl provides no justification for the diagram or why one should assume that cause and effect is represented. There are certainly no data brought to bear. Indeed, the point is to consider carefully the DAG before looking at the data for what *might* be learned about cause and effect. A natural question for us, therefore, is what conceptual sense the diagram makes. This is an undertaking in the same spirit as our earlier discussions of response schedules.

Imagine a Berkeley applicant named Kelly. The central policy question involves the role of gender.[15] What would be the admissions outcome if Kelly's gender were "set" to female, other factors held constant? And what would be the admission outcome if Kelly's gender were "set" to male, other factors held constant? The wording is a little awkward precisely because gender, as Pearl means it, is not something that can be manipulated. Indeed, the language is very telling; there is no appropriate verb. In contrast, one can set the minimum wage, build a logging road, determine the faculty-student ratio, give a patient medication, or apply herbicides.

---

[15] Actually "sex" is a more appropriate term than "gender." The policy issue has to do with a fixed biological attribute, not the full complex biological and social processes linked to that attribute. But it may be important to stay as close as possible to Pearl's actual example. So, gender it is.

And nature does not manipulate gender either, once fertilization has been achieved. Nature does not have the option of altering gender when a college senior applies to graduate school. But by now, all this is old news. The problems with fixed human attributes as causes were discussed at length earlier. In order to get more issues on the table, let's pretend for now that gender can be altered.

Gender is the sole determinant of Kelly's career objectives save for some error attached at random and in a fashion unrelated to gender.[16] Thus, encouragement from Kelly's parents and friends about career objectives, presumably folded into the errors, is unrelated to whether Kelly is male or female. Berkeley may discriminate, but Kelly's parents and friends treat a male college senior the same as a female college senior when careers are the issue. Thus, they will encourage or discourage any aspirations to be a nurse in the same manner whether Kelly is a he or a she.

Gender and career objectives fully determine the choice of the Berkeley department. Nothing else matters, and the process is deterministic. Thus, for example, Kelly's college major is irrelevant. And the choice of department cannot affect career objectives. Thus, Kelly is not allowed to decide to become a computer scientist as a result of first choosing, based on interest alone, to apply to the mathematics department. But these are, in some sense, quibbles that could be addressed with a better causal model. A far more unsettling issue is what direct and indirect effects might mean.

The direct effect of altering gender on the admissions outcome has to be determined holding department and career objectives constant. There is an indirect path from gender to admissions via department. And there is an additional link reflecting a "spurious association" because both gender and the errors affect career objectives and the admissions outcome.

It is very difficult to understand what holding constant means in this context.[17] For example, gender needs to be set with career objectives fixed. On the other hand, by setting gender, career objectives are supposed to be altered. This would seem to be a serious contradiction. Moreover, exactly how would career objectives be held constant? Would the graduate dean have to promulgate and enforce a rule that Kelly (and all students applying to Berkeley) be allowed only one set of career objectives once gender has been determined? Although it is far easier to imagine as a bureaucratic matter how department might be held constant, the same apparent contradiction surfaces. How can department be held constant while gender is set?

Despite these and other serious conceptual problems with the model, Pearl provides expressions to compute the direct effect of gender on admissions. The point is not that the model is inadequate or even internally contradictory. The point is that Pearl claims to be able to isolate the direct causal effects of

---

[16]Nowhere are we told what career objectives really are or how they are measured. So, one cannot be very specific about the distribution from which the errors are generated.

[17]Closely related issues are addressed in Freedman (1987).

gender anyway. Clearly, his procedures and the similar procedures of others are insensitive to whether the depiction of social and natural processes makes any subject matter sense.

In short, what Pearl really provides is a set of tools to (a) help researchers think far more clearly as causal models are specified, (b) help select a subset of candidate causal models, and (c) determine which causal effects are formally consistent with these models. Thus, Pearl's work is in much the same spirit as model selection and parameter identification procedures in statistics and econometrics. Claims that causal effects can be inferred from the observational data are overenthusiastic. You put cause in, and you can get cause out. Otherwise, you don't.

10.5.2 A Final Observation

The language of Pearl and many others can obscure that, beneath all multiple equation models, there is only a set of conditional distributions. And all that the data analysis can do by itself is summarize key features of those conditional distributions. This is really no different from models using single equations. With multiple equations, additional complexity is just laid on top. Including more equations per se does not bring the researcher any closer to cause and effect.

10.6 Meta-Analysis

Meta-analysis does not really fit within this chapter or perhaps even within this book. Regression analysis is not central to its mission. But regression analysis, is sometimes used in meta-analysis, and, more important, meta-analysis, is perhaps the latest in a long list of cure-alls for whatever ails policy-related research. Given the issues raised in earlier chapters, its claimed benefits need to be briefly addressed.[18]

Meta-analysis has two related goals. First, meta-analysis is supposed to be a more thorough and systematic way to conduct a formal literature review. Second, meta-analysis is sold as a method to increase the statistical power brought to bear on any estimation problem when there is more than one relevant study on which to draw.

> The first step in a meta-analysis is to extract the statistical results of numerous studies, perhaps hundreds, and assemble them in a database along with coded information about the important features of the studies producing these results. Analysis of this database can then yield generalizations about the body of research represented and relationships within it. (Lipsey, 1997:15)

[18]This section draws very heavily on Berk and Freedman (2003).

Researchers usually pay close attention to the response variables in each study because the intent is to combine them in a manner that reveals something not apparent from any single studies alone. Lipsey (1992), for example, assesses the effectiveness of a large number of juvenile delinquency treatment programs. Sherman and his colleagues (1997) examine a wide variety of other criminal justice interventions. Archer (2000) considers the role of sex differences in domestic violence. Meta-analysis is discussed in several accessible texts (e.g., Lipsey and Wilson, 2001) and anthologies (e.g., Cook et al., 1992). Statistical inference is usually a key feature of the exposition. We turn to that now.

Drawing heavily on the exposition of Hedges and Olkin (1985) but relaxing some of their assumptions slightly, the language of experimental studies with human subjects will be used. However, meta-analysis is certainly not limited to such studies.

Let responses for the experimental subjects be Y_{ij}^E and the responses for the control subjects be Y_{ij}^C. The subscript i indexes the study and the subscript j indexes a subject within a study. Thus, Y_{ij}^E is the response of the jth experimental subject in the ith study. There are a total of k studies, with n_i^E experimentals and n_i^C controls in the ith study.

For each study included in the meta-analysis, we assume the following:

(I) Y_{ij}^E are independent and identically distributed for $j = 1, \ldots, n_i^E$; these variables have common expectation μ_i^E and variance σ_i^2.

Likewise,

(II) Y_{ij}^C are independent and identically distributed for $j = 1, \ldots, n_i^C$; these variables have common expectation μ_i^C and variance σ_i^2.

Note that μ_i^E, μ_i^C, and σ_i^2 are unobservable parameters and that the variances in I and II are assumed to be equal. But there is more.

(III) The responses of the experimental and control subjects are independent.

Assumptions I and II force within-group independence and III adds the assumption of between-group independence. Finally, assume the following.

(IV) All of the included studies are independent of one another.

Now, let $\bar{Y}_i^E$ be the average response for the experimental subjects in study i, and $\bar{Y}_i^C$ be the average response for the control subjects. These averages may be computed for a given study and are commonly reported as part of any write-up of the analysis. It follows from I and II that, to a reasonable approximation,

$$\bar{Y}_i^E \sim N(\mu_i^E, \sigma_i^2/n_i^E), \qquad i = 1, \ldots, k, \tag{10.22}$$

and

$$\bar{Y}_i^C \sim N(\mu_i^C, \sigma_i^2/n_i^C), \qquad i = 1, \ldots, k. \tag{10.23}$$

For the ith study, define the "effect size" as

$$\eta_i = \frac{\mu_i^E - \mu_i^C}{\sigma_i}. \tag{10.24}$$

Finally, there is to be only one true effect size,

$$\eta_1 = \eta_2 = \cdots = \eta_k = \eta. \tag{10.25}$$

The estimated value of η_i for a given study is that study's effect size. For instance, if $\hat{\eta}_i = 0.30$, the intervention shifts the distribution of responses to the right by 30% of a standard deviation.

Assumptions I, II, and III *require* that treatment and control subjects for each study are drawn as independent random samples from two different populations with a common standard deviation. The standardization in Equation 10.24 removes any differences in scale. Thus, differing measurement units across studies do not matter. Equation 10.25 requires that there is but a *single* parameter value for the effect size over all of the studies. We are back in the world of standardized relationships.

Finally, the common effect can be estimated by computing a weighted average,

$$\hat{\eta} = w_1\hat{\eta}_1 + \cdots + w_k\hat{\eta}_k, \tag{10.26}$$

where

$$\hat{\eta}_i = (\bar{Y}_i^E - \bar{Y}_i^C)/\hat{\sigma}_i. \tag{10.27}$$

In Equation 10.26, $\hat{\sigma}_i$ represents the common standard deviation from the sample; the weights w_i adjust for differences in sample size across studies. Also, standard errors for $\hat{\eta}$ can be computed because the estimator is the product of a convenient and well-defined chance process.

But how likely is all this to square with how the data were actually generated? The experimental and control subjects will almost certainly not be drawn at random from populations with a common variance. It is also at least heroic to assume that *standardized* effects are constant across studies. For instance, why would 14 different studies of the impact of boot camp programs for first offenders each produce exactly a 1.5 standard deviation reduction in subsequent crime? Matters get even more sticky if the outcomes are somewhat different across studies, which is often the case: average length of time until a new arrest, number of crimes self-reported, number of felony convictions in a two-year follow-up, and so on. In that case, the standardization may also obscure the fact that different kinds of outcomes are being combined in a manner that may make little conceptual sense.

But if the common standardized effect assumption is heroic, the assumed independence across studies is an out-and-out fantasy. As Berk and Freedman (2001) observe,

> Investigators are trained in similar ways, read the same papers, talk to one another, write proposals for funding to the same agencies, and publish the findings after peer review. Earlier studies beget later studies, just as each generation of Ph.D. students trains the next. After the first few million dollars are committed, granting agencies develop agendas of their own, which investigators learn to accommodate. Meta-analytic summaries of past work further channel the effort. There is, in short, a web of social dependence inherent in all scientific research. Does social dependence compromise statistical independence? Only if you think that investigators' expectations, attitudes, preferences, and motivations affect the written word—and never forget those peer reviewers.

The basic model just described is often extended to allow for the possibility of different effect sizes. That is, Equation 10.25 no longer holds. Under a random effects model, the η_is are presumed drawn as a random sample from some population of ηs. Then, the goal is to estimate the grand mean μ of this population of ηs. However, as a practical matter, meta-analysis rests on a convenience sample of studies or the whole population of studies. Consequently, the random effects model simply does not apply.[19]

The random effects model can be reconfigured so that the ith study measures η_i, with an intrinsic error, the size of which is determined by Equations 10.22 through 10.24. Then, η_i differs from the grand mean μ by random error having a mean value of zero and constant variance across all potential studies. Such a "components-of-variance" model does not help. Why would these new assumptions be true? Which potential studies are being sampled, and what parameters are being estimated? Are we back into the world of superpopulation?

Even if it were possible to sensibly answer such questions, it is likely that each study's estimated effects vary from truth because of some intrinsic but differing bias. Enter regression analysis.

The observational unit is the study, with the response variable as the estimated effect size. Predictors can be almost any feature of the treatment, outcome, study subjects, study setting, or research design. The goal is to explain why effect sizes differ across studies. Statistical inference is driven by the sort of random sampling assumptions discussed in earlier chapters. However, with research

---

[19]The model now requires two kinds of random sampling: a random sample of studies and then a random sample of study subjects.

studies now as the unit of analysis, the random sampling assumption becomes especially puzzling. And one has to address all of the other issues associated with a credible regression analysis. Perhaps the most interesting question is why the technique is so widely used.[20]

Meta-analysis can be extended to include binary outcomes (e.g., live or die), but the basic problems remain. Meta-analysis can also be applied to randomized experiments. But the canonical model described above still does not play through unless the experimental and control subjects are sampled at random from a population that is much larger than the number of observational units actually assigned at random. If the full pool of potential subjects is used or even a substantial fraction of that pool, dependence between the sampled units automatically follows. Further details can be found in Berk and Freedman (2003).

In short, meta-analysis is certainly not the silver bullet that some of its proponents claim. Trying to do a systematic review of past studies is surely a good idea. And some of the discipline imposed by a careful coding and tabulating of studies can certainly be useful. But meta-analysis can stumble badly when it tries to combine studies with very different outcome measures just because they all can be put into standard deviation units. And it surely falls when it tries to undertake formal statistical inference using any of several models that depend on random sampling of subjects, studies, or both. Then, inferences are being made to some ill-defined or even imaginary population using estimates of unknown quality and standard errors that are likely to be very misleading. This is a ruse that can have real consequences.

10.7 Conclusions

The conclusions to this chapter can be easily written. Getting fancier can be helpful when there are very specific problems that are not well addressed within the usual linear regression framework and when there are alternative procedures that really do solve those problems. Logistic regression for binary outcomes is a good example. However, the vast majority of difficulties discussed in earlier chapters are typically not addressed with more complicated statistical techniques. Indeed, fundamental difficulties are largely ignored. And sometimes, important new complications are introduced.

One should also be skeptical about any claims that there is some technical fix in which weak data can be turned into strong conclusions. Thus, for example, one cannot use directed acyclic graphs to infer causal effects. Either causal effects are built in through information external to the data or they are not. If the goal is to find out what would happen if some variable were manipulated, the best strategy will usually be to go out and do it, and to do it within a

[20]For other commentaries, see Oakes (1990) or Petitti (1999).

solid research design. Likewise, if the goal is to generalize from a collection of estimated causal effects, formal meta-analysis will often obscure more than it enlightens. The underlying models depend on a random sampling of studies and observational units within studies. Although the usual literature reviews certainly have their problems as well, at least there is no technical razzle-dazzle conferring a credibility that is not really there. In short, fancier is not necessarily better; it will often be worse.

11 What to Do

A man has to know his limitations. (Dirty Harry)

Much of the material presented to this point has been critical of current practice. A great deal of the applied research used to inform public policy has been taken to task. But in the effort to raise concerns about practices that can be counterproductive, there have been relatively few suggestions about how research practices might be improved. In this chapter, we turn to such issues. So that there is no confusion: Regression analysis *can* be a very useful research tool when it is applied in combination with other approaches and when it is not asked to undertake tasks for which it is ill suited.

11.1 How Did We Get Into This Mess?

In the eyes of a growing number of knowledgeable observers, the practice of regression analysis and its extensions is a disaster. Consider de Leeuw's (1994:142) take on issues.

> In many quantitative disciplines, most typically econometrics, the appropriate statistical method is to assume a statistical model, then collect the data, then test the model by comparing the statistics with the model. If the model does not *fit* it is rejected. This is supposedly "sticking out one's neck," which is presumably

> the macho Popper thing to do. There are various things problematic with this prescription. They are now tedious to repeat, but here we go anyway. In the first place, if you follow the prescription, and your data are any good, your head gets chopped off. In the second place, because people know their head will get chopped off, nobody follows the prescription. They collect data, look at their data, modify their model, look again, stick out their neck a tiny bit, modify the model again, and finally walk around with a proud look on their face and a non-rejected model in their hands, pretending to have followed the Popperian prescription. Thus the prescription leads to fraud. The only reason it is still around is because some scientists take their models, and themselves, too seriously.

Yes, self-importance is no doubt a significant factor. But there is a lot more involved. This is not the place to undertake a sociology of current research practices. But to set the context for what follows, a few informal observations may be useful.

To begin, the primary technical literature on regression analysis and related procedures is typically quite careful about necessary assumptions and other constraints. Recall, for example, the discussion of meta-analysis. Hedges and Olkin (1985) are rather clear on what is required for the statistical models to perform as advertised. But somehow that information got lost in the translation into textbooks (e.g., Lipsey and Wilson, 2001) and then into practice. One can find a similar slippage in other expositions over a wide range of material. And it is certainly possible to do better. The introductory statistics textbook by Freedman, Pisani, and Purves (1998) is an outstanding example. Kennedy's text (1998) is an unusually sensible treatment of econometrics. And the text on applied regression analysis by Cook and Weisberg (1999) is clear, honest, and circumspect.

A related problem is that there is too often no equivalent of the Food and Drug Administration warning labels on the materials that researchers consult, or else those labels are too skimpy to be of much use. Researchers who learn their statistics on the fly by reading the manuals from major software packages would seem to be especially vulnerable. University classes based on such material certainly don't help. Nor do the many recent books that show how to apply various statistical procedures within a certain software package such as SPSS, STATA, or SAS (e.g., Rabe-Hesketh and Everitt, 2000) or programming languages such as S or R (e.g., Venables and Ripley, 2002). In all fairness, these books are not intended to teach statistics. Unfortunately, some practitioners seem to read them as if they are.

The professional practices of the statistical community have played into the dumbing-down process. Demanding theoretical work confers high status among statisticians. In order to obtain clean results, assumptions and simplifications are often employed that bear little relationship to real data or important empirical questions. If the most mathematically sophisticated statisticians do not seem to worry about whether their formulations correspond to the empirical world, why should practitioners? This has led one of my colleagues to observe that there seems to be an internal contradiction within the term *theoretical statistics*.

Such "mathematistry" (Box, 1976:797) also conveys that fancier models are somehow better models. Indeed, it is common in policy-related research to find peer reviews in which perfectly sound work is criticized simply because the statistical *tool du jour* is not employed. It is more important to be seen as working on the technical cutting edge than to get the empirical story right.

Making matters worse are the professional boundaries between theoretical and applied statistics, represented in book and journal titles, divisions within journals, competitions for grant money, and graduate courses in statistics. Fortunately, there is some evidence that, in the best statistics departments, the walls between theoretical and applied statistics are becoming more permeable.

And there is a deeper problem. The language used by statisticians depends fundamentally on abstractions from mathematical statistics: random variables, probability densities, sample spaces, probability limits, and the like. Mapping these concepts to real data can be difficult. An expected value is a mean of sorts, for instance, but loaded down with far more conceptual content. A histogram is both more and less than a probability distribution. A sampling distribution rests on a thought experiment that could never be implemented. Thus, there is often a disconnect between what statisticians are saying and what practitioners hear. And accurate expositions that are also accessible are very difficult to do. On the one hand, if one assumes that the reader has the necessary technical background, a very large number of practitioners are lost. On the other hand, if the requisite didactic material is included, a mini-textbook needs to be provided. Even if it is, there is no guarantee that it will be read.

But a lack of proper guidance for practitioners is not the only problem. For policy-related research, there is often a compelling need to "come up with something." The social issues may be great: getting people off the welfare rolls, reducing crime, cleaning up polluted streams, helping children from poor neighborhoods learn to read, and so on. Under such circumstances, the policy process is not likely to wait for the best answer, or even a good one. Decisions will be made based on the information available at that moment. Often, that information is incomplete or worse.

There is strong motivation, therefore, to deliver analyses that are better, but not necessarily much better, than what is currently available. That usually means setting the quality bar very low and having a good excuse for doing it. When such work is criticized, a common response is to raise the prospect of even worse research. "If I didn't do it, someone else would have." Implied is that the other party may have been even less able to deliver a quality product.

It is certainly true that no matter how low the bar is set, there will always be applied researchers who are capable of delivering something worse. However, capitulating to the threat of junk science has a very high, long-run price. At some point, the entire policy research enterprise is undermined. Policymakers will lose what ability they have to distinguish bad work, especially done on the cheap, from good work. Ideology and politics will then completely dominate the applied research process. The position taken here is that it is important to hold the line on research quality. If the people able to do good work choose not to, the game is surely lost.[1]

More venal motives no doubt figure in as well. As in any field, there are individuals whose main concern is self-promotion, whether it be built on empirical work or on new methods for solving heretofore unsolvable problems. The point, then, is packaging, not content. The many rewards that can follow from effective self-promotion, coupled with very little risk, provide ample incentives.

There is also the problem of arrogance. It seems all too common for applied researchers to believe that by learning how to run SPSS, they will, in the comfort of their offices, be able to routinely answer some of the most vexing policy questions of the day. Their track record to date belies such optimism, but belief in the power of regression models seems to continue unabated.

Finally, policy-related research formulated, undertaken, and ultimately shaped with a strong ideological agenda can be terribly destructive. If your heart is in the right place, your brain must be as well, or so the argument goes. In the extreme, such "advocacy research" seeks to transform sin into virtue.

In the face of so many forces making it difficult to do the right thing, the suggestions to follow may seem pretty weak. I offer them anyway. In these suggestions are whatever comparative advantage I may have. I begin with regression used for description.

11.2 Three Cheers for Description

Regression analysis is inherently a descriptive tool. As Snedecor and Cochran (1980:149, emphasis in the original) note,

> In mathematics Y is called a *function* of X, but in statistics the term *the regression of Y on X* is generally used to describe the relationship.

Regression analysis can almost always be safely used to construct descriptions of the data on hand. Regression may not necessarily be the best tool or even especially responsive to the key subject matter questions, but no harm likely will be done. And on the positive side, a great deal may be learned.

[1] Which is not to say that it won't be lost anyway.

11.2.1 What's Description?

Borrowing from information theory and Simon's (2001) accessible exposition, imagine a string of ninety 0's and 1's in a particular order. For example, the set of 0's and 1's might be (001001001001 . . . 001). One can think of the 0's and 1's as the data.

There is a simple way to summarize the pattern of 0's and 1's: "Repeat 001 thirty times." The summary contains all of the information in the data but characterizes it in an efficient and accessible manner. There is no need for talk of cause and effect or the role of chance. We have "just" a summary of the patterns in the data.

One can consider such summaries to be descriptions. A description is a "formula" through which the data can be reproduced. In this simple illustration, the summary is perfect in the sense that no information is lost. The data can be exactly reproduced from the description. In practice, matters are far more complicated. Even a very good description will only be able to approximately reproduce the data. Ideally, the information lost will be unimportant for the subject matter questions being addressed.

For example, one can show all of the average global temperature readings over the past 100 years or summarize those data with a regression line indicating that, on the average, the temperature has increased 0.01 degrees centigrade per decade. Likewise, one can show all of the earnings from a set of welfare recipients, some in a welfare reform program and some not, or through a regression analysis report that 11% of the program participants compared with 5% of the controls found jobs within six months. Both descriptions are incomplete. But both may be sufficient for the questions at hand.

With description characterized, we now can turn to some applications. In earlier chapters, considerable effort was made to address the ways in which descriptive results from a regression analysis could be effective in a variety of applied settings. We will consider some of these settings more systematically now.

11.2.2 Advocacy Settings

Formal disputes often arise over what the facts really are. Were black employees less likely to be promoted than similarly situated white employees? Does the quality of water from various reservoirs in a city substantially differ? Does air quality vary in a city depending on the economic and racial mix of a neighborhood? Are there important salary differences between male and female faculty members at a particular university, once differences in department and rank are taken into account?

A great deal can ride on the answers to these and a host of other factual questions. And the answers needed, at least at first, are essentially descriptive. Indeed, a solid descriptive answer will often settle the factual matter, and there, regression can often help.

Consider the earlier example of how the State of California allocated funds for new school construction. The legislation was rather clear on factors that should determine how the money was to be distributed. One could then use regression analysis descriptively to determine if, for the period of time in question, those factors (and certainly not race and income) were related to funding. In fact, such regression analyses essentially resolved the facts at issue in an otherwise very contentious matter. New procedures were then developed to more fairly target funds to the school districts that needed them most.

Statistical inference played no role. The data covered all of the school districts in the state for the several years that were at issue. Causal inference also played no role. The regressions were not meant to represent any causal mechanisms nor estimate what would happen if, say, median income in a school district was set to a particular value. Indeed, the idea that median income of a school district could be set to some value is silly on its face. However, ideas about cause and effect helped determine what variables were included in the analysis. Indeed, the legislation specified which features of school districts should determine funding. Speculations about possible causal relationships were stimulated by the results.

The general point, which will be addressed at more length shortly, is that possible causal relationships can surely be used to help inform descriptive analyses, and the descriptive analyses can help generate causal speculations. But regression models used for description are not meant to be a vehicle for causal inference in the way that structural equation modelers usually proceed. No "what-if" questions about causal effects are formally addressed. No causal machinery is represented.

Consider another example. In the City of Los Angeles, a lawsuit was filed charging that the police were using their K-9 units in a way that put minority residents in jeopardy. The charge was that the police were commonly letting their dogs attack minority suspects when there was actually no need for any use of force. Such attacks, moreover, often led to serious injuries requiring medical attention and even hospitalization.

A logistic regression analysis showed that the race of the defendant was unrelated to the odds of injury when similar cases were compared. However, it was also shown that, at the level of the police division (like a police precinct), there were more people bitten in divisions in which there were high proportions of minority residents. The official police response was that such patterns had an easy and legitimate explanation. Areas of the city with greater amounts of crimes for which the K-9 units were especially effective (e.g., burglaries when a search of a building might be necessary) were the very areas to which more K-9 units were sent. These areas typically had high proportions of minority residents. Then, as a matter of simple arithmetic, where there were more dogs, more people were bitten.

Yet a Poisson regression analysis showed that, although the number of people bitten was indeed associated with the frequency of certain kinds of crime, there remained large associations between the racial composition of a police division and the number of people bitten. Although the allocation of K-9 units was related to certain kinds of crime, there remained important associations with the racial and ethnic composition of police divisions. Clearly, the official police response was inadequate, and soon after, the City of Los Angeles agreed to settle the case. Soon after that, the police department altered the ways it trained its dogs and handlers and the way the K-9 units were allocated. The number of Los Angeles residents bitten by police dogs dropped dramatically, especially in minority neighborhoods.

Note that, once again, statistical inference was not especially relevant. The data were a population for the period of time dictated by the dispute. Causal ideas helped shape the analysis, and further speculations about possible causal effects were generated by the regression results. But the regression model was not a causal model.

11.2.3 Descriptive Regressions as Part of a Broad Research Program

Descriptive regression analyses can also be extremely useful as part of a larger research initiative in which a variety of research approaches and tools are used. That is, the analytic burden is spread around so that research tools are better matched with appropriate research questions. This is commonly the case in the environmental and health sciences. There have been, for instance, a very large number of regression analyses used to describe patterns of AIDS transmission and variables related to those patterns. For example, neighborhoods with a higher proportion of young, single people also tend to have higher rates of HIV infection. But such regressions are not causal models and cannot even explain by themselves why the relationships exist. That information derives from laboratory studies of the AIDS retrovirus: where it resides, how it functions, and how it may be transmitted. When combined with the regression results and other information on intravenous drug use and sexual practices, a plausible causal story can then be told. With regression analysis alone, it cannot.

Consider the earlier illustration of global increases in average temperature summarized by a regression of temperature on time. The goal was to summarize simply any temporal trends. The summary conveyed a very important fact: On the average, the planet has been getting warmer. Because the data represent a population, there was no need for any statistical inference. To what would such inferences be made? Model-based inference was also irrelevant because the regression equation was explicitly *not* a model. And just as clearly, no causal mechanisms were represented.

Regression analyses also show that the warming is strongly associated with the increase over time in greenhouse gases produced by a variety of human activities. Causal link? The regression analyses alone cannot say. But when such regression analyses are combined with laboratory studies of the chemical reactions thought to be relevant, sophisticated measurements from satellites and balloons showing the spatial distribution of temperature, the results of large-scale computer simulations, and well-established theory in chemistry and physics, a credible causal account emerges.

In short, descriptive regression analyses can be very instructive when used in concert with other research approaches. The weight of the research burden can then be shared so that the comparative advantage of each research method or tool can be exploited. The heavy causal lifting, for example, might more effectively be done with laboratory experiments than with regression models.

11.2.4 Spotting Provocative Associations

Sometimes, the scientific and policy questions being asked are causal ones, and, for any number of reasons, the investigator has to go it alone. Description by itself will not suffice, and there are no links to a broader research effort. What role can description play then?

Description can be very useful in revealing provocative associations that remain even after conditioning on a large number of potential confounders. For example, persistent findings of disparities in income for similarly situated male and female workers have spawned a number of useful studies into the underlying mechanisms. In one especially interesting and innovative effort, Nelson and Bridges (1999) use transcripts and other information from sex discrimination cases against business establishments to consider a range of possible causal mechanisms. And virtually all of the major randomized social experiments over the past several decades have been both stimulated and informed by earlier regression results: experiments on income subsidies for the poor, housing allowances for low-income families, gate money for prison inmates, welfare reform, educational television, coordination of mental health services, police interventions in domestic violence disputes, and a host of other important policy issues.[2]

But one must also face the real possibility of failure. There is, for example, an extensive literature on race and the death penalty in the United States. A key finding over the past several decades is that there tends to be a strong association between the race of the victim and the chances of being charged with a capital crime, holding constant a very large number of possible confounders: the race of the defendant, the setting in which the homicide occurred, whether there was another felony committed at the same time, the method of killing, the relationship between the victim and the perpetrator, the prior record of the defendant, the presence of eye witnesses or forensic evidence, and so on.

Over a number of studies in different jurisdictions, the regression results commonly show "race-of-victim effects," that is, the chances of a death penalty

[2]See, for example, Haveman (1977), Hausman and Wise (1985), and Sherman (1992).

increase if the victim is white. Is there a causal relationship? Not unless race can be manipulated. Are there different response schedules for victims of different races? Perhaps, but a regression analysis will probably not reveal it. One would have to specify what the two (or more) response schedules are and then be able to undertake a regression analysis consistent with those response schedules. Both steps are daunting. What a regression analysis might suggest is that something troubling is going on. What that something is, however, will probably have to be revealed by other methods.

For example, one explanation for race-of-victim effects begins with the observation that, given the limited resources, prosecutors must choose their legal battles carefully, and death penalty trials are both very costly and highly visible. It may be better to seek the death penalty in cases where public outrage is high, the background of the victim is sympathetic (e.g., not a drug dealer or gang member), there are credible witnesses ready to step forward, and a conviction will bring great credit (and votes) to the prosecutor. And in many jurisdictions, such cases may disproportionately have white victims. Race is little more than a marker for other factors that are really behind the decision to seek the death penalty. Alternatively, race is a context variable implying different prosecutor response schedules depending on the race of the victim.

Insofar as either account has merit, a causal story of some sort may emerge. Yet it is hard to imagine such complexity being captured explicitly in a regression model based on observational data. Nevertheless, persistent associations between the race of the victim and the chances of a capital charge suggest that something structural is going on linked to cause-and-effect relationships. And the implications of the persistent associations may be sufficiently compelling to motivate research efforts to understand how they come to be.

What should the research entail? Clearly, more observational studies analyzed by regression methods are not, by themselves, the answer. Experiments might help. For example, a set of retired prosecutors could be asked to review the paper records from a number of cases and decide for which cases they would seek the death penalty. Key features of those paper records, including the victim's race, could be altered at random.[3] Although the results of such an experiment would hardly be definitive, the findings might help to clarify matters a bit. If one could actually intervene in the prosecutorial process, much more useful studies could be launched.

But in some sense, doing the better research is a secondary point. There are many important cause-and-effect policy questions that cannot be answered in a compelling manner given current (and quite proper) legal and political constraints; just because a question is important does not mean that it can be answered. It would be better, then, to allocate scarce research resources

---

[3]A large number of studies in this spirit have been undertaken under the banner of "factorial surveys" (e.g., Rossi and Berk, 1997).

elsewhere. And, as noted above, sometimes that will not matter. The political and legal process may decide to act on whatever information it has. Thus, in some circumstances, "disparate" racial impact is sufficient by itself to require legal or legislative remedies. No causal explanation is required.

11.2.5 Some Other Benefits of Description

Regression analysis in a descriptive mode can be very liberating. One not does have to worry about how the data were generated as long as one also does not forget that the results are only formally applicable to the data analyzed. For example, there is no requirement of random sampling.

There is also no need to talk about the model being right in the statistical sense that all of the model's assumptions are being met. It does not matter if any of them are met. Absent statistical inference, correlations between the errors and the predictors, for example, do not formally matter. Indeed, the concept of bias is irrelevant. There is, likewise, no need to talk about the model being right in a causal sense. Response schedules and their implications for a causal model do not apply.

What matters is that the descriptions are useful. Once again, how the information from the data analysis will be applied to concrete problems is central. Indeed, it is not clear how one goes about constructing good descriptions unless there is some understanding of how the results might be used.

11.2.5.1 *Algorithmic Modeling*

With statistical inference and causal inference discarded, one is free to consider a wide variety of relatively new procedures that can have many of the same goals as regression analysis but that usually make no pretense about modeling either how the data were generated or how causal effects are produced. Breiman (2001b) calls such modeling "algorithmic" to emphasize that the enterprise is "only" a set of procedures to characterize how nature has associated predictor variables with response variables. Other terms commonly associated with algorithmic modeling are "data mining," "recursive partitioning," and "machine learning" (Hand et al., 2000).[4]

To get a sense of algorithmic approaches, consider recursive partitioning, which has the added didactic benefit of being closely related to conventional regression analysis. The idea is simple enough. The goal is to break up the data into subsets of cases that are as similar as possible on some response variable of interest. Perhaps the best known technique is Classification and Regression

[4]These terms do not represent fully overlapping sets of techniques. The literature on recursive partitioning tends to be dominated by statisticians, and the literature on machine learning tends to be dominated by computer scientists. The favored procedures differ as well.

Trees (CART), developed by Breiman, Friedman, Olshen, and Stone (Breiman et al., 1984).[5]

Imagine trying to predict the grade point average (GPA) of a set of college students during their freshman year. One begins with a training data set in which there are a number of possible predictors. The goal is to use the relationships between the predictors and the response to partition the data so that all of the freshman GPAs in each subset are as much alike as possible.

To keep the exposition simple, suppose there are only two predictors: high school GPA and total SAT I score. Suppose one first considers the possible role of the high school GPA. The key task is to find the best break point for high school GPA (e.g., at a GPA of 3.0) that divides the data into two groups, each of which is as homogeneous as possible on freshman GPA. For many routines, this means minimizing the within-group sum of squares. Suppose that leads to a group defined by having a high school GPA less than 3.0 and a group defined by having a high school GPA of 3.0 or higher. In regression language, we pick a break point for high school GPA so that the residual sum of squares for freshman GPA is as small as possible. Alternatively, we can say that a function of the prediction error is as small as possible.[6] The same procedure is applied then to the total SAT I score. Again, a break point is defined that minimizes the residual sum of squares for freshman GPA. Now there are two residual sums of squares, one for each bifurcated predictor.

The variable with the smaller residual sum of squares defines the first split of the data. Suppose it is high school GPA, and the break point is 3.0. All students with a high school GPA greater than 3.0 go into one group, and all students with a high school GPA equal to or less than 3.0 go into another group.

Now *within* each of the two groups defined by high school GPA, one repeats the process for both predictors. That is, one computes the best break point for high school GPA and the best break point for total SAT I score. The break points do not have to be the same for the higher and lower high school GPA groups defined in the prior step. For the higher high school GPA group, the SAT break point might be 1350, and for the lower high school GPA group, the SAT break point might be 1190. But in both cases, these are the breaks that minimize the residual sum of squares for freshman GPA (for the higher or lower GPA group, respectively). Then, as before, the variable used to define the next split will be the one for which the break produces the smallest residual sum of squares. The process then continues until the subsets produced have fewer cases than some predetermined threshold (e.g., 10), until the decreases in the residual sum of squares are too small to matter, or some other criterion. The

[5]Actually, the first CART-like procedures were developed by Morgan and Sonquist (1963), both social scientists.

[6]Be clear, however, that the partitioning of the data on hand has nothing to do with actual forecasting either into the future or into another data set. The results, however, can certainly be used for forecasting with a new set of data.

sequential splits of the data can be displayed to look a bit like an inverted tree; hence, the term "tree-based" models. The final collection of subsets is often called the "terminal nodes" of the tree or the "leaves" of the tree.

Tree-based methods are easily and commonly applied to categorical outcomes as well, using other criteria for determining the break points and the order in which the predictors are used. For example, if the outcome is binary, the Gini Index criterion is popular. For a given node, the Gini Index value is $p(1 - p)$, where p is the proportion of "successes" in that node. Thus, if the binary outcome is whether a prison inmate assaults another inmate or correctional staff, p for "successes" in a node could be the proportion of inmates who commit such an assault.

The goal at each step is to pick the best break point for each predictor, and then the best predictor, such that the combined value of the Gini Index for the two "daughter" nodes is as small as possible. Like other popular fit criteria for categorical outcomes, the Gini Index is at its maximum for a given node when $p = .5$ and falls off symmetrically to 0 as p approaches 0 and 1; the Gini Index makes good intuitive sense as a measure of node "impurity." So, in the prison example, one would want to pick a predictor and its appropriate break point such that p is as close as possible to 1 for one of the two subsets, and p is as close as possible to 0 for the other subset. One daughter node has a very large proportion of high-risk offenders, and the other daughter node has a very small proportion of high-risk offenders.[7]

In practice, there are a number of complications with tree-based models. A key problem is that, as one moves down the inverted tree, some of the partitions may not help much. The fitting criterion does not substantially improve. For example, the residual sum of squares for two daughter nodes may not be much smaller than the residual sum of squares for the parent node. One response is to "prune" some of the lower tree branches so that the model is simplified without much degradation in performance. The data analyst tries to construct the simplest model that still fits well. Formally, there is often a complexity penalty attached to the fitting criterion that increases with the number of terminal nodes.

Another problem is overfitting. Here, cross-validation procedures can help. Recall that cross-validation applies the model constructed from a training data set to a new "test" data set to see how much the model's performance degrades. A more recent approach for classification and regression trees, called "bagging" (for "bootstrap aggregation"), constructs a number of trees from a set of bootstrap samples and then averages across the results. Prediction performance into a new data set can improve (Breiman, 1996), in part because overfitting is

[7]Tree-based methods can include categorical, ordinal, and quantitative predictors. The categorical predictors can have more than two categories. Ordinal and quantitative predictors are handled in the same manner when optimal break points are determined. For categorical predictors, all possible allocations to two classes are examined. For categorical responses, more than two categories are usually permitted, although some difficult new issues can arise as a result.

addressed. A still more recent approach, called "random forests" (Breiman, 2001a), randomly samples the data bootstrap style and then, at each step, selects randomly a subset of predictors. Results are presented as averages across a large number of trees produced in this fashion. Initial tests suggest that random forests compares very favorably with the best alternatives developed by computer scientists (e.g., "Adaboost," Freund and Schapire, 1996) and seems better grounded in statistical theory.[8]

Yet another problem is how to make the results accessible to users. For example, how might one communicate in quantitative terms which predictors are most "important"? When predicting into a new data set, one approach is to determine how much the predictions degrade if the values of a given predictor are shuffled at random. The increase in prediction error is the measure of importance. Prediction error can be computed for each predictor and used to compare the predictive "skill."

Tree-based methods are but one kind of algorithmic modeling. Although the goals of other methods are usually much the same, the algorithms can be quite different.[9] Breiman (2001b) claims that, in general, algorithmic modeling will, compared with conventional modeling, produce a better fit and more accurate predictions. It is too early to determine the relative merits of algorithmic modeling and the kinds of modeling discussed in this book. But it is a good bet that, for some important classes of applications in which description and/or prediction are paramount, algorithmic models will dominate. One such class may be applications in which there are a very large number of cases and a very large number of predictors.[10]

11.2.5.2 *Usefulness*

Any discussion of regression analysis as description necessarily raises the question of usefulness. Because one can no longer talk about a model being correct or not, the most common yardsticks measure the benefits from real use. More generally, usefulness has been cited as a key evaluation criterion at many points in earlier discussions. Even badly flawed models can perhaps be justified as useful. But what might "useful" imply?

---

[8]When results are presented as averages over trees, a tree representation of the results is no longer possible. The relationship to conventional regression analysis is far more distant. Some special summary statistics need to be computed to characterize the results.

[9]There are a variety of regression procedures that use smoothers of one sort or another to link predictors to a response: projection pursuit, the ACE and AVES algorithms, and the generalized additive model (Hastie and Tibshirani, 1990). Neural nets (Ripley, 1996), which is essentially a highly nonlinear regression model with lots of parameters, is another approach. These regression procedures can be understood as algorithmic in conception and are best justified as exploratory and descriptive techniques. However, they are often not included under the algorithmic banner.

[10]For a good introduction to algorithmic modeling, see Mitchell (1997), Zhang and Singer (1999), Christianini and Shawe-Taylor (2000), Witten and Frank (2000), or Hastie et al. (2001).

There are really no surprises. First, the analysis has to be responsive to the empirical questions being asked. This point seems obvious but in practice is often overlooked. The recent controversy surrounding the U.S. census is a good example.

The overall census undercount is small, less than about 5%. But the undercount is larger for certain racial minorities and for the urban areas where many live. Because census counts are used to distribute federal funds and to allocate congressional seats, these undercounts can matter. In response, a serious proposal was made to collect special survey data with which to "correct" the usual census count. The stated goal was to make the census more accurate. Many statisticians (but certainly not all) argued that the proposed methods would reallocate population to at least partly redress earlier claims of underrepresentation, but without actually making the census more accurate. In fact, the adjustments made it less accurate. Clearly, if the goal was to make the census more accurate, the modeling exercise was not useful.[11]

Being responsive also means allocating research effort where the real policy concerns are. It is important, in Box's words (1976:975), to distinguish between mice and tigers. If policy issues are about tigers, worrying a lot about mice is unresponsive. However, it will often not be apparent to the data analyst which is which unless real subject matter expertise is brought to bear.

To illustrate, there was great celebration recently among many environmentalists in Los Angeles when new building codes were adopted requiring that, for all new residential and commercial construction, environmentally friendly means had to be in place to handle runoff from winter storms. Ideally, the water would be allowed to percolate into the ground rather than rushing into storm drains. A substantial amount of good policy research, particularly by civil engineers, went into this effort. However, the new codes did not address the existing "hardscape" of Los Angeles from where the vast majority of runoff will come in the foreseeable future.

The mouse-tiger distinction has another important set of implications. The size of the beast helps to determine the kinds and sizes of errors that can be tolerated. Several years ago, the U.S. Department of Justice sued a large foreign car manufacturer for the failure of its managerial employees to pay taxes on the "executive automobiles" leased to them at well below market rates. The company responded with a survey using "willingness-to-pay" techniques and a number of regression analyses to estimate the value to their managers of the leased automobiles. There were many potential problems with the estimates, but with an anticipated tax bill in the millions of dollars, there was no point in worrying a great deal about methodological flaws costing the government or the car company a few thousand dollars. To do so would have been unresponsive.

[11]This has become a huge debate with critical policy implications. One can get a sense of the issues from Freedman and Navidi (1986) and the commentary that follows, and from a special issue of *Jurimetrics* (Goldman et al., 1993) devoted to census adjustments. See also Breiman (1994), Freedman and Wachter (1994), and Belin and Rolph (1994).

Second, the descriptive results should prejudge as little as possible so that potentially useful information is not lost. Again, to draw on earlier chapters, providing a table of regression results without also providing a number of regression diagnostics makes it difficult to properly interpret the findings. It can be important to see, for example, residual plots, influence figures, and added variable plots.

Unfortunately, bare-bones regression tables are common. Recall the University of California report discussed above on the "predictive validity" of SAT scores (Geiser and Studley, 2001). Using freshman GPA as the response, the report claimed that SAT I scores explained no additional variance in the response after high school GPA and SAT II scores were taken into account. But in that report, there were only a few cross-tabulations and very sparse regression tables surrounded by pages of policy-laden prose. There was a Web site where more details could be found, but if regression diagnostics were seriously used, they were not reported. It was, therefore, impossible to make fully informed judgments about the findings (although for reasons addressed in earlier chapters, there were ample grounds for skepticism).

Third, useful descriptions are accessible. This is partly a matter of careful labeling of variables, tables, and figures. But it is also a matter of aesthetics. This is not the place to consider what makes for good graphs (see, e.g., Cleveland, 1993), but one obvious issue is to strike a balance between the amount of information contained and overwhelming clutter. Accessibility also depends on teaching. Writing for a policy audience will often require a substantial amount of didactic material geared for the intended readership. When writing a report for state or federal legislators, one is really writing for their legislative aides, whose statistical training is at the very least rusty (but usually better than their bosses').

Good descriptions come with full disclosure as well. The source and nature of the data need to be apparent. Any decisions that may have substantially affected the results need to be explained. Deletion of outliers is one illustration. If there is more than one possible set of results that is reasonably credible, they all need to be presented or at least discussed. Using again the University of California report, the relevant population about which decisions had to be made was the pool of applicants. The data apparently came from all University of California freshmen who entered the university from the fall of 1996 through the fall of 1999. The reader is never told what fraction of the total number of applicants were ultimately admitted. One cannot determine, therefore, what the potential for sample selection bias really is.[12]

---

[12]But note that if the censoring is on the response variable, freshman GPA at the University of California, the chances of serious selection biases are good. One might also argue that the research design is simply unresponsive to the key policy question: For the high school students who apply to the University of California system, how well *do* the SATs predict college performance? It is, after all, the pool of *applicants* for which admissions decisions have to be made.

Finally, there are a number of less apparent features of usefulness that are relevant. In particular, descriptive analyses can serve as pilot studies for future work or as a means to refine the questions being asked. Trying to analyze even a weak data set for which statistical inference and causal inference are not justified can sharpen thinking.

For example, a recent study conducted under the auspices of Reefwatch (http://www.reefwatch.asn.au) attempted to estimate the impact of establishing no-fishing zones on fish populations living among coral reefs. One complication was that because some species of fish are highly mobile, they may readily swim outside of the preserve and be caught. It was not at all clear, therefore, that no-fishing zones would effectively protect all species of fish. To get an initial sense of the possible benefits of no-fishing zones, a site that had been protected was compared with a site that had not been protected. There were many more species of fish, and more fish overall, in the protected site. However, in this region, fishing is often done using underwater explosives or poisons that temporarily stun the fish. In either case, the reefs themselves can be fundamentally damaged. So, it was not clear whether the smaller fish populations in the unprotected sites resulted from the direct removal of fish, damage to the fish habitat, or both. And if a damaged fish habitat was the primary culprit, one might allow fishing as long as there was no collateral damage to the coral. It became apparent as the regression analysis of the data was undertaken that future studies would have to compare sites that varied in fishing methods. A very simple descriptive study turned out to be extremely useful.

In summary, good description is the bread and butter of good science and good policy research. Regression analyses can play a very important role in this enterprise. They should not be dismissed as "mere" description. As Herbert Simon (2001:36) notes, "The primordial acts of science are to observe phenomena, to seek patterns (redundancy) in them, and to redescribe them in terms of the discovered patterns, thereby removing redundancy."

11.3 Two Cheers for Statistical Inference

Statistical inference can be very informative when there is a well-defined and real population to which instructive inferences can be drawn. Statistical inference can be useful as well when a strong case can be made for the model used in model-based sampling. And in either case, obtaining estimates of the uncertainty due to sampling error can also be very handy.

Two important prerequisites have been discussed: (a) The data must have been generated by random sampling, a naturally occurring close approximation, or a well-described natural process; and (b) the regression model must be correct. There is no need here to repeat the arguments. Suffice it to say, for both prerequisites, the burden falls heavily on the investigator to make the case. Often, this will be very hard to do, and the usual hand waving is typically a ruse.

Because, in practice, even well-designed probability samples are usually implemented imperfectly, and virtually all regression models are wrong, the usefulness of statistical inference will usually be a matter of degree. How many errors of what kinds and sizes can be tolerated in order to get a sufficiently useful approximation of the information desired? Unfortunately, there are no easy answers. But sensible practice can at least reduce exposure. Here are a few commonsense suggestions, some of which have been around for years but are honored mostly in the breach.

- It is essential to avoid the many common misinterpretations of significance tests and confidence intervals. There is no need to rehash these here; there is no need for déjà vu all over again.
- It is a good idea to use formal statistical tests very sparingly. The many technical and logical problems with formal tests are well known, and their status as scientific ritual has been widely discussed. It is especially important to avoid the use of formal tests for determining how good or bad a model may be (e.g., misspecification tests). Among the many difficulties is the strong temptation to accept the null as true when it cannot be rejected. The same issues arise when researchers use hypothesis tests to decide when to drop variables from a regression model.
- The literal use of p-values more generally is risky either as evidence against the null hypothesis or implicitly in the construction of confidence intervals. In much policy-related research, a large number of p-values are computed, often in a cascading manner. Earlier p-values and explorations of the data inform later analyses for which new p-values are computed. Such practices give a false sense of precision; the p-values and confidence intervals are likely to be far too small.
- If significant exploratory work is required, it is usually wise to treat it as such, and efforts to properly represent uncertainty should be postponed until a new data set for confirmatory analyses can be obtained. Cross-validation procedures can also be very useful in this regard. If both of these strategies are impractical, and if no more than a modest amount of exploration has been undertaken, a useful fallback position is to heavily discount any computed p-values. Although none of the existing formal procedures for multiple comparisons is able to capture the many creative ways researchers manage to capitalize on chance, some of the more conservative adjustments can often be usefully applied. For example, with the Bonferroni procedure, the critical value for rejection of the null hypothesis is divided by the number of post hoc tests undertaken. Thus, if there are ten such tests, the new critical value might be $.05/10 = .005$. A wide variety of adjustments for multiple tests are discussed in any number of intermediate-level statistics texts (e.g., We and Hamada, 2000: Section 1.7).

- In this same spirit, the many different algorithms available for model selection, such as stepwise regression, must be understood as exploratory. Any p-values used in the procedures, let alone those applied to a "final" model, are very likely to be far too small.
- The use of statistical inference as part of a meta-analysis is usually a bad idea. As argued earlier, the model required has almost no correspondence to how the worlds of science and policy research really function or to much of anything else for that matter. Very misleading conclusions can result.

Even if these pitfalls can be avoided, there remain two practical problems. First, how close does the data generation process have to be to one of the ideals for statistical inference to be credible? Second, how close to correct does the regression model have to be for statistical inference to be credible? If both approximations are good, there are a number of constructive options.

11.3.1 Working With Near-Random Samples

In a great many situations, the approximation to random sampling is laughable. Convenience samples or quota samples are not even close. There is no point, then, in haggling over price, and statistical inference risks serious nonsense.

Far more interesting and subtle issues arise when the data should have been generated by random sampling, designed either by the researcher or by nature, but the sampling process is partly degraded. Perhaps the most common and most thoroughly studied instance occurs when response rates for survey samples fall well below 100% (Groves, 1989: Chapter 4). There is a lively debate about how low the response rates can get (they have been dropping over the past several decades) before analysis of the data is not worth the trouble. And not surprisingly, there is no simple answer. A lot depends on the use that will be made of the data, how accurate the results need to be, how heterogeneous the population is, and what sorts of biases have been introduced. Nevertheless, there are at least three important lessons.

First, it is vital to gain as much understanding as possible about *why* the cases are missing. If, by some bit of good fortune, the missing cases are a random sample of the rest, then the only consequence is a smaller sample (which will usually mean less statistical power). But it will be unusual indeed for a researcher to be able to convincingly demonstrate that the cases were lost at random. This is not the place to review the large and interesting literature on missing data, but if one can make a strong argument about the mechanisms by which cases were lost, and if one has good information on those mechanisms, there are a number of constructive strategies that, in principle, can be implemented (Little and Rubin, 1987).[13] But as always, hand waving will not do.

Second, it is sometimes possible to improve matters by adjusting the data for empirically demonstrable biases. It is common in survey research to weight the data so that certain distributions better reflect those distributions in the population. Sometimes, this is called "poststratification" (Thompson, 2002: 124-125). For example, if a sample has 40% African Americans, and the population from which the data were randomly drawn has 80% African Americans, the data can be weighted so that in later analyses, each African American case gets twice the relative weight it would normally have. The key, then, is having useful information on the population. The most common source of such information is the U.S. census, but if the samples are drawn from formal organizations such as large manufacturers, school districts, or labor unions, there often are also helpful benchmarks available on the population.

However, even when such information can be obtained, one can only adjust for the variables for which the population distributions are known. The biases in the degraded sample may be related to other variables. For example, it is common to require parental consent before high school students are permitted to fill out a research questionnaire. There is ample evidence that the parents who either refuse to let their children cooperate or who simply don't bother to give permission are often very different from the parents who allow their children to fill out the questionnaire (Esbensen et al., 1999; Henry et al., 2002). It is a good bet, therefore, that the two sets of children are different as well. Unfortunately, it is usually not clear exactly how they are different. Adjusting by the usual background variables is unlikely to correct all of the important biases.

Third, it is sometimes instructive to undertake sensitivity analyses. Absent weights from the population, weights can be used that represent the best-case and worst-case scenarios. For example, if a low response rate sample from a rural area has 10% of the cases with household earnings below the poverty line, a likely worst-case scenario might be that 50% of the population is below the poverty line. Weighting can be applied accordingly.

The problems can become even more difficult if the issue is not just bias but lack of independence. One complication is that dependence in the sampling process will typically not be apparent in the data alone. Usually, concerns about independence come from external information about the sampling process. And then, any remedies will depend on certain kinds of identifiers in the data that may not be available.

For example, a sample of schoolchildren will likely have dependence built in if the cases are obtained by sampling classrooms at random and then taking a random sample of children within each. But unless the cluster

---

[13] Little and Rubin (2002) discuss missing cases and incomplete cases under the rubric of missing data.

sampling approach is known and there are classroom identifiers in the data, the dependence will likely go unnoticed. If the dependence is recognized, the classroom identifiers can be used to estimate the amount of dependence, from which adjustments to the standard errors can be made.

Analogous information will sometimes be available in natural settings. Thus, water samples taken from a set of storm drains will usually be labeled by time, date, and location. These are, in effect, the clustering units, and it may be possible to make the case that with adjustments for clustering within these units, the samples are effectively random.

In short, when the sample is not too far from random, and when there is information about the likely biases and data dependencies, useful inferences sometimes can be made.

11.3.2 Working With Data From Nature

When the data are being treated as a realization of some natural process, the issues are much the same. The key is knowing how the data have been degraded. And with that knowledge, the same strategies may prove useful.

For example, there has been for some years considerable controversy over projections to the middle of the 21st century of the legal liabilities of asbestos manufacturers and installers for the asbestos-related diseases of their employees and others who have come in contact with their products. Although the epidemiological models for such diseases are sometimes judged to be sufficiently credible by agencies like the Occupational Safety and Health Administration (OSHA, 1986), liabilities depend on who seeks compensation.

Matters are complicated by the fact that some individuals who might legitimately seek compensation do not, and some who have no legitimate claim do; there is no one-to-one correspondence between contracting an asbestos-related disease and suing an asbestos manufacturer or installer. As a result, there have been a number of efforts to construct models of the "propensity to sue" to supplement the existing epidemiological models. So far, these efforts have not been very convincing. For example, a key assumption is that the mix of asbestos-related diseases does not change over time. Yet there is already evidence that the most serious diseases are becoming less common.

11.3.3 Working With a Nearly Correct Model

There are also useful approaches if the model is likely to be almost right. An obvious place to begin is to examine how robust the p-values are to a range of reasonable alterations in the data or the model. For example, influential observations might be dropped to see if the results change in important ways. Or, suspect observations that were discarded might be included. The same strategy can be applied to variables of marginal importance or transformations undertaken that arguably were not needed. Clearly, the hope is that the p-values will be relatively stable. As noted above, however, greater levels of instability can be tolerated if not too much is riding on them alone.

Another often overlooked point: All decisions about the model and what to make of it should be undertaken with substantial subject matter knowledge. Estimates of uncertainty can provide useful information that should be weighed together with other inputs. In particular, one always needs to consider whether the results and their subject matter implications make sense. Out of context, it is difficult to be very specific, but it is often a terrible error to delegate all analysis decisions to a statistical recipe or even (especially) to a statistician.

To illustrate, in a study of sentences for federal crimes undertaken by researchers in a federal agency, the impact of certain variables on sentence length seemed far too large. Even though the p-values were tiny, a consultant knowledgeable about the federal penal code and associated sentencing guidelines simply could not believe the results. When he dug into the regression analyses further, he found that the code for missing data was treated as a legitimate sentence. That missing-value code was 99.

To take another illustration, a spatial regression analysis was undertaken by another federal agency to show that the concentrations of selenium in a local water supply were too high to remediate. As such, a clean-up was prohibitively expensive. But a geologist from a private consulting firm noted that the regression model produced selenium concentrations that were, on the average, far too high. They did not make geological sense. Selenium can naturally enter the water supply due to soil erosion caused by heavy rains. But the selenium concentrations from natural causes are usually not problematic. On closer inspection of the regressions and the data, a statistician called in to help observed that very few data points were driving the results. These happened to come from agricultural wells heavily contaminated with irrigation runoff. Again, subject matter knowledge really made a difference.

11.4 One Cheer for Causal Inference

Causal inference is always difficult, even under the best of circumstances. Perhaps the key obstacle is that causal inference rests on a conceptual foundation preceding the construction of a causal model and estimation of the model's parameters. One has to offer a causal story up front that even skeptics can take seriously. There is no recipe for how to tell such a story because it usually must integrate existing subject matter theory and past empirical studies. In a great many policy areas, the theory is weak and the extant empirical research inconclusive. What's a causal modeler to do?

The best existing answer seems to be to experiment. Randomized experiments surely have their interpretative problems (Berk, 1990; Smith, 1990;

Rosenbaum, 2002a), and some observers make a good case that for many important policy questions, randomized experiments are unresponsive (Heckman, LaLonde, and Smith, 1999; Heckman, 2001). For example, randomized experiments may disrupt the environment in which the program is being tested. As a result, the effects estimated do not apply to the environment in which the program might actually be implemented. Still, one can usually obtain an unbiased estimate of the average difference between various intervention outcomes coupled with statistical inference that will likely be on sound technical footing (see, e.g., Rosenbaum, 2002: Chapter 2). And alternative methods are often worse.

Strong quasi-experiments can also be very useful. Interrupted time series designs and regression discontinuity designs, in particular, have been applied with some success (e.g., Berk and de Leeuw, 1999).

But in some sense, true experiments and strong quasi-experiments bypass the issues that have been raised in earlier chapters. For us, the main question has been what one can learn about cause and effect from regression when one only has observational data.

First, there are several points discussed at length in earlier chapters that are worth a brief restatement.

- Credible causal inferences cannot be made from a regression analysis alone; it is still true that correlation is not causation. The sole output from a regression analysis is a way to characterize the conditional distribution of the response variable, given a set of predictors.
- Standardized coefficients do not represent the causal importance of a variable.
- Contributions to explained variance for different predictors do not represent the causal importance of a variable.
- A good overall fit does not demonstrate that a causal model is correct.
- There are no regression diagnostics through which causal effects can be demonstrated.
- There are no specification tests through which causal effects can be demonstrated.
- There are no mathematical formalisms through which causal effects can be demonstrated.
- Causal inference rests first and foremost on a credible response schedule. Without a credible response schedule, causal inference is moot.
- Absent a nearly right model, there are so many potential problems with causal models that existing remedial strategies are easily overwhelmed.

Given a credible response schedule and a regression model that is nearly right, regression diagnostics, specification tests, and mathematical formalisms can sometimes be helpful. There are four additional tools that can sometimes be helpful as well. Each rests in part on a simplification of the problem; aspirations are reduced.

But be forewarned; although each of the four approaches has been developed by talented individuals, none of them would claim to have fundamentally solved the problem of getting proper estimates of causal effects from observational data. Each approach still rests in part on important and untestable assumptions. Advances? Probably yes. Solutions? Surely no.

In an attempt to cut the problem down to size, each of the four strategies focuses primarily on estimating the causal effects of a single intervention on a single response (although generalizations exist). All other variables are typically (a) irrelevant because they are unrelated to the response, (b) not a source of bias because they are unrelated to the intervention, or (c) confounders related to both the intervention and the response. Thus, all variables but the intervention and the response are usually of no legitimate subject matter concern or are treated as a nuisance.

There are now, therefore, only two causal processes that need to be addressed: selection effects and treatment effects. The former represent the impact of the confounders on which observational units are exposed to which interventions. The latter represent the impact of the interventions on the outcome. Although one is still doing regression analysis, this formulation is some distance from the usual regression analysis applications.

To make this more concrete, consider the question of whether welfare benefits affect the likelihood that male children will stay in school. Rich (1999:89-90) suggests that there are at least three possibilities. Transfer payments may lower the incentive for parents to remain in the labor force, and hence, the parents are more likely to provide poor role models. Then, their children may be more likely to drop out of school. Alternatively, the increase in family income may reduce the need for the household's children to work. As a result, they may be more likely to stay in school. Finally, if the welfare benefits are reduced when a child is employed, there may be an incentive to seek illegal income, which, in turn, would reduce the likelihood of staying in school.

Even considering just low-income families, the analytical problem for this study was that households that receive welfare benefits differ from those that do not on a host of factors: skills, motivation, access to transportation, availability of child care, health, and so on. All of these plausibly could affect the likelihood that a child would remain in school.

Rich (1999:93-94) considers four possible responses for male children 14 to 20 years of age living at home:

1. not enrolled in school and employed,
2. enrolled in school and not employed,
3. not enrolled in school and not employed,
4. enrolled in school and employed.

A multinomial logit model followed, conditioning on as many variables as possible. The estimated treatment effects were not impressive. It is, of course, easy to suggest important predictors that were not available. But it may have been possible to do better using some combination of the following procedures. Then, a key would have been to focus on selection effects and treatment effects only.

11.4.1 Special-Purpose Estimators

Coupled with the argument that the gold standard of randomized experiments is not really so golden after all (e.g., Cronbach, 1982; Heckman, 1995) have come a number of suggestions about how useful estimates of various intervention effects can be obtained, using techniques responsive to the particular features of a study, that give the data analyst some real leverage. An instructive illustration is procedures derived for "broken" randomized experiments (Bernard et al., 1998).

A broken randomized experiment occurs when some experimental and/or control subjects do not comply with the treatment condition to which they are randomly assigned. For this situation, Angrist et al. (1996) provide an instrumental variable estimator, embedded in the Neyman-Rubin formulation of causal effects, from which consistent treatment effect estimates for key subsets of subjects may be obtained. An important feature of the estimated effects is that they can have clear causal interpretations. Another important feature is that the necessary assumptions represent assertions about the actual behavior of the study subjects. The real world is invited to participate in the analysis. Then, there are relatively straightforward sensitivity analyses that can be undertaken.

Consider a relatively simple example to get a general sense of the issues. Let

$$y_i = \alpha_0 + \alpha_1 t_i + \epsilon_i, \tag{11.1}$$

where y_i is a response of interest, t_i is an indicator variable coded 1 if subject i actually experiences the treatment condition and 0 if subject i actually experiences the control condition, and ϵ_i is a random error whose properties will be considered shortly. In many policy applications, α_1 (the relationship between the treatment experienced and the response) is a key parameter.

Then, let

$$t_i^* = \beta_0 + \beta_1 a_i + \upsilon_i, \tag{11.2}$$

where a_i is a manipulable assignment variable coded 1 or 0 determining whether subject i is assigned to the treatment condition or the control condition respectively, and υ_i is a random error whose properties will also be considered shortly.

The latent variable t_i^* is the inclination of subject i to comply with the treatment or control condition assigned. More specifically,

$$t_i = \begin{cases} 1 & \text{if } t_i^* > 0 \\ 0 & \text{if } t_i^* \leq 0, \end{cases}$$

where the use of 0 as the threshold is arbitrary and in practice has no important consequences.[14] Note that t_i^* is not observable and does figure importantly in what follows. It is a motivating construct. In practice, one works with the relationships between a_i, t_i, and y_i.

Suppose the value of a_i is determined by random assignment. Then, a_i is uncorrelated with (indeed independent of) υ_i. Also suppose that $\beta_1 \neq 0$; the intervention assigned to subject i affects the likelihood that a subject will actually experience the treatment or control condition. Finally, suppose that a_i is uncorrelated with ϵ_i; the treatment assigned to subject i can affect the response y_i only through a link between a_i and t_i.

It follows by definition that a_i is an instrumental variable.[15] Therefore, it can be used in the conventional way to obtain a consistent estimate of α_1. A least squares estimate of α_1 will be biased and inconsistent insofar as t_i and ϵ_i are correlated. Such a correlation is likely because omitted variables contained within υ_i will often be related to omitted variables contained within ϵ_i (or even be some of the same omitted variables). Omitted variables affecting the inclination to comply might well be related to omitted variables affecting the response. For example, if the treatment is job training and the response is wages, unemployed individuals who are more motivated to show up for the job training classes to which they were randomly assigned might also give a better impression in job interviews.

To see how the instrumental variable estimator is constructed, begin by letting

$$y_i = \gamma_0 + \gamma_1 a_i + \nu_i. \tag{11.3}$$

Because of random assignment, the random error ν_i is uncorrelated with a_i. If the response of any given subject is unrelated to the treatment assigned to other subjects (SUTVA), unbiased estimates of β_1 and γ_1 are easily computed (thanks to random assignment). The estimate of γ_1 is a key feature of an "intention-to-treat" analysis of randomized experiments. It can represent the causal effect of the *assigned* intervention on the outcome, but it neglects, therefore, the fact that for some subjects the intervention assigned is not the intervention actually experienced.

In many policy settings, an estimate of α_1 is at least as important as an estimate of γ_1. The parameter α_1 links the treatment actually experienced to the response. Because the treatment actually experienced is here not randomly

[14] It is absorbed in the intercept.

[15] Random assignment is not formally necessary but here ensures the requirement that a_i is uncorrelated with υ_i.

assigned, the receipt of treatment t_i is not likely to be "ignorable." However, because a_i operates through t_i, $\gamma_1 = \alpha_1 \beta_1$. Hence, $\alpha_1 = \gamma_1 / \beta_1$, which, after replacing γ_1 and β_1 with their estimated values, is the instrumental variable estimator of α_1.

Angrist et al. (1996) stress that, even with random assignment, the IV estimate of α_1 depends on assumptions that cannot be directly tested. For example, suppose there are individuals who would never accept the randomly assigned intervention; no matter what, they always behave as if they were members of the control group. For these individuals, $\beta_1 = 0$, and then any association between a_i and y_i is not through t_i. If there are relatively many such individuals in the study, the IV estimate of α_1 could be quite misleading. Note also that even though such noncooperating subjects randomly assigned to the treatment could often be easily identified (if the intervention experienced is measured as well as the intervention assigned), they would be hard to identify when placed in the control group. With respect to the control condition experienced, they would look the same as subjects in the control group who would cooperate fully with the study.

But there is more to the story. It is often desirable in policy settings to give an estimate of α_1 and γ_1 clear causal interpretations. For that, additional assumptions are required that are best understood in the context of a particular application.

Building on Angrist et al. (1996) and several studies, Bernard et al. (2003) analyzed a broken randomized experiment on the educational impact of school vouchers. Some households that were given vouchers for private schools did not use them. Some households sent their children to private schools even though they were not given vouchers.

The analysis rests on constructing four strata:

1. *Compliers:* those who would use an awarded voucher to send their child to a private school and not send their child to a private school without having gotten an awarded voucher;
2. *Never Takers:* those who would not send their child to a private school whether or not they were randomly awarded a voucher;
3. *Always Takers:* those who would send their child to a private school whether or not they were randomly awarded a voucher;
4. *Defiers:* those who, if awarded a voucher, would not send their child to public school, but if not awarded a voucher, would.

The formal assumptions mentioned above for instrumental variable estimation were grounded in specific statements about how the experiment was implemented. Perhaps more interesting, an assumption was made that there were no defiers among the households studied. For this study, that is probably a reasonable behavioral assumption. Then, because, by definition, there could be no causal effects for the never takers and always takers (the treatment experienced cannot be altered), the causal effects estimated only applied to the compliers. The instrumental variable estimate of the causal effect of the treatment actually experienced was for compliers only. Generalization of the findings to a realistic population of households, should a real school vouchers program be implemented, is probably ill advised.[16]

By grounding the necessary assumptions in statements about behavior, the analysis highlights a point made many times in earlier pages: Assumptions made so that a statistical analysis is manageable are statements about how nature is supposed to operate. Here, the benefit is that clear interpretations of causal effects follow and meaningful sensitivity analyses can be undertaken. At the same time, the particular estimator used and the interpretations made depend fundamentally on the special features of the study in question. For example, random assignment plays a key role. Although the perspective taken and the logic employed have very broad applicability, the instrumental variable estimator and its causal interpretation do not. And randomized experiments broken by noncompliance are a very small fraction of all policy-relevant studies.

A related set of special-purpose estimators come from studies of active interventions in labor markets. Heckman and his colleagues (1999) provide an extensive menu of options.[17] In biomedical applications, the work of Robbins and his colleagues serves a similar function (Robbins, 1997, 1999). Once again, a key idea is to take better advantage of special features of the data, what is known in detail about the intervention, and information on selection into the treatment groups.

The regression-discontinuity approach mentioned earlier is one illustration. Suppose prison administrators want to know if there is any deterrent impact on misconduct in prison if inmates are housed in more restrictive settings. Suppose, as a routine administrative matter, prison inmates are placed into different security levels solely by a "classification score." The classification score is computed by formula from various background characteristics of the inmate: age, age when first arrested, evidence of gang activity, sentence length, and so on. There are then several thresholds to determine placement. Inmates with scores above the highest threshold, for instance, are placed in the highest security level. Inmates with scores below the highest threshold but above the threshold just beneath it are placed in the next highest security level, and so on.

One can then obtain an unbiased estimate of the effect of security level on inmate misconduct by simply conditioning on the classification score: Misconduct is taken to be a function of security level and classification score only. No other covariates need be considered (Rubin, 1977; Berk and de Leeuw, 1999;

[16]There were also problems with missing data that had to be addressed in the analysis. Those are not considered here.

[17]The background literature is vast. See, for example, Heckman and Robb (1985) and Heckman and Hotz (1989).

Heckman et al., 1999). However, this example of a special-purpose estimator will provide unbiased estimates of causal effects only if the covariate on which the conditioning rests fully determines the treatment received.[18] Here, inmates must be placed by the classification score alone. Although assignment procedures of this sort are used in a wide variety of situations (e.g., awarding college scholarships on the basis of National Merit Scholarship Test results), they are hardly commonplace.

Other special-purpose estimators capitalize on a variety of instrumental variable estimators (indeed, the regression-discontinuity approach can be conceptualized in this manner), information contained in panel data, randomly sampled individuals from the same population over time, and a number of other particular features of the data and the intervention. One major contribution of this literature is that the assumptions to which nature must conform are often well described. A careful researcher should not be misled. In addition, when it is possible to make the case that nature has cooperated in the manner required, the estimators deliver. But special-purpose estimators work as advertised only in the right settings, and these settings apply only to a relatively small fraction of the policy situations in which estimates of causal effects are desired.

11.4.2 Propensity Scores

The basic idea behind propensity scores is deceptively simple (Rosenbaum and Rubin, 1983b). One regresses the categorical (or binary) variable for treatments received on the variables thought to affect selection. Logistic regression is commonly used. The predicted values of that regression can be expressed as the predicted probabilities of assignment to the various treatments. These probabilities are called "propensity scores." One can then condition on the propensity scores when the relationship between the treatments and the response is estimated. If all of the variables related to selection and the response are included in the construction of the propensity scores, and if those variables are measured without error, conditioning on the propensity scores in the second step will produce unbiased estimates of the average treatment effects. The conditioning can be done through a regression model or in a more robust way by matching (Smith, 1997).

The study of intervention effects by conditioning on propensity scores has enjoyed some popularity. One study, for example (Berk et al., 1986), examined whether a short stay in a residential shelter for battered women reduced subsequent risk. There was a selection equation addressing factors thought to affect the decision to enter a shelter. Propensity scores from this initial analysis were used as controls when the impact of a shelter stay was estimated. Seeking refuge in a shelter reduced later violence, but only when the victim was prepared

[18]The functional form of the regression equation also has to be correct.

to end the relationship. However, the credibility of that conclusion depended fundamentally on getting the selection model pretty close to right, and there was really no way for that to be determined.[19]

Using propensity scores, when applicable, can greatly simplify the causal modeling process. One major strength is that the process by which subjects are exposed to the intervention is distinguished from the process by which the responses are generated. This can help clarify the key assumptions and make various model diagnostics easier to apply. For example, once propensity scores are computed, a model for the treatment effects may have only two predictors: the propensity scores and the treatment indicator. The data are then rather easily explored with the help of graphical methods. At the same time, all of the usual problems with regression analysis remain; everything depends on how good the model really is.

11.4.3 Sensitivity Analysis of the Selection Process

Partly in response to such difficulties, Rosenbaum in particular (Rosenbaum and Rubin, 1983a; Rosenbaum, 2002a: Chapter 4; Rosenbaum, 2002b) has argued for routine use of sensitivity analyses focused on the selection process. Again, the basic idea is straightforward, although proper implementation can be a little tricky. One manipulates the estimated odds of receiving a particular treatment to see how much the estimated treatment effects can vary. What one wants to find is that the estimated treatment effects are robust to a plausible range of selection biases.

Consider again the example of the null findings for the impact of welfare benefits on the likelihood that a male child will stay in school. Suppose households with male children between the ages of 14 and 20 who were not inclined to stay in school had estimated odds of 2 to 1 of receiving welfare payments. Under these circumstances, suppose that no treatment effects were found. What would the estimated treatment effect be if the odds of receiving payments were 4 to 1? That is, what would happen to the estimated treatment effects if families with male children uninterested in school were even more likely to receive welfare benefits? The underlying concern would be that the selection model had underestimated the likelihood that welfare families had children who were already at high risk of being school dropouts. If, under the 4 to 1 ratio, important treatment effects were still not found, the null findings would take on additional credibility.

Rosenbaum recommends trying a variety of scenarios in an effort to determine how robust any findings are (for a related approach, see Berk and

[19]Like so much of the work on estimating causal effect from observational data, this, too, is subject to a heated debate, at least over important details (Rubin and Thomas, 1996; Heckman et al., 1997).

de Leeuw, 1999). When the findings change importantly, the researcher can consider whether selection biases of that magnitude are likely for the data on hand. If so, the findings are of little use.

It seems hard to argue with the underlying intent of Rosenbaum's sensitivity analyses. But hands-on experience with the procedures seems still to be rather limited. And there are skeptics (Robbins, 2002).

11.4.4 Bounding Treatment Effects

Recall the earlier exposition of counterfactuals in causal inference. Suppose y is a binary response coded 1 or 0. Then, let t be a binary variable coded 1 if the treatment is received and 0 if not. Finally, there is a hypothetical treatment t^* coded 1 for the treatment condition and 0 for the control condition. Thus, for example, $(y|t = 0, t^* = 1)$ is the response if the treatment were delivered to subjects who were, in fact, in the control group.

Consider a prison example. Suppose that the binary outcome is whether or not an inmate engages in some form of reportable misconduct while in prison (e.g., fighting, refusing to report for a work assignment) and the intervention is placement in a high-security institution versus some other institutional placement (e.g., a forestry camp). Now

$$\begin{aligned}(y = 1|t^* = 1) &= p(y = 1|t^* = 1, t = 1) \times p(t = 1) \\ &\quad + p(y = 1|t^* = 1, t = 0) \times p(t = 0). \qquad (11.4)\end{aligned}$$

Equation 11.2 shows that the proportion engaging in misconduct if placement is into a high-security facility depends on the proportion engaging in misconduct for those who were actually placed in a high-security facility and the proportion engaging in misconduct for those who were not. The second expression of the right-hand side is counterfactual: One cannot observe what would happen in a high-security placement for those who were placed in other settings.

For the "what if" when placement was not into a high-security facility, one has

$$\begin{aligned}p(y = 1|t^* = 0) &= p(y = 1|t^* = 0, t = 1) \times p(t = 1) \\ &\quad + p(y = 1|t^* = 0, t = 0) \times p(t = 0). \qquad (11.5)\end{aligned}$$

Equation 11.5 shows that the proportion engaging in misconduct if placement is not into a high-security facility also depends on the proportion engaging in misconduct for those who were actually placed in a high-security facility and the proportion engaging in misconduct for those who were not. The first expression of the right-hand side is counterfactual: One cannot observe what would happen in the absence of high security for those who were placed in that setting.

Although the counterfactuals cannot be observed, it is possible to consider what the causal effect might be under various assumptions about the outcomes for the counterfactuals. For example, one might assume that, had the inmates not placed in high security actually been assigned there, they would have engaged in the same amount of misconduct as those who were actually assigned to high-security facilities. On its face, this assumption makes little sense. Prison placement practices commonly try to sort inmates by levels of risk for misconduct and then house the inmates at great risk in the high-security facilities. Unless prison screening practices have no predictive power, inmates placed in high-security facilities will be meaningfully different from those who are not. For example, the inmates in high-security settings may be more likely to be young gang members with long criminal records, and these may be the very individuals who, past experience indicates, are most likely to get into trouble.

It would be very useful if it were possible to get a better handle on the consequences of different assumptions about the counterfactuals. In the body of work associated with Charles Manski (1990, 1994) and James Robins (1989),[20] the idea of bounding causal effects using assumptions about counterfactuals is given a rigorous treatment. The goal is not to provide a single numerical estimate for the causal effect but a plausible range under alternative assumptions in which the effect will fall. The easiest approach is to construct the widest possible range.

Suppose there were evidence that high-security placements reduce misconduct. Assume now that none of the inmates assigned to lower security housing would have failed if they had been placed in a high-security facility, and that all of the inmates assigned to high-security housing would have failed had they been placed elsewhere. This would produce the largest possible effect of the high-security intervention.

The smallest possible effect could be computed by reversing the logic. Now, all of the inmates who were not assigned high-security housing would have failed if they had been, and none of the inmates assigned to high-security housing would have failed had they been housed elsewhere. The actual treatment effect of a high-security placement must fall between these two bounds. Unfortunately, bounds of this type are likely to be very large relative to the precision needed by policymakers. But at least there is a truthful assessment.

The bounds can be made tighter if a researcher is prepared to make assumptions affecting the counterfactuals. In Manski and Nagin (1998), for example, the bounding procedure is applied to the juvenile justice system, for which the interventions are confinement in a residential treatment facility or diversion to a nonresidential program. The outcome is recidivism. Two processes are hypothesized by which judges decide which juveniles to place in which treatment. For the "optimization model," judges know for each offender the probability of recidivism under the two interventions, and they sentence the offender to the intervention with the greater probability of success. Under the "skimming model," judges are able to divide offenders into a high-risk group and a low-risk

[20] See also Balke and Pearl (1993).

group and then assign the high-risk group to the more restrictive setting and the low-risk group to the less restrictive setting. Compared with the largest bounds under no assumptions, both models produce smaller intervals.

The overall stance taken by the bounding approach is surely sensible. Insofar as plausible scenarios can be constructed for the process by which cases are assigned to treatments, the bounding approach can be useful. But everything depends on those scenarios, which require a considerable specificity. Unless the policy community demands extensive and convincing documentation for all of the assumptions applied, there is enormous potential for abuse.

11.4.5 Some Forecasts

Many of the most important limitations of drawing causal inferences from observational data were known over a generation ago when causal modeling was first introduced into policy research. Researchers may have hoped that useful results would be forthcoming nevertheless. The difficulties experienced were merely a nuisance that, with proper statistical techniques, could be eliminated or at least rendered too small to make an important difference. What followed was a large experiment in the doing of science. Over several decades, causal models were applied to all manner of policy questions, often by researchers who were unaware or unmindful of what credible results require. Perhaps now the data from that science experiment are in. The original concerns, and new ones that have surfaced, turn out to be very important. They are pervasive, difficult to handle, and can have fatal impacts on research credibility.

There have been four constructive responses that could well become more important in the future: an acknowledgment among many very sophisticated observers that most current practice is badly flawed; the development of specialized tools that, for some particular problems, can help; a recognition that stronger research designs and better measurement are essential for stronger causal inferences; and, in some circles, a dramatic reduction in expectations about what can be learned from causal modeling. It is also likely that it will take a decade or more for routine practice to catch up.

11.5 Some Final Observations

11.5.1 A Police Story

On November 2, 2000, the mayor of the City of Los Angeles signed a consent decree negotiated between the City of Los Angeles and the U.S. Department of Justice. In response to charges of police misconduct and corruption, the consent decree sought "to promote police integrity and prevent conduct that deprives individuals of their rights, privileges or immunities secured or protected by the Constitution or law of the United States."

Starting June 1, 2001, and for each subsequent quarter over five years, the chief of police was required to submit to the local police commission, with a copy to the inspector general, a set of required "audits" of specified police activities. The audits were to be undertaken by a new entity within the police department substantially funded by the city. The new "audit unit" was charged with collecting, archiving, and analyzing the relevant data.

Oversight of the Los Angeles Police Department (LAPD) was well funded and well supervised. A technical consultant was hired to help LAPD collect and organize the required data. A generous contract was awarded to an out-of-state management consulting firm to represent the federal court and do the monitoring required. The costs to the LAPD of collecting and storing the necessary data were handled with internal LAPD funds supplemented by the city. All this unfolded under the close scrutiny of the mayor, city council, city police commission, the union representing the police officers, media, and various stakeholders. One would think that all of the relevant forces were aligned so that useful information would be produced.

One controversial concern that, in part, triggered federal oversight was the claim that the LAPD employed "racial profiling," in which police officers were stopping and questioning pedestrians and motorists primarily because of their apparent racial or ethnic identity. A component of the consent decree required that the police department begin collecting systematic data on the race or ethnicity of citizens in all police stops.

The police department's stated policies were clear.

> The Department shall continue to prohibit discriminatory conduct on the basis of race, color, ethnicity, national origin, gender, sexual orientation, or disability in the conduct of law enforcement activities. The Department shall continue to require that, to the extent required by federal and state law, all stops and detentions, and activities following stops or detentions, by the LAPD shall be made on the basis of legitimate, articulable reasons consistent with all standards of reasonable suspicion or probable cause. (Internal memorandum, Los Angeles Police Department, 2001)

The empirical question was whether these policies were being violated. The key data were to come from new forms completed by any police officer who made a traffic or pedestrian stop. On these forms were to be recorded the following information for each individual stopped:

1. whether the individual was a pedestrian, driver, or passenger;
2. gender;
3. apparent descent [racial/ethnic background];
4. apparent age;

5. incident number;
6. initial reason for stop;
7. whether the driver was required to exit the vehicle;
8. whether a patdown or frisk was required;
9. whether the detainee was asked to submit to a consensual search;
10. if there was a warrantless search, the search authority;
11. whether a search was actually conducted;
12. what was searched;
13. what was discovered/seized;
14. action taken;
15. date;
16. time;
17. reporting district;
18. officer's serial number (for two officers if necessary);
19. officer's police division number (for two officers if necessary);
20. officer's name (for two officers if necessary).

Note that the exact location of the stop is not recorded. The only spatial data are for the police division, each of which covers a large area that can be very heterogeneous with respect to the background of the citizens served.

Suppose now that in a particular police division, 44% of the individuals stopped by police were labeled African American. Is that a lot or a little? Does it represent good or bad police practice? Does the LAPD engage in racial profiling or not?

An initial issue is how seriously to take the racial/ethnic information reported. But even if the "apparent descent" of the drivers can be taken at face value, overall racial/ethnic breakdowns would seem to be of little value without something with which they could be compared. Yet there was no provision made to collect any baseline data.

The obvious choice of using census data to characterize the citizens in a police division does not help much. For vehicular stops, the relevant baseline for each incident is the mix of motorists at the location where the stop occurred. Especially if these are major thoroughfares, the mix of motorists will likely be quite different from the mix of local residents. The same arguments apply to pedestrians, especially near mass transit stations and bus stops. And the spatial unit of a police division is very coarse to begin with. In short, the matter of "compared to what?" cannot be intelligently answered.

Even if the baseline problem had been properly addressed, one would still need data to determine whether such apprehensions are justified as good police work. Many would argue that racial profiling is defined by the use of racial/ethnic markers unjustified by sound police practice. Suppose that by some sensible yardstick, young, male Hispanic Americans are disproportionately apprehended. But what if such traffic stops produced a large number of arrests for carrying concealed weapons or trafficking in narcotics? This might well be the case if the individuals arrested were typically gang members.

In fact, useful comparison data could have been collected for both issues if the address of the stop were recorded. For example, surveillance cameras are now used at a number of intersections in Los Angeles to record for individuals who drive through red lights the driver's face, license plate, and vehicle type. Citations are then sent to the address at which the vehicle is registered. The same technology could easily be used to help determine the mix of drivers using a particular street. And low-tech observational methods could be used to collect relevant data on pedestrians.

Data also could be collected on current success rates of police officers. One strategy would be to collect data on success rates of officers designated by the LAPD as unusually skilled; these officers would be allowed to determine what defined good police work. For example, one indicator might be the proportion of pedestrian stops leading to an arrest and conviction. Then, officers whose stops of minorities were comparatively unproductive could be identified. And it is perhaps these officers who might be guilty of racial profiling. One could also compare the productivity of LAPD officers with police officers in other cities. Although such productivity comparisons are certainly not flawless, they at least allow some analysis of whether local police practices have a demonstrable law enforcement rationale.

Clearly, important data are not being collected. And the data that ultimately will be available will have significant problems. One can predict, nevertheless, that there will be hundreds of pages of regression output addressing racial profiling. Reports from those analyses will be laden with p-values, hypothesis tests, and lots of causal talk. Indeed, there is ample precedent for such work in earlier research on the topic. This brings us back to where we started more than 200 pages ago.

11.5.2 Regression Analysis as Too Little, Too Late

Very near the beginning of this book, a simple observation was made that informed much of what followed. Regression analyses typically do nothing more than produce from a data set a collection of conditional means and conditional variances. Nearly everything beyond these conditional means and variances rests on information, often as formal assumptions, external to that data set. The point made was that because so much rests on that external input, the input better be good.

It should now be clear that much of the imported information depends on how the data were generated. Consequently, if that information is to be useful, the data generation process needs to be well understood and consistent with the needs of the researcher. A critical implication is that a lot of time, energy, and material resources need to be invested at the front end, well before regression analysis is applied. And if current practice is a fair yardstick, up-front investments have commonly been inadequate. If the goal is to characterize some important features of a set of observational units, measure well. If the goal is to generalize from the data, get a probability sample of sufficient size. If the goal is to learn what the response would be to some intervention, intervene. Most of the time, collecting good data cannot be done on the cheap. Fallback positions can often be useful, but aspirations need to be reduced accordingly.

Many investigators proceed as if fancy statistical procedures can compensate for failures to invest in proper data collection. Moreover, back-end patches are often cheap and, if executed with virtuoso skill, confer rich professional rewards. All this happens without any need to leave a comfortable, well-appointed office.

Alternatively, there is the back-end patch called theory. In many of the natural sciences, the information contained in theory can sometimes legitimately save the day. For the social sciences, especially when applied to very specific policy issues, what theory there is often does not help much. Commonly, there is little more than a tentative taxonomy with some arrows between key categories. There is little that would help in constructing a convincing response schedule. And when there is formal theory complete with mathematical relationships, the assumptions required often turn the theory into a Kiplingesque Just So Story.

Improvement in policy-related research depends on acknowledging the limitations of current practice, reducing aspirations and claims accordingly, better matching what regression analysis can do with useful empirical questions, and investing far more heavily in the front end. Acknowledging the limitations of current practice would be a good start.

References

Akaike, H. (1974) "A New Look at the Statistical Model Identification." *IEEE Trans.* AC 19: 716-723.

Angrist, J., Imbens, G.W., and D.B. Rubin (1996) "Identification of Causal Effects Using Instrumental Variables" (with discussion). *Journal of the American Statistical Association* 91: 441-472.

Archer, J. (2000) "Sex Differences in Aggression Between Heterosexual Partners: A Meta-Analytic Review." *Psychological Bulletin* 126 (5): 651-680.

Atkinson, A. C. (1985) *Plots, Transformations, and Regression: An Introduction to Graphical Methods of Diagnostic Regression Analysis.* Oxford: Oxford University Press.

Balke, A., and J. Pearl (1993) "Bounds on Treatment Effects in Studies With Imperfect Compliance." Technical Report R-199-J, UCLA Cognitive Systems Laboratory.

Barnett, V. (1982) *Comparative Statistical Inference*, second edition. New York: John Wiley.

Belin, T.R., and J.E. Rolph (1994) "Can We Reach Consensus on Census Adjustment?" (with commentary). *Statistical Science* 9: 486-537.

Berk, R.A. (1977) "Discretionary Methodological Decisions in Applied Research." *Sociological Methods & Research* 5: 317-334.

Berk, R.A. (1983) "An Introduction to Sample Selection Bias in Sociological Data." *American Sociological Review* 48 (3): 386-397.

Berk, R.A. (1988) "Causal Inference for Sociological Data," in *Handbook of Sociology*, edited by N. Smelser. Newbury Park, CA: Sage Publications.

Berk, R.A. (1990) "What Your Mother Never Told You About Randomized Field Experiments" in *Community Based Care of People With AIDS: Developing a Research Agenda*, AHCPR Conference Proceedings. Washington, D.C.: U.S. Department of Health and Human Services.

Berk, R.A., Baek, A., Ladd, H., and H. Graziano (2003) "A Randomized Experiment Testing Inmate Classification Systems." *Criminology & Public Policy*, 2: 215–242.

Berk, R.A., and J. de Leeuw (1999) "An Evaluation of California's Inmate Classification System Using a Generalized Regression Discontinuity Design." *Journal of the American Statistical Association* 94 (448): 1045-1052.

Berk, R.A., and D.A. Freedman (2003) "Statistical Assumptions as Empirical Commitments," in *Punishment and Social Control*, edited by T.G. Blomberg and S. Cohen. New York: Aldine de Gruyter.

Berk, R.A., Newton, P.J., and S.K. Fenstermaker (1986) "What a Difference a Day Makes: An Empirical Study of the Impact of Shelters for Battered Women." *Journal of Marriage and the Family* 48: 481-490.

Berk, R.A., Weiss, R.E., and Boger, J. (1993) "Chance and the Death Penalty" (with commentary and rejoinder). *Law & Society Review* 27: 89-110.

Berk, R.A., and R.E. Weiss (1996) "Assessing the Capriciousness of Death Penalty Charging." *Law & Society Review* 30: 607-626.

Berk, R.A., Western, B., and R.E. Weiss (1995) "Statistical Inference for Apparent Populations," in *Sociological Methodology*, Volume 25, edited by P.V. Marsden. Oxford: Blackwell Publishers.

Bernard, J., Du, J., Jill, J.L., and D.B. Rubin (1998) "A Broader Template for Analyzing Broken Randomized Experiments." *Sociological Methods & Research* 27: 285-317.

Bernard, J., Frangakis, C.E., Hill, J.L., and D.B. Rubin (2003) "A Principle Stratification Approach to Broken Randomized Experiments." Journal of the American Statistical Association.

Besharov, D.J., and P. Germanis (2001) *Rethinking WIC: An Evaluation of the Women, Infants, and Children Program*. Washington, D.C.: AEI Press.

Bickel, P.J., and K.A. Doksum (2001) *Mathematical Statistics: Basic Ideas and Selected Topics*, Volume 1, second edition. New York: Prentice Hall.

Bickel, P.J., and J.W. O'Connell (1975) "Is There a Sex Bias in Graduate Admissions?" *Science* 187: 398-404.

Blaug, M. (1980) *The Methodology of Economics*. Cambridge, UK: Cambridge University Press.

Blumstein, A., Cohen, J., and S.E. Martin (1983) *Research on Sentencing: The Search for Reform*, Volumes I and II. Washington, D.C.: National Academy Press.

Bollen, K.A. (1989) *Structural Equation Modeling With Latent Variables*. New York: John Wiley.

Bollen, K.A. (1995) "Apparent and Nonapparent Significance Tests," in *Sociological Methodology*, Volume 25, edited by P.V. Marsden. Oxford: Blackwell Publishers.

Boudett, K.P., and D. Friedlander (1997) "Does Mandatory Basic Education Improve Test Scores of AFDC Recipients?" *Evaluation Review* 21: 568-588.

Bowden, R.J., and D.A. Turkington (1984) *Instrumental Variables*. Cambridge, UK: Cambridge University Press.

Box, G.E.P. (1976) "Science and Statistics." *Journal of the American Statistical Association* 71: 791-799.

Box, G.E.P., and D.R. Cox (1964) "An Analysis of Transformations." *Journal of the Royal Statisical Society, Series B* 26: 211-252.

Box, G.E.P., Hunder, W.G., and J.S. Hunter (1978) *Statistics for Experimenters*. New York: John Wiley.

Breiman, L. (1994) "The 1991 Census Adjustment: Undercount or Bad Data." *Statistical Science* 9: 458-475.

Breiman, L. (1996) "Bagging Predictors." *Machine Learning Journal* 26: 123-140.

Breiman, L. (2001a) "Random Forests." Working Paper, Department of Statistics, University of California, Berkeley.

Breiman, L. (2001b) "Statistical Modeling: Two Cultures" (with discussion). *Statistical Science* 16: 199-231.

Breiman, L., Friedman, J.H., Olshen, R.A., and C.J. Stone (1984) *Classification and Regression Trees*. Monterey, CA: Wadsworth and Brooks/Cole.

Breslow, N.E. (1984) "Extra-Poisson Variation in Log-Linear Models." *Applied Statistics* 33: 38-44.

Brown, L.D., Eaton, M.L., Freedman, D.A., Klein, S.P., Olshen, R.A., Wachter, K.W., Wells, M.T., and D. Ylvisaker (1999) "Statistical Controversies in Census 2000." *Jurimetrics* 39: 347-375.

Bryant, P.G., and O.I. Cordero-Braña (2000) "Model Selection Using the Minimum Description Length Principle." *American Statistician* 54: 257-268.

Bryk, A.S., and S.W. Raudenbush (2002) *Hierarchical Linear Models: Applications and Data Analysis Methods*, second edition. Thousand Oaks, CA: Sage Publications.

Campbell, D.T., and J.C. Stanley (1963) *Experimental and Quasi-Experimental Designs for Research*. Chicago: Rand McNally.

Cheng, G. (1999) "Forest Change: Hydrological Effects in the Upper Yangtze River Valley." *Ambio* 28(5): 457-459.

Chilès, J., and P. Delfiner (1999) *Geostatistics: Modeling Spatial Uncertainty*. New York: John Wiley.

Christianini, N., and J. Shawe-Taylor (2000) *An Introduction to Support Vector Machines*. Cambridge: Cambrige University Press.

Cleveland, W.S. (1979) "Robust Locally Weighted Regression and Smoothing Scatter Plots." *Journal of the American Statistical Association* 74: 829-836.

Cleveland, W.S. (1993) *Visualizing Data*. Murry Hill, NJ: AT&T Bell Laboratories.

Cochran, W.G. (1983) *Planning & Analysis of Observational Studies*. New York: John Wiley.

Cohen, J. (1988) *Statistical Power Analyses for the Behavioral Sciences*, second edition. Hillsdale, NJ: Lawrence Erlbaum Associates.

Cohen, J. (1994) "The Earth Is Round ($p < .05$)." *American Psychologist* 49: 977-1003.

Cook, D.R. (1998) *Regression Graphics: Ideas for Studying Regressions through Graphics*. New York: John Wiley.

Cook, D.R., and S. Weisberg (1994) "Transforming a Response Variable for Linearity." *Biometrika* 81: 731-737.

Cook, D.R., and S. Weisberg (1999) *Applied Regression Including Computing and Graphics*. New York: John Wiley.

Cook, T.C., Cooper, D.S., Hartmann, H., Hedges, L.V., Light, R.I., Loomis, T.A., and F. M. Mosteller (1992) *Meta-Analysis for Explanation*. New York: Russell Sage.

Cronbach, L.J. (1982) *Designing Evaluations of Educational and Social Programs*. New York: Jossey-Bass.

Currie, J., and M. Kivelson (2000) "Gender Equity Affecting Senate Faculty at UCLA; Report of the Gender Equity Committee." UCLA, October 10.

Davison, A.C., and D.V. Hinkley (1997) *Bootstrap Methods and Their Applications*. Cambridge: Cambridge University Press.

Dawid, A.P. (2000) "Causal Inference Without Counterfactuals" (with commentary). *Journal of the American Statistical Association* 95: 407-448.

de Leeuw, J. (1994) "Statistics and the Sciences," in *Trends and Perspectives in Empirical Social Science*, edited by I. Borg and P.P. Mohler. New York: Walter de Gruyter.

Donohue, J.J., and S.D. Levitt (2001) "The Impact of Legalized Abortion on Crime." *Quarterly Journal of Economics* CXVI: 379-420.

Duncan, O.D. (1975) *Introduction to Structural Equation Modeling*. New York: Academic Press.

Duncan, O.D. (1984) *Notes on Social Measurement: Historical and Critical.* New York: Russell Sage Foundation.

Edgington, E.S. (1986) Randomization Tests, second edition. New York: Marcel Dekker.

Efron, B., and R.J. Tibshirani (1993) *An Introduction to the Bootstrap.* New York: Chapman Hall.

Esbensen, F., Miller, M.H., Taylor, T.J., He, N., and A. Freng (1999) "Differential Attrition Rates and Parental Consent." *Evaluation Review* 23: 316-335.

Feller, W. (1968) *An Introduction to Probability Theory and Its Applications*, Volume 1, third edition. New York: John Wiley.

Freedman, D.A. (1981) "Bootstrapping Regression Models. " *Annals of Statistics* 9: 1218-1228.

Freedman, D.A. (1983) "Significance Tests in a Nonstochastic Setting." In *A Festschrift for Eric L. Lehman*, Belmont, CA., Wadsworth.

Freedman, D.A. (1985) "Statistics and the Scientific Method," in *Cohort Analysis in Social Research: Beyond the Identification Problem*, edited by W.M. Mason and S.E. Fienberg. New York: Springer Verlag.

Freedman, D.A. (1987) "As Others See Us: A Case Study in Path Analysis" (with discussion). *Journal of Educational Statistics* 12: 101-223.

Freedman, D.A. (1991) "Statistical Models of Shoe Leather," in *Sociological Methodology, 1991*, edited by P.V. Marsden. Oxford: Basil Blackwell.

Freedman, D.A. (2001) "On Specifying Graphical Models for Causation, and the Identification Problem." U.C. Berkeley Department of Statistics Preprint Series #601.

Freedman, D.A., and D. Lane (1983) Significance Testing in a Nonstochastic Setting." In A Festschrift for Eric L. Lehman, pp. 185–208. Belmont, CA: Wadsworth.

Freedman, D.A., and W.C. Navidi (1986) "Regression Models for Adjusting the 1980 Census" (and commentary). *Statistical Science* 1: 3-39.

Freedman, D.A., Pisani, R., and R. Purves. (1998) *Statistics*, third edition. New York: W.W. Norton.

Freedman, D.A., and K. Wachter (1994) "Heterogeneity and Census Adjustments for the Intercensal Base." *Statistical Science* 9: 476-485.

Freund, Y., and R. Schapire (1996) "Experiments With a New Boosting Algorithm," in *Machine Learning: Proceedings of the Thirteenth International Conference*. San Francisco: Morgan Kauffman.

Garrett, C.J. (1985) "The Effects of Residential Treatment on Adjudicated Delinquents: A Meta-Analysis." *Journal of Research on Crime and Delinquency*, 45: 287-308.

Geiser, S., and R. Studley (2001) "UC and the SAT: Predictive Validity and Differential Impact of the SAT I and SAT II at the University of California." Oakland: University of California, Office of the President.

Gifi, A. (1990) *Nonlinear Multivariate Analysis*. New York: John Wiley.

Glymour, C., and G. Cooper (eds.) (1999) *Computation, Causation, and Discovery*. Cambridge: MIT Press.

Goldman, S., Feinberg, S.E., Rolph, J.E., Freedman, D.A., and K. W. Wachter (1993) "Adjusting the Census of 1990: An Exchange." *Jurimetrics* 34, 1.

Gourieroux, C., and E. Monfort (1994) "Testing Non-Nested Hypotheses," in Z. Griliches and M. Intrilligator (eds.), *Handbook of Econometrics*, Volume 4. Amsterdam: North Holland.

Granger, C., and P. Newbold. (1986) *Forecasting Economic Time Series*. New York: Academic Press.

Graubard, B.L., and E.L. Korn (2002) "Inference for Superpopulation Parameters Using Sample Surveys." *Statistical Science* 17: 73-96.

Gray, M.W. (1993) "Statistical Arguments in Courts Concerning Faculty Salaries" (with commentary). *Statistical Science* 8: 144-179.

Greene, W.H. (2000) *Econometric Analysis*, fourth edition. New York: Prentice Hall.

Groves, R.M. (1989) *Survey Costs and Survey Errors*. New York: John Wiley.

Hamilton, J.D. (1994) *Time Series Analysis*. Princeton, NJ: Princeton University Press.

Hand, D.J., Blunt, G., Kelly, M.G., and N.M. Adams (2000) "Data Mining for Fun and Profit" (with commentary). *Statistical Science* 15: 111-131.

Hansen, M., and B. Yu (2001) "Model Selection and Minimum Description Length." *Journal of the American Statistical Association* 96: 746-774.

Hastie, T., Tibshirani, R., and J. Friedman (2001) *The Elements of Statistical Learning: Data Mining, Inference, and Prediction*. New York: Springer-Verlag.

Hastie, T.J., and R.J. Tibshirani (1990) *Generalized Additive Models*. New York: Chapman Hall.

Hausman, J.A., and D.A. Wise (1985) *Social Experimentation*. Chicago: University of Chicago Press.

Haveman, R.H. (ed.) (1977) *A Decade of Federal Antipoverty Programs*. New York: Academic Press.

Heckman, J. (1979) "Sample Selection Bias as a Specification Error." *Econometrica* 46: 931-961.

Heckman, J. (1990) "Varieties of Selection Bias." *American Economics Review* 80: 313-318.

Heckman, J. (1995) "Assessing the Case for Randomized Social Experiments." *Journal of Economic Perspectives* 9: 85-110.

Heckman, J. (1999) "Causal Parameters and Policy Analysis in Economics: A Twentieth Century Retrospective." *The Quarterly Journal of Economics*, February: 45-97.

Heckman, J. (2001) "Micro Data, Heterogeneity, and the Evaluation of Public Policy: Nobel Lecture." *Journal of Political Economy* 109: 673-723.

Heckman, J., and V.J. Hotz (1989) "Choosing Among Alternative Nonexperimental Methods for Estimating the Impact of Social Programs: The Case of Manpower Training." *Journal of the American Statistical Association* 84: 862-874.

Heckman, J., Ichimura, H., Smith, J., and P. Todd (1997) "Characterizing Selection Bias Using Experimental Data," invited lecture at the Latin American Econometric Society.

Heckman, J., LaLonde, R.J., and J.A. Smith (1999) "The Economics and Econometrics of Active Labor Market Programs," in *Handbook of Labor Economics*, Volume III, edited by O. Ashenfelter and D. Card. New York: Elsevier Science/ North-Holland.

Heckman, J., and R. Robb, Jr. (1985) "Alternative Methods for Evaluating the Impact of Interventions," in *Longitudinal Analysis of Labor Market Data*, edited by J. Heckman and B. Singer. New York: Cambridge University Press.

Hedges, L.V., and I. Olkin (1985) *Statistical Methods for Meta-Analysis*. New York: Academic Press.

Henry, K.L., Smith, E.A., and A.M. Hopkins (2002) "The Effect of Active Parental Consent on the Ability to Generalize the Results of an Alcohol, Tobacco, and Other Drug Prevention Trial to Rural Adolescents." *Evaluation Review* 26: 645-655.

Hoenig, J.M., and D.M. Heisey (2001) "The Abuse of Power: The Pervasive Fallacy of Power Calculation for Data Analysis." *American Statistician* 55: 19-24.

Holland, P.W. (1986) "Statistics and Causal Inference." *Journal of the American Statistical Association* 81: 945-960.

Hollis, M., and E. Nell (1975) *Rational Economic Man: A Philosophical Critique of Neo-Classical Economics*. Cambridge, UK: Cambridge University Press.

Hsiao, C. (1986) *Analysis of Panel Data*. Cambridge: Cambridge University Press.

Johnston, J. (1984) *Econometric Methods*, third edition. New York: McGraw Hill.

Joyce, T. (2001) "Did Legalized Abortion Lower Crime?" *NBER Working Paper*, No. W8319.

Kaplan, D. (2000) *Structural Equation Modeling: Foundations and Extensions*. Thousand Oaks, CA: Sage Publications.

Kaye, D.H., and D.A. Freedman (2000) "Reference Guide on Statistics," in *Reference Manual on Scientific Evidence*, second edition. Washington, D.C.: Federal Judicial Center.

Kennedy, P. (1998) *A Guide to Econometrics*, fourth edition. Cambridge: MIT Press.

Kish, L. (1987) *Statistical Design for Research*. New York: John Wiley.

Kraemer, H.C., and S. Thiemann (1987) *How Many Subjects?* Newbury Park, CA: Sage Publications.

Kreft, I., and J. de Leeuw (1998) *Introduction to Multilevel Modeling*. Thousand Oaks, CA: Sage Publications.

Lal, M. (2001) "Climate Change—Implications for India's Water Resources." *Indian Journal of Water Resources* 27: 240-257.

Leamer, E.E. (1978) *Specification Searches: Ad Hoc Inference with Non-Experimental Data*. New York: John Wiley.

Levin, H.M., and P.J. McEwan. (2001) *Cost-Effectiveness Analysis*, second edition. Thousand Oaks, CA: Sage Publications.

Lieberson, S. (1985) *Making It Count: The Improvement of Social Research and Theory*. Berkeley: University of California Press.

Lindgren, G., Zettergvist, L., and G. Holmstedt (1993) "Estimation of Quantiles in Airborne Pollution: Measuring Pollution around Gas Furnaces," in *Statistics for the Environment*, edited by V. Barnett and K. F. Turkman. New York: John Wiley.

Lipsey, M.W. (1992) "Juvenile Delinquency Treatment: A Meta-Analysis Inquiry Into the Variability of Effects." Pp. 83-127 in *Meta-Analysis for Explanation*, edited by T.C. Cook, D.S. Cooper, H. Hartmann, L.V. Hedges, R.I. Light, T.A. Loomis, and F.M. Mosteller. New York: Russell Sage.

Lipsey, M.W. (1997) "What Can You Build With Thousands of Bricks? Musings on the Cumulation of Knowledge in Program Evaluation." *New Directions for Evaluation* 76 (Winter): 7-24.

Lipsey, M.W., and D.B. Wilson (2001) *Practical Meta-Analysis*. Thousand Oaks, CA: Sage Publications.

Little, R.J.A., and D.B. Rubin (2002) *Statistical Analysis With Missing Data*, second edition. New York: John Wiley.

Long, J.S. (1997) *Regression Models for Categorical and Limited Dependent Variables*. Thousand Oaks, CA: Sage Publications.

Lott, J.R., and J. Whitley (2001) "Abortion and Crime: Unwanted Children and Out-of-Wedlock Births." *Yale Law School Working Paper*, No. 254.

MacKenzie, D. L. 1991. "The Parole Performance of Offenders Released from Shock Incarceration (Boot Camp Prisons): A Survival Time Analysis." *Journal of Quantitative Criminology*, 7(3): 213-236.

Mallows, C. (1973) "Some Comments on C_p." *Technometrics* 15: 661-676.

Maltz, M.D. (1984) *Recidivism*. New York: Academic Press.

Manski, C.F. (1990) "Nonparametric Bounds on Treatment Effects." *American Economic Review Papers and Proceedings* 80: 319-323.

Manski, C.F. (1994) "The Selection Problem," in *Advances in Econometrics, Sixth World Congress*, edited by C. Sims. Cambridge, England: Cambridge University Press.

Manski, C.F., and D.S. Nagin (1998) "Bounding Disagreements About Treatment Effects: A Case Study of Sentencing and Recidivism," in *Sociological Methodology*, Volume 28, edited by A.E. Raftery. Boston: Blackwell Publishers.

McCullagh, P., and J.A. Nelder (1989) *Generalized Linear Models*, second edition. New York: Chapman and Hall.

Millard, S.P., and N.K. Neerchal (2001) *Environmental Statistics With S-Plus*. New York: CRC Press.

Mitchell, T.M. (1997) *Machine Learning*. New York: McGraw Hill.

Morgan, J.N., and J.A. Sonquist (1963) "Problems in the Analysis of Survey Data, and a Proposal." *Journal of the American Statistical Association* 58: 415-434.

Nelson, R.L., and W.P. Bridges (1999) *Legalizing Gender Inequality: Courts, Markets and Unequal Pay for Women in America*. Cambridge, UK: Cambridge University Press.

Neyman, J. [1923] (1990) "On the Application of Probability Theory to Agricultural Experiments. Essay on Principles. Section 9." Translated and edited by D.M. Dabrowska and T.P. Speed. *Statistical Science* 5: 465-471.

Oakes, M. (1986) *Statistical Inference: A Commentary for the Social and Behavioral Sciences*. New York: John Wiley.

Occupational Safety and Health Administration, Department of Labor, U.S. Government. (June 20th, 1986) "Occupational Exposure to Asbestos, Tremolite, Anthophyllite, and Actinolite: Final Rules." *Federal Register* 29 CFR Parts 1910 and 1926.

Pearl, J. (2000) *Causality: Models, Reasoning and Inference*. Cambridge, UK: Cambridge University Press.

Petitti, D.B. (1999) *Meta-Analysis, Decision Analysis, and Cost-Effectiveness Analysis*, second edition. New York: Oxford University Press.

Pybus, O.G., Charleston, M.A., Gupta, S., Rambaut, A., Holmes, E.C., and P.H. Harvey (2001) "The Epidemic Behavior of the Hepatitis C Virus." *Science* 292: 2323-2325.

Rabe-Hesketh, S., and B. Everitt (2000) *A Handbook of Statistical Analyses Using STATA*, second edition. New York: Chapman Hall.

Rice, J.A. (1995) *Mathematical Statistics and Data Analysis*, second edition. Belmont, CA: Duxbury Press.

Rich, L.M. (1999) "Family Welfare Receipt, Welfare Benefits Levels, and the Schooling and Employment Status of Male Youth." *Social Science Research* 28: 88-109.

Ripley, B.D. (1996) *Pattern Recognition and Neural Networks*. Cambridge, UK: Cambridge University Press.

Robbins, J.M. (1989) "The Analysis of Randomized and Nonrandomized AIDS Treatment Trials Using a New Approach to Causal Inference in Longitudinal Studies," in *Health Service Research Methodology, A Focus on AIDS*, edited by L.L. Sechrest, H. Freeman, and A. Mulley. Washington, D.C.: U.S. Public Health Service.

Robbins, J.M. (1997) "Causal Inference From Complex Longitudinal Data." *Latent Variable Modeling and Applications to Causality: Lecture Notes in Statistics* 120: 69-117.

Robbins, J.M. (1999) "Association, Causation, and Marginal Structural Models." *Synthese* 121: 151-179.

Robbins, J.M. (2002) "Comment" (on "Covariance Adjustment in Randomized Experiments and Observational Studies"). *Statistical Science* 17: 309-321.

Roe v. Wade, 410 U.S. 113 (1973).

Rosenbaum, P. (2002a) *Observational Studies*, second edition. New York: Springer-Verlag.

Rosenbaum, P. (2002b) "Covariance Adjustments in Randomized Experiments and Observational Studies" (with discussion). *Statistical Science* 17: 286-327.

Rosenbaum, P., and D.B. Rubin (1983a) "Assessing Sensitivity to an Unobserved Binary Covariate in an Observational Study With a Binary Outcome." *Journal of the Royal Statistical Society, Series B* 45: 212-218.

Rosenbaum, P., and D.B. Rubin (1983b) "The Central Role of the Propensity Score in Observational Studies for Causal Effects." *Biometrika* 70: 41-55.

Rosenberg, M. (1968) *The Logic of Survey Analysis*. New York: Basic Books.

Rossi, P.H., and R.A. Berk (1997) *Just Punishments: Federal Guidelines and Public Views Compared*. New York: Aldine de Gruyter.

Rubin, D.B. (1977) "Assignment to Treatment Group on the Basis of a Covariate." *Journal of Educational Statistics* 2: 34-58.

Rubin, D.B. (1986) "Which Ifs Have Causal Answers." *Journal of the American Statistical Association* 81: 961-962.

Rubin, D.B. (1990) "Comment: Neyman (1923) and Causal Inference in Experiments and Observational Studies." *Statistical Science* 5: 472-480.

Rubin, D.B., and N. Thomas (1996) "Matching Using Estimated Propensity Scores: Relating Theory to Practice." *Biometrics* 52: 249-264.

Schmidt, F.L. (1996) "Statistical Significance Testing and Cumulative Knowledge in Psychology: Implications for Training Researchers." *Psychological Methods* 1: 115-129.

Schwartz, G. (1978) "Estimating the Dimension of a Model." *Annals of Statistics* 6: 461-464.

Scrucca, L. (2000) "Fitting Extra-Poisson Variation in Poisson Models Using *ARC*." Department of Statistics, Universita degli Studi de Perugia, Italy.

Sherman, L.W., Gottfredson, D., MacKenzie, D., Eck, J., Reuter, P., and S. Bushway (1997) *Preventing Crime: What Works, What Doesn't, What's Promising?* Washington, DC: U.S. Department of Justice.

Sherman, L.W. (1992) *Policing Domestic Violence*. New York: Free Press.

Simon, H.A. (2001) "Science Seeks Parsimony, Not Simplicity: Searching for Patterns in Phenomena," in *Simplicity, Inference, and Modeling: Keeping It Sophisticatedly Simple,* edited by A. Zellner, H.A. Keuzenkamp, and M. McAleer. Cambridge, UK: Cambridge University Press.

Smith, H.L. (1990) "Specification Problems in Experimental and Nonexperimental Social Research," in *Sociological Methodology, 1990*, edited by C.C. Clogg. Washington, DC: American Sociological Association.

Smith, H.L. (1997) "Matching With Multiple Controls to Estimate Treatment Effects in Observational Studies," in *Sociological Methodology, 1997*, edited by A.E. Raftery. Oxford: Blackwell Publishers.

Snedecor, G.W, and W.G. Cochran (1980) *Statistical Methods*, seventh edition. Ames: Iowa State University Press.

Spirtes, P., Glymour, C., and R. Scheines (1993) *Causation, Prediction, and Search*. New York: Springer-Verlag.

Thompson, S.K. (2002) *Sampling*, second edition. New York: John Wiley.

Venables, W.N., and B.D. Ripley (2002) *Modern Applied Statistics With S*, fourth edition. New York: Springer-Verlag.

Walker, A.M., Loughlin, J.E., Friedlander, E.R., Rothman, K.J., and N.A. Dryer (1983) "Projections of Asbestos-Related Disease 1980-2009." *Journal of Occupational Medicine* 25: 409-425.

Weiss, R.E., Berk, R.A., and C. Lee (1996) "Assessing the Capriciousness of Death Penalty Charging." *Law & Society Review* 30(3): 607-626.

White, H. (1984) *Asymptotic Theory for Econometricians*. New York: Academic Press.

Williams, D.A. (1982) "Extra-Binomial Variation in Logistic Linear Models." *Applied Statistics* 31: 144-148.

Witten, I.H., and E. Frank (2000) *Data Mining*. New York: Morgan and Kaufman.

Wu, C.F.J., and M. Hamada (2000) *Experiments: Planning, Analysis, and Parameter Design Optimization*. New York: John Wiley.

Wu, D. (1973) "Alternative Tests of Independence Between Stochastic Regressors and Disturbances." *Econometrica* 41: 733-750.

Zellner, A., Keuzenkamp, H.A., and M. McAleer (eds.) (2001) *Simplicity, Inference, and Modeling: Keeping It Sophisticatedly Simple*. Cambridge: Cambridge University Press.

Zhang, H., and B. Singer (1999) *Recursive Partitioning in the Health Sciences*. New York: Springer-Verlag.

Index

About the Author

Richard Berk is Professor in the Departments of Statistics and Sociology at the University of California, Los Angeles. He also holds the position of Visiting Faculty Member at the Los Alamos National Laboratories. Professor Berk is an elected fellow of the American Association for the Advancement of Science and the American Statistical Association and has served on the Committee on Applied and Theoretical Statistics of the National Research Council, the National Center for Atmospheric Research Scientific Advisory Committee for the Climate Modeling Program, and the Social Science Research Council's Board of Directors. He has been awarded the Paul F. Lazarsfeld Award by the Methodology Section of the American Sociological Association. He is a founding editor of the *Evaluation Review*, a position that he still holds.